Multicultural polic
state: a comparison ~~of two~~
European societies

2020
£6
17/02

Multicultural policies and the state: a comparison of two European societies

Edited by

Marco Martiniello

*Comparative Studies in
Migration and Ethnic Relations 5*

European Research Centre on Migration and Ethnic Relations
Utrecht University, The Netherlands
1998

Printed in The Netherlands
Copy-edited and typeset by Oxford Publishing Services, Oxford

ISBN 90 75719 07 8

European Research Centre on Migration and Ethnic Relations
(ERCOMER)
Utrecht University
Heidelberglaan 2
3584 CS Utrecht
The Netherlands

Contents

Figure

Tables

Abbreviations and acronyms

BCS	British Crime Survey
CCME	Churches Commission for Migrants in Europe
CEIFO	Centre for Research in International Migration and Ethnic Relations (Sweden)
CGKR	Centre for Equal Opportunities and the Fight Against Racism
CIEMI	*Centre d'Informations et d'Etudes sur les Migrations Internationales*
CIMO	Centre for Interculturalism and Migration Research
CRC	community relations council/commission
CSC	*Confédération des Syndicats Chrétiens*
CVP	*Christelijk Volkspartij* (Flemish Christian Social Party)
ERA	Education Reform Act
ETA	*Euzkadi ta Askatsuna* (Basque: Basque Nation and Liberty; nationalist organisation)
FDF	*Front des Francophones*
FGTB	*Fédération Générale du Travail de Belgique*
FIS	*Front islamique du salut*
FN	*Front National*
FNSP	*Fondation Nationale des Sciences Politiques*
INBEL	*Institut Belge d'Information et de Documentation*
IRA	Irish Republican Army
ISOR	*Interdisciplinair Sociaal-wetenschappelijk Onderzoeksinstituut Rijksuniversiteit Utrecht*
KCM	*Koninklijk Commissariaat voor het Migrantenbeleid*
MERCI	*Mouvement Européen pour la Reconnaissance des Citoyens, en ce compris ceux issus de l'Immigration*
MTV	Music Television
NCWP	New Commonwealth and Pakistan
NOP	National Opinion Poll

ONS	Opinion National Survey
OETC	*Onderwijs in Eigen Taal en Cultuur* (education in own language and culture)
PC	*Parti Communiste*
PCI	*Partito Communista Italiano*
PRL	*Parti Réformateur Libéral*
PS	*Parti Socialiste*
PSC	*Parti Social Chrétien*
PSI	*Partito Socialista Italiano*
PTB	*Parti du Travail de Belgique*
QMW	Queen Mary and Westfield College, London
SACRE	Standing Advisory Council for Religious Education
SCORE	Standing Conference on Racial Discrimination in Europe
SP	*Socialistische Partij*
SRG	Single Regeneration Grant
SS	Schutzstaffel (Nazi paramilitary organisation)
SUA	*Socialistische Uitgeverij Amsterdam*
UKACIA	UK Action Committee on Islamic Affairs
ULB	*Université Libre de Bruxelles*
UNESCO	United Nations Educational, Scientific, and Cultural Organisation
VLB	*Vrije Universiteit Brussel*

COMPARATIVE STUDIES
IN MIGRATION AND ETHNIC RELATIONS

Maykel Verkuyten (Senior Editor)
Malcolm Cross & Louk Hagendoorn (Editors)

This series of books is intended to fill a vacuum in current publishing on migration and ethnic studies. It remains the case that most contributions to the field are restricted to *national* coverage. All the books in this series will have some wider *comparative* purpose. This will either be achieved by addressing an important theme from different national perspectives or by the inclusion of truly comparative studies. The books focus on Western, Central or Eastern Europe, but may from time to time include titles covering material from elsewhere.

Books in the series are intended to be of value to students of migration, nationalism, race relations and ethnic studies from a variety of social science disciplines as well as to established researchers and others. They are available only in paperback and are intended to represent excellent value for money.

Titles

* *Nationalism, ethnicity and cultural identity in Europe*
  edited by Keebet von Benda-Beckman and Maykel Verkuyten

* *Turks in European cities: housing and urban segregation*
  edited by Sule Özüekren and Ronald van Kempen

* *Exclusion and inclusion of refugees in contempory Europe*
  edited by Philip Muus

* *Multicultural policies and the state: a comparison of two European societies*
  edited by Marco Martiniello

Full details of the CSMER book series and other ERCOMER publications are available from ERCOMER and on our Website: http://www.ercomer.org

DISTRIBUTOR:

Lavis Marketing
73 Lime Walk, Headington
Oxford OX3 7AD – UK

Fax: +44 (0)1865 750079
Tel.:   +44 (0)1865 767575
Email: lavismarkt@aol.com

Acknowledgements

This volume is one of the outcomes of a Belgo-British seminar held in Brussels in January 1995 and jointly organised by the British Council and the Centre d'Étude des Migrations et de l'Ethnicité (CEDEM) of the University of Liège.

I am very grateful to the British Council for its support in organising the seminar. It was a real pleasure to work with the staff of the British Council in Brussels and especially with Ms Depoorter and Mr Churchill.

Other institutions have supported this event: the Fonds National de la Recherche Scientifique, le Ministère de la Culture de la Communauté française de Belgique and the University of Liège. I would like to thank them too. Thank you also to the participants, the audience and the contributors.

Thanks finally to Eileen Sheehan who translated Bastenier's paper, to Adrian Favell who revised some of the chapters and to Jacqueline Leroy.

This book is for Bearje.

Introduction

Marco Martiniello

The dramatic changes that have occurred worldwide in the last decade have put an end to an era of relative stability and certainties about the future and opened the way to a new era of complex instability and acceleration of history. Whereas the cold war era was characterised in Western Europe by a shared trust in the idea of social, economic, political and cultural progress and by a clear identification of the enemy, the new world disorder (Hobsbawm 1995) is characterised by a collapse of the landmarks and certainties of the previous period. To many, the world seems more complex and more unpredictable than ever before. New hopes and new projects are often sought to make sense of the global changes that have been taking place and that our intellectual tools have often fallen short of understanding, let alone predicting, rooted as they are in the nation state experience.

Let us take the example of the impact of globalisation on the capitalist economy to underline some of these difficulties. It is often argued that this process would lead to a 'global globalisation', modifying profoundly not only the sphere of economics but also the spheres of culture and of politics. The liberal prophets of world capitalism put forward the extraordinary opportunities offered by the global market, which in their view should lead to more social equality and justice and to some sort of globalised economic and social well-being. Needless to say, this prediction does not match current developments. Not only is the economic gap between the world's rich and poor regions widening, but poverty and deprivation in rich countries are also progressing rapidly and affecting a growing portion of the population. Capitalist globalisation certainly increases the world's wealth, but it does not necessarily imply a drastic change in the redistributive patterns of this wealth between regions and individuals. These processes remain largely inegalitarian.

Another expected consequence of the globalisation of the capitalist economy would be the emergence of a homogeneous world culture invented by global corporations for their own profit and spread out all around the world through the new information technologies. There is indeed a strong tendency towards the homogenisation of mass culture in which global corporations play a central role. To a certain extent, this leads to the emergence of a McWorld (Barber 1995) and a 'McDonaldization' of society (Ritzer 1993) in which the principle of fast-food restaurants (McDonald's) is coming to dominate more and more sectors of the world economy and culture: fast music (MTV), fast computers (Macintosh), fast entertainment (Hard Rock Cafe). But this is only one part of a complex picture. As a matter of fact, the McWorld is counterbalanced by the (re)assertion of various forms of ethno-cultural particularisms, some of which are diametrically opposed to the logic of the global market and its universalist aspirations. In other words, there seems to be a tension between cultural homogenisation and cultural heterogenisation (Appadurai 1990). The latter process is not only at the core of new nationalist movements in many parts of the world, including Western Europe (Caplan and Feffer 1996) but also of all sorts of religious fundamentalist movements and of ethnic and national minorities' claims. According to Barber, the present era can be characterised by an opposition between the McWorld and jihad, defined as 'a bloody holy war on behalf of partisan identity that is metaphysically defined and fanatically defended' (Barber 1995: 9). For Huntington, our world can be defined by a 'clash of civilisations', a conflict between conflicting universalisms (Huntington 1996). Others, observing the political debates in the United States, defend the hypothesis of a war of cultures taking place to define the future of the USA (Hunter 1991). These theses are certainly problematic. They nevertheless help us qualify the thesis of the emergence of a global culture based on 'fast consumerism'. New nationalisms, new ethno-cultural movements, new bigotry, new identity politics may well be more than temporary epiphenomena of globalisation. They could well be the result of a quest for new projects, new certainties to compensate for the loss of the landmarks of the cold war era. They also question the possibility of using the word culture in the singular, even if it is a global culture. Is not diversity a fundamental characteristic of any human society?

Furthermore, it is often claimed that the globalisation of the capitalist economy would lead to a globalisation of the principles of individualism, individual freedom and human rights and, consequently, would facilitate the generalisation and strengthening of a democratic global polity replacing obsolete nation states. Again, this hypothesis seems shaky in the face of recent worldwide political developments. If the rhetoric of human rights and democracy is widespread, it is not universally accepted. In some parts of the world, it is seen as a weapon of Western neoimperialism. When we turn to the practice of democracy, problems are more obvious, even in Western societies. Bill Clinton was re-elected by fewer than 25 per cent of eligible US citizens, and many crucial decisions for the future of the European Union are taken by non-elected civil servants and politicians. These are only two examples of the limitations of democracy in supposedly solid democracies. In other parts of the world where democracy is younger, things are often even worse. The questions then arise of: How to improve the functioning of democracy in the Western World? Is the globalisation of the capitalist economy going to promote democracy or, on the contrary, increase its problems?

As to the nation state, its powers have certainly been eroded either by transnational regional integration processes like, for example, the European Union or by sub-nationalisms and regionalisms. Even though the role of the nation state is changing and it is by no means the only locus of political regulation in the post-cold war era, it still has a role to play in current political life to the extent that many people still identify with their nation state. Nationalism and its correlate, the nation state, are still powerful myths, despite the fact that all human societies can be said to be multicultural and, I would also add, multi-ethnic. *De facto* diversity of values, religions, behaviour and material cultures is the norm, despite the emergence of powerful tendencies towards homogenisation of mass culture. In reality, no state coincides perfectly with a single nation. Each state produces its own national identity, but minority groups, either national minorities or ethnic groups, can nevertheless have different ethnicities and identities beyond the dominant one and try to assert their specificity within any given nation state.

In his famous latest book, the Canadian political philosopher Will Kymlicka (1995a) distinguishes two major types of multicultural societies, namely 'multination' states and 'polyethnic' states. In the former, cultural diversity arises from the incorporation of previously self-governing cultural units into a larger state. This newly formed state therefore hosts a variable number of national minorities. In 'polyethnic' states, cultural diversity is mainly the result of large-scale migration which leads to the formation of ethnic groups. This distinction is certainly useful to describe diversity both in Belgium and in Britain.

There are huge differences between the historical processes of national incorporation and migration in Britain and Belgium. Belgium is much smaller in size and in population. It is a small continental country at the core of Europe with direct borders with the main European powers of France and Germany. Its national unity has always been problematic (Dieckhoff 1996) and its European commitment has been taken for granted from the outset of the European integration process. Despite the Channel tunnel, Britain remains a group of islands that is somewhat proud of its insularity, though the latter does seem to be decreasing. Its European commitment has always been problematic, whereas its national unity was not considered to be as problematic as in Belgium, despite the coexistence of four nations in the United Kingdom (Kearney 1991). Northern Ireland is obviously a specific case and cannot easily be compared with the Belgian situation. Another difference is linguistic. Despite the survival of minority languages like Welsh, or some Scottish dialects, linguistic unity is a reality in Britain. Even the Scottish nationalists campaign in English. The situation is clearly different in Belgium. Each national group speaks its own language, the only bilingual area being the federal capital city, Brussels. As for recognition of the national groups, Belgium is now a federal state made of communities and regions each enjoying a detailed set of powers. Nevertheless, the idea of having different currencies or different legal systems in the country, as with Scotland, would be seen as a divisive factor. On the contrary, in Britain federalisation is often resisted, whereas national autonomy is becoming increasingly important within the unitary United Kingdom framework, as recent referenda on partial devolution in Scotland and Wales suggest. As for migration patterns, there are two main differences between Britain and Belgium. Both societies became immigration countries but adopted different migration mechanisms. Britain gave preference to migration first from Ireland and then from the colonies and former colonies. Therefore, a huge majority of immigrants in Britain were British subjects, even though they were socially seen as racially different. On paper, they had the rights of full citizens, but in reality they faced strong discrimination. Belgium, however, decided not to import a labour force from the colonies but gave preference to the temporary immigration of foreign workers from southern Europe and North Africa. Until recently, most migrants in Belgium were not citizens and, consequently, were deprived of the main political rights.

Nevertheless, beyond these differences both Britain and Belgium are today both 'multination' and 'polyethnic' states. The English, Welsh, Scots and Northern Irish in the case of Britain, the Flemings, Walloons and 'Germanophones' in Belgium constitute the main national groups. As far as ethnic immigrant groups are concerned, Asians and West Indians are the most important groups in the United Kingdom, while Italians, Moroccans and Turks are the most numerous groups in Belgium.

There are other common features between Britain and Belgium. Both countries were important colonial powers even though, in absolute terms, the Belgian colonies did not compare with the size and wealth of the former British Empire. Both countries had to face a severe economic decline after the Second World War and decolonisation, after having been for a long time among the wealthiest societies in the world. They have not yet fully recovered. Both countries are also kingdoms, even though the role of the crown is far from being the same in Belgium and Britain. Furthermore, there is a strong tradition of working class mobilisation and protest in both societies.

The British and Belgian examples highlight that the traditional models of the nation inherited from last century do not match the actual composition of the population and its diversity. The idea of the nation state, which developed through the nineteenth and twentieth century and which was based on the assumption that each nation should have its own state, was above all a project of society and provided a myth on the basis of which this project should have concretised. With the (re)assertion of subnational and ethnic immigrant identities, it has become partially obsolete, even though it can still be very strong as a mobilising principle. As a matter of fact, nationalistic political projects seem sometimes to develop while we are simultaneously witnessing a consolidation of *de facto* cultural diversity. Obviously, this creates a tension in which the debate on multiculturalism has emerged. In Belgium, like in Britain, the issues of 'national minorities' and 'ethnic immigrant groups' have traditionally not been merged. In Belgium, the usage of the expression 'multiculturalism' is less widespread than it is in Britain. The concept of the integration of migrants has for a long time been preferred, despite the many problems it poses (Martiniello 1992). In Britain, the US influence seems more obvious and this explains partly why the expression multiculturalism has been discussed earlier than in Belgium. In any case, the different wordings refer to the same fundamental issues: how to deal with the increase of ethno-cultural diversity stemming from migration? Should we accommodate cultural diversity? To what extent? How is it reshaping the whole society and its identity?

In this context, multiculturalism has recently been discussed as a project of the post-national society, or as an alternative to the nation state model. It is seen as an ideology, as a politically correct version of racism, as a set of state policies aimed at fighting past and present discrimination against ethnic minorities, as a resource for the social mobility of the ethnic minorities' leaders, as forms of cultural expression and as forms of political mobilisation aimed at taking into account the cultural and identificational diversity of modern states. For its advocates, multiculturalism provides the only means of avoiding the ethnic and ethno-cultural fragmentation of modern states by allowing each group living within the borders of a state some recognition within a broader and shared set of political institutions. On the contrary, some challengers argue that multiculturalism will increase the 'Balkanisation' of the society and lead to some sort of generalisation of apartheid. Other challengers argue that multiculturalism is just a smoke screen used not to address efficiently the main problems in our societies, namely socio-economic inequality, if not to reproduce this inequality (Ålund and Schierup 1991). In any case, multiculturalism is thus much more than the simple statement that we are living in culturally diverse societies as shown by the demographic indicators.

The aim of this book is to discuss some of the main issues related to multiculturalism in a critical and comparative manner. It does not advocate a single theoretical stand. Rather, it recognises the necessity to cross the artificial borders between academic disciplines, or at least to promote a dialogue between them, especially on the topic of this volume, which needs a joint effort of all disciplines in order to improve our knowledge. The authors come from various disciplines such as sociology, anthropology, political science and linguistics. They were not given theoretical guidelines to respect but were simply asked to address freely one of the four issues that form the four parts of the present volume.

In the first part, the variety of views on multiculturalism and multicultural societies are discussed in general terms. In Chapter 1, John Rex presents a broad descriptive overview of Belgium and Britain, which he sees as doubly multicultural: a first dimension of multiculturalism derives from the existence of national minorities in the two states, a second from the immigration experience that characterised both countries during the last century and even earlier. In Chapter 2, Steven Vertovec exposes the variety of meanings that the word multiculturalism can take for different social and political actors. In his view, even though this plurality of meanings can often lead to some misunderstandings, the concept can remain useful provided adequate caution is exercised. After these two chapters, which frame the concept of multiculturalism – at least in some of its meanings – in a positive way, the last two chapters of this first part essentially present two critiques of multiculturalism. In his contribution based partly on theoretical insights and partly on an empirical study of 'multicultural' education in Belgium, Eugeen Roosens advocates the use of the concept of multi-ethnicity instead of multiculturalism to characterise the Belgian interaction or non-interaction between non-migrant and migrant. He does so within a somewhat primordialist and essentialist approach to ethnicity. This is precisely the core of Nira Yuval-Davis's criticism of multiculturalism in Chapter 4. In her view, multiculturalist discourse and ideology can lead to the essentialisation not only of ethnic groups but also of gender groups. The consequence of all this is that multiculturalism can reinforce the dominated position of women as well as of ethnic minorities in society.

The second part of the volume examines state action in the field of multiculturalism and the integration of migrants and ethnic minorities. In his contribution on integration politics in Belgium (Chapter 5), Jan Blommaert goes beyond an analysis of integration policies to explore the political rhetoric and discourses on integration and multiculturalism. He uncovers all the ambiguities of this notion in Belgian politics. In Chapter 6, Malcolm Cross presents a critical view of British anti-discrimination policies and shows how in the British case, ethnic differentiation is the result of the absence of a truly pluralist conception of society.

The third part of the book deals with the political mobilisation, participation and representation of ethnic minorities in formal politics. Marco Martiniello examines these issues in the case of Belgium where they are just emerging (Chapter 7). Until very recently, ethnic minorities were non-existent in formal politics, but the situation is changing with the emergence of some ethnic origin politicians, especially in Brussels. In Chapter 8, Shamit Saggar shows how the representation of ethnic minorities is linked to parties' strategies to maintain their power. He also addresses the existence of a specific minority agenda in politics, which is certainly a major issue for any account of multiculturalism.

The subject of religious diversity is examined in the last part of the book. Albert Bastenier analyses the importance of religion for the formation of an ethnic awareness among Moroccan immigrants and their descent by using qualitative empirical data collected in Brussels. By focusing on South-Asian religions, Steven Vertovec presents a critical account of how religious diversity has been accommodated in Britain.

Some important issues usually associated with multiculturalism, such as education and the school curriculum, political correctness or the arts could not be covered. The present volume nonetheless presents some of the complex problems encountered by two European states in their move from a limited multiculturalism related to their multinational character to a more general multiculturalism connected with the definitive settlement of migrants on their soil mainly after the Second World War. Though no contributor states that diversity resulting from migration, whether cultural or in terms of identities, is to be dealt with in the same manner as diversity linked to the multinational character of the two societies, they all make the case that diversity is to a certain extent unavoidable and that it is not necessarily incompatible with democratic principles and citizenship.

Part I

Conflicting views on multiculturalism and the multicultural society

Multiculturalism and political integration in Europe

John Rex

The United Kingdom and Belgium are both multinational states that have been faced since the 1950s with new immigration from geographically and culturally distant territories. The aim of this chapter is to draw a comparison between the two countries in the light of a wider consideration of the problem of multiculturalism and political integration.

Multinational states

The United Kingdom

The United Kingdom is in fact less than completely united. It is governed centrally from Westminster in London, England, but Wales, Scotland and Ireland have relative degrees of autonomy from this centre.

(a) Wales

Wales is the least independent of these territories. It has a nationalist political party, Plaid Cymru, which in principle aspires to independence but succeeds in gaining the election of only a handful of Members of Parliament. In practice, it is distinguished by the possession of a separate language spoken by a minority of the population, among its Christian population by the predominance of Non-Conformist (Methodist, Baptist and Presbyterian) churches, by the perpetuation of a somewhat distinct culture reflected in the artistic festival, the eisteddfod, as well as in certain sports such as rugby union football. It is also part of the economic periphery of the United Kingdom and a large part of its population have migrated to England in search of work. In these circumstances, the most contentious issues have concerned the demand of nationalists for some acknowledgement of the Welsh language in education and in the public services as well as in place and street names.

There is no separate Welsh parliament and most government departments are simply part of overall United Kingdom administration. The British Labour Party gains most Welsh seats in the British Parliament and in local councils, reflecting the fact that class affiliation is more important for Welsh workers than nationalism, but Welsh Labour MPs and Plaid Cymru unite in demanding the diversion of investment to Wales, and even the until recently ruling Conservative Party has found it necessary to promote this kind of investment. Another form of protest against their peripheral economic status lies in objection and resistance to the purchase or building of holiday cottages for the English.

Apart from these sources of possible political tension, Welsh cultural achievements remain distinctive and enjoy a certain prestige throughout the United Kingdom. Choral singing reaches a high level and this, together with the other arts, is reflected in the annual competition, the eisteddfod, which includes a ceremony of the chairing of a poet as the 'bard' (a purely cultural and symbolic role), rugby union football, a game which in England is largely played by the upper and middle classes, is played by all classes in Wales, reducing soccer to a minor role. National emotions are expressed perhaps more than anywhere else in the moving singing of the national song or anthem, *Land of our Fathers*, when the Welsh rugby team plays at Cardiff Arms Park. Such symbolic cultural expressions, whether in the arts or sport, do not, however, have any great political significance, and, despite their distinct political and cultural history and their now peripheral economic position, the Welsh do not have a strong nationalist movement, and Wales is, and is likely to remain, part of the United Kingdom. This is expressed in terms of royal symbolism in the fact that the senior son of the monarch is given the title of Prince of Wales and is enthroned in a ceremony in the ancient Welsh town of Caernavon.

(b) Scotland

The Scottish nation shares some of the characteristics of the Welsh, but nationalism, the demand for autonomy and cultural distinctiveness from the English are far stronger.

In terms of the symbolism of the monarchy, the union of Scotland and England is strong, but the monarch of the United Kingdom has to be monarch of both England and Scotland. He or she is received in Edinburgh by a hereditary Scottish duke and is expected to change his or her religion in Scotland where the established religion is Presbyterianism rather than Anglicanism. In this way, an effective symbolic balance is achieved.

Like Wales, Scotland has a relatively peripheral economic status and many Scotsmen have migrated to England or to the Old (White) Commonwealth. The largest political party is the British Labour Party, which holds most of the Scottish seats in the Westminster Parliament.

There is, nonetheless, a Scottish National Party, which is much stronger than Plaid Cymru in Wales and which demands independence much more clearly than does Plaid Cymru. This party also fights strongly for economic investment in Scotland, together with the Labour Party, but its position has been greatly strengthened by the fact that the new British oil industry is concentrated in the seas about Scotland.

Scotland's legal system is distinct from that of England and many of the social service departments are controlled in Scotland by a separate Scottish Office. The educational system is almost completely distinct from that in England. The ideal of a relatively powerful Scottish parliament enjoying the power of taxation is now supported not only by the Scottish Nationalists but by the Labour and Liberal Parties. This is opposed by the British Conservatives who insist upon the political union and on the value of a single economy.

The Scots clearly have a distinct culture, with a distinct form of Christian religion; they have their own distinctive dialect and accent when talking English and a relatively small minority seeks to perpetuate Gaelic as a folk language. On formal occasions they wear a distinctive male dress, the kilt, and the tartan patterns of the ancient clans are widely worn. In terms of cultural achievements, they have their own artists, writers and poets, and the work of the poet Robbie Burns is celebrated in all classes at the annual Burns 'nicht' (night). Whiskey is a national drink as well as being the most famous of Scotland's exports. So far as sport is concerned, the Scots do not play cricket in the English County Championship and it is largely the upper and middle classes who play and support rugby union. The most popular national game is soccer, there is an entirely separate Scottish Football League, and Scotland competes separately from England in international competitions. In all of these ways one may say that Scotland has a 'distinct society' and culture, and though this distinctiveness is not necessarily political, it is more separated from English society and culture than is Wales and it does have stronger political overtones.

Nationalism has, however, also to contend with internal divisions. There is a clear division between the industrial South and the rural culture of the Highlands; there are important class divisions between the industrial proletariat and bourgeois and aristocratic elements in the population; there is a surviving minority Roman Catholic tradition going back to before the time of the Union with England, reinforced by the arrival of Irish immigrants; finally, even soccer support is divided between the Catholic Celtic football club and Rangers, a team deliberately created to assert Protestantism against the Catholics. All these factors tell against a united Scottish nationalism.

Undoubtedly, however, Scottish nationalism is based on a greater distinctiveness and a greater militancy than is the case with nationalism in Wales, even though there are factors such as outward migration to England and the role of the Labour Party that bind England and Scotland together. At the same time, while this nationalism is politically expressed, it has hardly been expressed in a violent form.

(c) Northern Ireland

The main point to be noticed about Northern Ireland is that it was created only following the attainment of independence by the Republic of Ireland in 1921. Six counties in the island of Ireland were separated off from the new independent state and remained part of the United Kingdom. Inevitably the politics of Northern Ireland came to rest upon the opposition of two types of 'Unionism'. The majority in the six counties wished at all costs to maintain the union with England as part of the United Kingdom, but a large minority of about one-third of the population demanded reunification with the South.

There are some pro-British Unionists in Ireland who would claim that their political and religious history is an ancient one, but this point cannot be pressed too far. The majority among them are the descendants of settlers from Scotland and England, who were implanted in Ireland and given land in order to maintain the Union. The problems of Northern Ireland have to be seen, in part at least, therefore, as those of a colonialist and settler society (even though the descendants of these settlers may have lived in Ireland for several centuries).

The cultural divisions of Northern Ireland reflect this political history and are reinforced by it. The religions of the various parties to the national conflict are different and they come, indeed, to be called, not simply Unionists, who want union with Britain, and United Ireland Nationalists, but Protestants and Catholics. Most Protestants are Presbyterians, but there is also a Church of Ireland associated with the Anglican Church in England. The Presbyterians defend the economic interest of their members in Ireland and do so by insisting on the Union with Britain, while the very *raison d'être* of the Church of Ireland is that Union itself. Such politically based religions then become markers of distinctiveness and political loyalties and also provide a framework for the development of residential neighbourhoods and largely separate schools and other social services.

Ireland is a peripheral economic entity in the British isles (including the Republic of Ireland) and Northern Ireland is a peripheral area in the United Kingdom. Emigrants from both territories have migrated to England, Scotland, the old Commonwealth and the United States in search of work. Nonetheless, unlike Scotland, Northern Ireland has not reproduced the English class based division between Conservative and Labour. Such divisions are subordinated to the nationalist and unionist agendas, even if Unionists support the Conservatives in the British Parliament and the Social Democratic Party is allied with Labour.

The Social Democratic Party represents the interests of the Catholic nationalist minority in the North and has sought to do so by peaceful means, by voting in Parliament, or in street demonstrations. In 1968 they consciously adopted the civil rights agenda of Martin Luther King in the United States. Almost immediately, however, their movement was taken over by those for whom nationalism was more important than civil rights, and the Social Democratic Party itself had to adopt a nationalist agenda, working for some kind of united Ireland by peaceful means. They were, however, challenged in the nationalist Catholic community by those prepared to use more militant and violent means.

Traditionally, the politically and religiously organised communities celebrate their history and their conflict with each other by street demonstrations. For the Protestants, a central event is the Apprentice Boys' March in Derry/Londonderry celebrating the victory of William of Orange in the late seventeenth century and many Protestants are members of so-called Orange orders who organise their own marches and festivals. The Presbyterian churches are intimately connected with these orders and are divided only between the more orthodox Presbyterians and the Free Presbyterian Church led by Reverend Ian Paisley, which is openly militant politically and hostile to Catholicism and nationalism.

Militant nationalists and Catholics who do not support the scrupulously peaceful methods of the Social Democrats are organised in a political party, Sinn Fein, which contests elections and gains about 15 to 20 per cent of the vote, and in the Provisional Irish Republican Army (IRA), which resorts to armed struggle and terrorism. The IRA has reduced Northern Ireland to a state of low civil war since 1968 and, even though there are now peace talks in progress, the possibility of continued armed conflict has been there, and, not surprisingly, a cease-fire was called off by the IRA in February 1996 and a highly successful bombing attack was made on the City of London. It might be wrong, however, to suggest that the IRA simply initiated a rebellion *ab initio*. They faced a situation in which Catholics and Nationalists were attacked by Unionists and in which some of the Unionist groups created their own paramilitary organisations. They also found themselves fighting against the police and the British army, even though both of these claimed only to be enforcing the peace.

There is no point in speculating here on the possibility of a negotiated solution to Northern Ireland's problems. What does concern us is the kind of society the political conflict presently creates.

Negatively, there is little possibility of maintaining the Union in the way it is maintained *vis-à-vis* Scotland. The Royal Family and senior members of the British government can only visit Northern Ireland under conditions of maximum security. Nor can there be an effective autonomous assembly. In the past, such an assembly was dominated by the Unionist/Protestant majority and worked in its interests. The most that can be hoped for is the sort of power sharing assembly in which the minority share in the actual processes of government. But this, too, has been tried and failed. Clearly, what has to be negotiated is a peace and a society in which leaders who have fought each other even by violent means develop a shared agenda for the future of Ireland. The odds at the moment are much against this.

The paramilitaries still hold their arms and, though their party allies have only a small minority vote, when there is violence, many who would not themselves support such violence would still not betray the terrorists to the police and would provide safe houses for them, whether because of political sympathy or fear of intimidation.

Interestingly, on the cultural level, there are factors which unite not merely the Northern Irish communities but Northern Ireland and the Republic. Both the Catholic and the Anglican Churches are organised on an all Ireland basis and the archbishops of both churches have their cathedrals in Armagh in Northern Ireland. In sport, the Irish rugby union team represents both the Republic and Northern Ireland. There are also many other ways in which an all-Irish culture is expressed. Such a shared symbolic culture, however, is not likely of itself to have political consequences any more than are cross confessional groups of youth among Christians.

Other multinational states

Before turning to the comparison with Belgium, it will be useful to look at a number of cases in which multinationalism is evident since some of these may be more relevant to the Belgian case than the United Kingdom.

The first of these is Spain, where one encounters both Catalan and

Basque nationalism. The Catalan case is in some ways similar to that of the Welsh or the Scots. The Catalan nationalist parties were in a pragmatic alliance with the socialist government in Madrid and negotiated with it about aspects of cultural and administrative autonomy. They also have to recognise that they must speak not merely for native Catalans but for inward migrants from other parts of Spain whom they see as counting as Catalans by virtue of residence. The Basque case is more reminiscent of Ireland. Basque nationalists divide on the degree of autonomy/independence they seek and in their attitude to the violent ETA movement. There are strong parallels between ETA and the IRA. In both cases there are many issues short of political independence for which nationalists may fight. They include especially issues of language, education and administrative autonomy.

The other most relevant case is not European. It is that of Canada and the present province of Quebec. Canada, unlike the United Kingdom and like Belgium, claims to have two founding nations and, though one conquered the other, it has sought to create a bilingual and bicultural as well as a federal nation. Some of the Quebecois parties have aimed at political independence for what is now the province of Quebec and have appropriated the case of the Francophones across Canada and put it to the service of Quebecois nationalism. The demand for complete independence by the *Parti quebecois* falls only just short of obtaining an electoral majority in Quebec and is strong enough to be able to negotiate with a federal government, itself enjoying some support in Quebec. Thus far, the Quebecois have not been in a position to make a unilateral declaration of independence, but it is possible that, if they had a clear electoral mandate for independence, some of their leaders would adopt this course. If independence were taken in this way, the problem which would arise would be whether Quebec would be able to achieve economic autarchy or renegotiate its economic links with Canada and the wider world. The Canadian government has gone far in recognising Quebec as a 'distinct society', but would not be willing voluntarily to concede independence.

For the moment, both Canada and Quebec have to work out what kinds of societies and nations they are. Canada, of course, recognises the relative autonomy including powers of taxation of the various provinces and, crosscutting this, it concedes that all cultural and national groups should preserve their own linguistic and cultural heritage within a bilingual society. Quebec, on the other hand, has the problem of relating its Anglophone minority and other non-French speaking immigrants to a Francophone society. Even within the present situation, the Quebec government has sought radical solutions to these problems and has aimed to produce a distinct culture and a Francophone state. For the moment therefore, the Canadian state and, within it the state of Quebec, are in a state of tension and it cannot be said with certainty whether the federal state will remain.

Switzerland is the other country with two or three national and linguistic groups living together under a single government. It has dealt with this by a radical form of decentralisation in which relatively linguistically distinct regions and cantons are accorded a great deal of autonomy and there is no sign of the Swiss state breaking up.

Finally, in this section we should note that most other West European states have some problems of multinationalism and internal nationalist movements (for example the Corsicans, Bretons and Basques in France) but have been able to contain these within modern national economies and within a common citizenship. It also should be noticed that regional divisions sometimes tend to take on a significance as forms of near nationalism, as in Italy, where some political parties manipulate the southern regions to their own advantage, while the Northern League seeks to further the interests of the north against these tendencies.

Belgian multinationalism

Belgium is a country like Canada that has two founding nations, although they are more equal in power than the French and the English are in Canada. It is thus possible to speak of the two nations of Wallonia and Flanders, regionally located and speaking predominantly French and Flemish. In principle, the country is bilingual and its cities have both French and Flemish names. In practice, however, many Belgians are not bilingual and few Walloons are prepared to call Liège, Luik, and few Flemish call Antwerp, Anvers.

There are, of course, important crosscutting divisions which divide people in Wallonia and Flanders and which unite some Walloons with some Flemish. The country as a whole includes both Catholics and Protestants, and capitalist entrepreneurs and employees. These crosscutting conflicts act as a brake on the purely national conflict and the central Belgian government is bound to be based upon some kind of coalition. Moreover, in a modern industrial economy Walloons and Flemings may well find themselves having to enter into economic relations with one another. Though there may be a degree of economic autarchy in the two regions, there therefore has to be some overall centralised direction of the economy.

All that has been said above refers to Wallonia and Flanders outside the Brussels area. Brussels, however, is neither Walloon nor Flemish, neither French nor Flemish speaking, even though there may be a kind of French cultural and linguistic ascendancy, reinforced by the fact that the international civil servants in Brussels are more likely to speak French and English than Dutch or Flemish and this may well produce resentment and resistance on the part of the Flemish. Nevertheless, there can be no question of autonomous regions in Brussels. It has to be bilingual and it has to be the seat of a modern economy and polity.

There is no exact parallel to the position of Brussels in the other countries we have discussed. What it means is that, however much autonomy and economic autarchy there may be in the separate regions, there is also at the centre a shared set of institutions. Moreover, if Belgium were to break into two countries, there would have to be a separate solution for Brussels.

The one absolutely unique feature of the Brussels situation is that it is not merely the capital of Belgium but the effective administrative capital of Europe. This raises the question of the relation of Wallonia, Flanders and, indeed, Brussels itself, to Europe. So far as Wallonia and Flanders are concerned it may well appear that separate participation in Europe as regions rather than indirectly as parts of Belgium might appeal to Walloon and Flemish nationalists as it does to some Scottish, Irish or Basque nationalists. What would lose its appeal in Europe would be a movement in Wallonia for union with France or in Flanders for union with the Netherlands. This might give some cultural satisfaction, but the political and economic cost would be unpredictable.

So far as Brussels is concerned, it is conceivable that if a European federal state came into being, and if Wallonia and Flanders separated, Brussels might simply become a capital region like Washington DC or Canberra. In the European case, such a capital region would need to be not merely bilingual and bicultural but multilingual and multicultural.[1]

Perhaps all that has been said above is based upon a doomsday scenario. It is quite possible, however, that Belgium will survive. If it does, it will have to work out some kind of system of political, economic and cultural autonomy for its separate national regions as well as a bilingual culture to support shared institutions in Brussels.

New immigration in multinational states

Discourse about multiculturalism in Belgium almost always focuses primarily on the question of multinationalism rather than on the position of recent immigrants. In Britain, the multinational question is usually referred to as a constitutional question, while the term multiculturalism refers to the existence of separate cultures among immigrants from relatively geographically dispersed regions with sharply different cultures from the British. In both cases, however, new immigrants with newly different and distant cultures and forms of organisation do pose a problem. We should now consider this problem and the way it has to be dealt with in two multinational societies.

Immigrant minority cultures in the United Kingdom

In Britain two kinds of immigrants receive little political attention. These include, first, those such as Americans and Japanese who work temporarily or permanently in Britain on behalf of their nationally-based companies. They are positively welcome because their presence is a sign that inward investment is taking place. Second, there are immigrants from other West European countries. They are not much discussed because the problems they face and present are small compared with those of coloured immigrants and those from markedly different cultural, linguistic and religious backgrounds. How to refer to these groups is a matter of etiquette and political correctness. Commonly, in England they are all referred to as black, although there is a range of skin colours to be found among them, which is why the politically incorrect term 'coloured' is preferred here. Another useful term widely used in Canada is 'visible minorities'.

Clearly, there is a problem in all European countries of the rights of these coloured culturally distant visible minorities. They seem to become natural targets for attack either because of xenophobia or because they serve as the easiest scapegoats in time of trouble. In Britain they first became singled out under some euphemistic guise such as 'New Commonwealth' immigrants for special measures of immigration control. But, severe though that control became, the original immigration from the Caribbean, the Indian subcontinent and East Africa, which occurred in the 1950s and 1960s, meant that Britain had minority populations of this descent and had to develop appropriate policies towards them. Moreover, if they were not to become permanent second-class citizens, measures had to be taken to ensure that they had the equality of opportunity that belonged to citizens. It should be noted that in the British situation these coloured immigrants *were* citizens on arrival. They were not, like the Turks in Germany and many other immigrants elsewhere, merely *guestworkers*. Of these citizens, therefore, a leading spokesman on behalf of the Labour government in 1966 said, 'Without immigration control, integration is impossible, but immigration control without integration is morally indefensible' (morally indefensible, that is, in a society in which all citizens were held to be equal) (Rex and Tomlinson 1979).

The model the British chose for their policies was derived from a study of US institutions set up to achieve equality for black Americans. Such institutions were established through a series of Race Relations Acts passed in 1965, 1968 and, finally, in 1976. Surprisingly, however, they were applied not merely to the Afro-Caribbean people, whose history and experience paralleled that of black Americans migrating to the north from the Deep South, but also to Asians whom Americans saw as a quite distinct group in the United States.

In any case, elaborate institutions were set up at government and local government level to prevent direct and indirect discrimination on grounds of race or ethnic group membership, and these institutions are without parallel in any other European country. This is not to say that racial discrimination no longer exists. It clearly does and there are also very high levels of anti-black and anti-Asian violence committed by white people in Britain, but at least a beginning has been made to ensure equality for this class of immigrant citizens.

By the end of the 1960s, however, it became apparent that there were two problems which had to be dealt with. One was the question of equal treatment; the other was that of allowing cultural diversity. The first was the more important question so far as Afro-Caribbean immigrants were concerned, because, on a cultural level, they were actually quite close to the British, speaking English and practising Christian religions, albeit in creolised forms. The Asian immigrants on the other hand, while they also suffered discrimination and had to fight for equality, had the additional problem that they spoke different languages, adhered to one of the non-Christian world religions, and had their own family practices and other customs.

The most usual response to cultural diversity in Europe, but most deliberately in France, was to insist on the cultural assimilation of immigrants. They were expected to abandon their old ways and become culturally like their hosts. This was the initial response in Britain when a body called the Commonwealth Immigrants Advisory Service, speaking of education, said that immigrants should not expect that their cultures would be perpetuated in the educational system. This, however, was not the general policy ideal eventually promulgated by the Home Secretary, Roy Jenkins, in 1968, when he defined integration as 'not a flattening process of uniformity, but cultural diversity coupled with equal opportunity in an atmosphere of mutual tolerance' (Rex and Tomlinson 1979). Three goals were set here: (1) equality of opportunity, which the institutions set up to deal with racial discrimination would achieve; (2) the acceptance of cultural diversity; and (3) the education of host people as well as immigrants in cultural tolerance.

Dealing with the first two of these, I suggested that it implied two coexisting value systems or cultures (Rex 1986, 1996). The first, which I called the shared political culture of the public domain, would be unquestionable and would rest upon the idea of equality of opportunity in economic and political matters. The second was the existence in a more private communal domain of separate languages, separate religions and separate family practices.

This attempt to explicate the notion of a democratic multicultural society, however, raised many difficulties of which three perhaps deserve special mention. First, it is not the case that the complex set of institutions of the host society constituted simply one among many cultures. They did set the terms of immigrant settlement and any immigrant would have to learn to live within them for at least part of his/her life, even though they should all be expected to conform to the ideal of allowing equality of opportunity. One aspect of this was that it was hard to see why special multicultural institutions should be set up alongside those of the welfare-state through which conflicting class interests were reconciled. Second, it was clear that the educational system straddled both the private and the public sphere. It was concerned with primary moral socialisation, but it was also concerned with preparing pupils for participation on equal terms in a highly competitive world. There was a question therefore of whether special multicultural classes might actually stand in the way of the achievement of equality. Third, there was the question of what actually constituted the culture of an immigrant minority group. This I was frequently told was not some kind of fixed essence presided over by elderly male leaders and that we therefore had to allow for diverse responses, for change, and for some degree of defection from these minority cultures. It was therefore necessary in speaking of private communal cultures to give due recognition to all these factors. A sensitive multicultural policy therefore had to be based upon a complex sociological account of possible forms of ethnic mobilisation (Rex 1996).

The third element in the Jenkins formula was that of mutual tolerance. Another way of putting this is that when immigration occurs in a democracy, democratic values have to be reinforced to counter any tendency towards xenophobia. This is what antiracist movements and antiracist policies in Britain have sought to achieve. Interestingly, the major report on multicultural education in Britain (the Swann Report) (Department of Education and Science 1985) directed its main attention to the education of the white majority child to learn to tolerate cultural differences rather than stigmatising them.

Those who speak loosely of multiculturalism in Britain do not necessarily refer to the sort of ideal situation I have described. Some simply accept diversity of culture as inevitable but regard it as a set of markers of inequality and hierarchy (Honeyford 1988). On the other hand, there are those who believe that a truly multicultural society has to be one in which existing national culture is abandoned or replaced by some kind of cultural hotchpotch or amalgam. Between these two possibilities there is, I think, a much more moderate view of multiculturalism, which to some extent informs policy and which most immigrant minority members would accept. This is that, for several generations at least, minority cultures, albeit in a complex form, have value for three reasons: (1) they provide a kind of psychological home and a form of emotional support which prevents migrants living in a state of anomie; (2) they provide the organisational forms through which minorities are enabled to fight collectively for their rights; and (3) they may include some values that have objective validity and might serve to enrich the culture of societies of settlement.

All of the above refers to political arguments about multiculturalism in Britain. They do not suggest a cut and dried model, but they do show that, in dealing with immigrants, Britain has placed the question of multiculturalism on the political agenda alongside of, though separate from, the problems of the constitution of the multinational state.

Immigrant minority cultures in Belgium

Perhaps the first thing to be noted about Belgium is that it has been highly successful in assimilating other European immigrants including manual workers. In particular, when it had a labour gap it filled it with Italians especially in the coal mines and other heavy industries. The children of these immigrants were easily assimilated, especially in Wallonia where they learned French and some of them were socially mobile. They were also assimilated in Flanders and in Brussels. Belgium did not apparently have an 'Italian problem'.

Unlike Britain, Belgium did not draw on its former colonies for immigrants. There are very few immigrants from Zaire. When it did have to look beyond Europe it turned to Francophone North Africa, particularly Morocco. These immigrants settled especially in Brussels. There they enjoyed the advantage of having had some familiarity with French, but the disadvantage of coming from poor backgrounds and having alien cultures and the alien religion of Islam.

Preoccupied as it was with the multinational problem and having previously only had to deal with European immigrants who were culturally close, like the Italians, the governments of Belgium, Wallonia, Brussels and Flanders had no clear policies towards these immigrants. In both the Francophone community and the Flemish community, moreover, they were seen as a potentially dangerous underclass and became an object for xenophobia. In the Flemish community, moreover, past experience of Francophone domination produced a particularly strong nationalist and xenophobic response to these immigrants. The success of Vlaams Blok standing on an anti-immigrant platform put anti-immigrant racism firmly on the political agenda. If part of the response in the mainstream was to consider the development of adequate policies to promote equality, multiculturalism and multicultural tolerance, there were also those who sought to head off the challenge of the Vlaams Blok by partially adopting its attitudes and policies. An anti-immigrant theme and anti-immigrant political representation were also evident in the politics of Wallonia.

It remains to be seen whether Belgium will develop adequate policies in relation to its new immigrants. Its preoccupation with its multinational problem may well prevent this. Yet, experience is being gathered by trades unionists, social workers and teachers of the real problems immigrants face and it is this experience that will provide the basis for an anti-racist movement and for a multicultural policy along the lines for which some have been arguing in Britain. But any movement for multiculturalism and antiracism will have to contend with what is at present a rising tide of racism and xenophobia directed towards immigrants. This is a shared problem across Europe and it is to be hoped that democratic and antiracist social scientists will play a role in proposing creative solutions for the integration of immigrants and their descendants into European national societies.

Note

1. As to the German speaking part of Belgium, in principle, the same options would be open to it as to Wallonia and Flanders, namely retaining a federal relationship with one or both of these, seeking regional independence, or becoming a German *Land*.

Multi-multiculturalisms

Steven Vertovec

The terms 'multicultural' and 'multiculturalism' are ubiquitous today. Throughout the world, they are read or heard in parliamentary debates and political party manifestos, in the statements of ethnic group leaders, in local government strategies and budgets, in educational and social scientific publications, in popular media and in commercial marketing. Further, within the past ten years, specialists in an increasingly broad range of professions have felt the need to rethink their field with reference to these terms and the myriad issues that accompany them. This is exemplified by the proliferation of the terms in book titles. A bibliographic search reveals several dozen recent books about multicultural education, with an increasing amount on multiculturalism and libraries, the media and general resources (see, for instance, the 546-page guide by Boyd 1995). There are also many new 'multicultural readers' in literature, feminism and history. Beyond these fields, the following titles are provided to emphasise how far the terms have travelled into diverse realms:

- *Counselling and psychotherapy: a multicultural perspective* (Ivey and Ivey 1993)
- *Pastoral care: an antiracist/multicultural perspective* (Duncan 1988)
- *Dance: a multicultural perspective* (Study of Dance Conference 1986)
- *Textile arts: multicultural traditions* (Singer and Spyraw 1989)
- *Voices of wisdom: a multicultural philosophy reader* (Kessler 1992)
- *Better science: working for a multicultural society* (Ditchfield 1987)
- *Medical practice in a multicultural society* (Fuller and Toon 1988)

- *Child health in a multicultural society* (Black 1989)
- *Multicultural health care and rehabilitation of older people* (Squires 1991)
- *Unresolved grief: a practical, multicultural approach for health professionals* (Gunzburg 1993)
- *Marginality: the key to multicultural theology* (Lee 1995)
- *Multicultural mathematics* (Nelson et al. 1993)
- *Multicultural pharmaceutical education* (Bleidt 1993)
- *Managing substance abuse in a multicultural society* (Gordon 1994)
- *Communication disorders in multicultural populations* (Battle 1993)
- *Mindscapes of management: use of individual differences in multicultural management* (Maruyama 1994)
- *Multicultural public relations* (Banks 1995)
- *Marketing in a multicultural world* (Costa and Bemossy 1995)
- *Multiculturalism: criminal law* (Australian Law Reform Commission 1991)
- *Kid pix around the world: a multicultural computer activity book* (Chan 1993)

In some spheres, the term's usage has even reached a kind of absurdity, for it is invoked – presumably to add some contemporary acceptability – with reference to matters that by their nature involve a plurality of peoples and cultures. Examples here include the Australian Olympic Committee's promise that the Sydney 2000 games will be the first multicultural Olympics, and the report published by a group of experts, who were assembled under the aegis of UNESCO to 'investigate' and 'celebrate' international cultural diversity, entitled *The multicultural planet* (Laszlo 1993).

The increased usage of the terms 'multicultural' and 'multiculturalism' in a wide range of contexts and by a variety of actors certainly marks a significant and widespread 'change of semantics, a change of the codes in which society is describing itself' (Radtke 1992: 2). But given such a wide range of actors and arenas, it is apparent that multiculturalism currently means no single thing – that is, it represents no single view of, or strategy for, contemporary complex societies. 'The concept of 'multiculturalism', observe Ella Shohat and Robert Stam (1994: 47), 'is polysemetically open to various interpretations and subject to diverse political force-fields.' Is there any implicitly agreed understanding? What are the differences in conceptualisation? What are the consequences of differential usages? This chapter provides a preliminary exploration of these questions and indicates some areas for enquiry and policy development.

Common tenets?

'Multiculturalism', in all its uses, has something to do with ethnic pluralism.[1] The condition of ethnic pluralism permeating a particular society is certainly nothing new – indeed, William H. McNeill (1986) stresses that it has been the norm, rather than an aberration, throughout the history of civilisations (Smith 1994). Roman citizenship, *convivencia* in early medieval Andalusia, the *millet* system of the Ottomans, the ghettos of eastern Europe, and the institutions of colonial pluralism described by Furnivall (1948) were all arguably forms of managing multiculturalism.

The meanings and overlapping discourses of 'multiculturalism' described below, having arisen mainly in the 1970s, achieved predominance throughout the public spheres of Australia, North America and Europe in the 1980s. The causes and processes through which the term arose are likely to be complex and context specific. Yet at least two general developments in this period can be seen as largely contributory: (a) among postwar immigrant and ethnic minority groups the achievement of high levels of education and advanced forms of organisation and lobbying (Rex and Drury 1994), and (b) the new social movement concerns of an emergent 'postmodern left' (blending Marxism and deconstructionism) in university faculties (Robbins 1991). Following the Civil Rights Movement of the 1960s, both of these led to increasingly outspoken criticisms of forms of discrimination and the entrenchment of (ethnically, racially, culturally, gendered) homogeneous power structures. 'Multiculturalism' is one umbrella term that arose by way of advocating alternatives.

In the broadest senses, ideas underlying – and the people invoking – the terms 'multicultural' and 'multiculturalism' are differentiated by a binary division into orientations which Pierre-André Taguieff (1990) has labelled 'heterophilia' (in which a multiplicity of different cultures in any single society is desired and praised) and 'heterophobia' (in which such multiplicity is feared and rejected). People who invoke 'multiculturalism' in the former, positive manner would likely agree that the term is meant to summarise and promote ideals of tolerance, the right of ethnic minority groups to maintain aspects of cultural heritage and language; equal treatment, equal access and full participation with regard to matters of law, employment, education, social services, economic activity and political representation; rights to collective expression; and commitment by all, regardless of ethnic background, to a constitution or state and its rule of law. People who invoke 'multiculturalism' in a negative way commonly view the term as representing ideas that threaten core ideals (such as republican citizenship, 'academic freedom' or 'the melting pot'). Therefore, in their eyes, the term represents a recipe for the destruction of national identity and the breakdown of social cohesion. Within both of these general orientations – yet more so in the advocates' camp – there are numerous, identifiably distinct (although not mutually exclusive) discourses in which the meanings, emphases, strategies and visions surrounding the terms 'multicultural' and 'multiculturalism' differ (Castles 1987; Kobayashi 1993; Vertovec 1996c).

Distinct discourses: 'multiculturalism as...'

The following sections are not intended as an exhaustive account of developments or of possible ways of discussing the meanings of multiculturalism. Rather, they are intended to demonstrate the ways in which 'multiculturalism' in itself means no one thing (and therefore questioning any sense of an '-ism'; cf. Goldberg 1994a). Below, several discourses are identified and some observations about each are offered.

Demographic description

One prominent discourse invoking the term 'multicultural' is that describing a condition of ethnic diversity, usually following a recent historical period of mass immigration. Here, the presence of people whose origins are in another place is often said to make this or that country a '*de facto* multicultural society'. A conflation of 'culture' and 'race' is often obvious in this discourse: commonly in Britain, multiculturalism refers to matters surrounding the population of Afro-Caribbeans and South Asians, seldom Jews, Polish, Italians, Turkish or Greek Cypriots.

This is a discourse based, as well, on an implicit (and false) reckoning that before the period of immigration, the country was ethnically or culturally homogeneous. It begs the question of critical threshold: after the influx of *how many* people does the society change into a multicultural one? An assumed 'numbers game' linking immigrants/ethnic minorities and a 'cultural threat' is characteristic of the anti- 'multiculturalist' British political right. Such views were voiced by Winston Churchill MP (grandson of the famous prime minister), who painted a lurid picture of a Britain endangered by too many Muslim immigrants: Mr Major promises us that 50 years from now, spinsters will still be cycling to communion on Sunday mornings, he said (*Guardian*, 29 May 1993), 'more like the muezzin will be calling Allah's faithful to the High Street mosque!'

Broad political ideology

In 1968, the British Home Secretary Roy Jenkins made a famous speech in which he advocated a model of integration 'not as a flattening process of uniformity but of cultural diversity, coupled with equal opportunity in an atmosphere of mutual tolerance'. This view – arising as an alternative to models of both exclusion and assimilation – could be seen as the foundation of a broad political ideology of multiculturalism. Its general tenets are an acceptance of ethnic pluralism as a long-term feature of society, and a recognition that ethnic minority communities will retain their own languages and cultures. Politicians' task, then, was to formulate and safeguard these ideals in law and public institutions.

A key feature of this task, John Rex (1986, 1991) has described, involves identifying the nature of, and the relation between, the public and private spheres. This should involve fostering commonality (shared laws, and open economy and equal access to state provisions) in the former and ensuring freedom (here, for ethnic minorities to maintain their own traditions) in the latter. The discourse of multiculturalism in this sphere led, logically, to the discourses and frameworks involving policy and institutional restructuring.

Socio-political policy

The policy discourse surrounding multiculturalism especially involves identifying structural factors contributing to discrimination, disadvantage and exclusion; and formulating and implementing policies that facilitate equality of opportunity and outcome. A large part of this policy in the UK involves anti-discrimination measures, which are mostly on grounds of 'race' rather than culture or religion (following the Race Relations Act 1976 and the establishment of the Commission for Racial Equality). Ethnic monitoring in employment and public services, too, falls within this kind of discourse. Other key aspects of policy here include:

(a) *Accommodation* of ethnic minority needs in social, health, legal and judicial services. Examples include the allowance of ritual slaughter of animals for Muslims and Jews, traditional clothing for Asian girls in schools or Asian women employees, turbans instead of motorcycle helmets or construction-site hard-hats for Sikhs (Parekh 1991);

(b) *Provision*, including state funds (particularly via Sections 11 and 57 of the 1966 Local Government Act), for language training, translation, interpreting facilities (in courts, healthcare facilities, social services) and linguistic assistance in schools; and for special 'community' workers, centres and organisations; and

(c) *Education*, perhaps the largest and main sphere directly invoking multiculturalism by way of policy (see Lynch et al. 1992). The central philosophy here, it is usually thought, is twofold: (1) to raise the self-esteem of the ethnic minority child, and (2) to create the basis for social understanding in the classroom which, it is hoped, will extend beyond this setting once children grow into adulthood.

Institutional restructuring

Once social and political policies were formulated in the name of multi-culturalism, local and national institutions had to be created or restructured in order to operationalise policies aimed at fostering or safe-guarding ethnic minority equality, access and participation. Foremost among these institutional measures have been:

(a) *Consultation* through providing frameworks in which ethnic minority communities can speak on their own behalf. Having grown out of grassroots friendly societies and other groups established to assist immigrants, the local authority voluntary liaison committees of the mid-1960s were superseded by community relations councils (also councils for racial equality, committees for community relations). These were coordinated throughout Britain by the National Commit-tee for Commonwealth Immigrants, which was itself replaced by the Community Relations Commission, later the Commission for Racial Equality. On the local level, most community relations councils (CRCs) have now been supplanted by race relations units and/or a range of *ad hoc* bodies and other consultative forums for ethnic minority organisations. The traditional roles of all these councils and boards set up on behalf of migrant minorities have been simultaneously as social welfare advisors, legal watchdogs and policy advocates;

(b) *Organisation* of ethnic minority groups has proliferated throughout Britain, especially during the 1980s when local government initiatives promoting multiculturalism exhibited a 'new political drive towards pluralistic welfare provision' (Reeves 1989: 183) by extending public resources to a range of ethnic groups (Kalka 1991). In this way, a vision of multiculturalism held sway according to which certain (pre-sumed uni-cultural) communities would be ensured of equality, respect – or at least tolerance – and continuity of tradition by local government financing or other support of specific identity-based organisations; and

(c) *Training* for public sector workers, including social workers, health-care practitioners, and police. The idea here has been to foster sensi-tivity to the values and practices of ethnic minorities by teaching about customs. While certainly doing much good (for instance, Muslims are less frequently offered pork on hospital or school menus), the training courses and materials have sometimes amounted to no more than 'curious collations of facts and speculations that have sometimes passed for guides to practice in a multicultural society' (Johnson 1994: 313). Such collations may serve to distance ethnic minorities further by stressing their 'otherness', rather than serving to emphasise their status as co-citizens.

Resourcing cultural expression

Yet another discourse or set of programmes – in line with the ideal of fostering the maintenance and reproduction of ethnic minority traditions – has involved the extension of public resources for community cultural activities. This is the mode Audrey Kobayashi (1993: 206) calls '"red boots" multiculturalism: folk dancing, cultural festivals and ethnic restaurants' (Schierup and Ålund 1987. Also, see below for some criticisms of cultural funding priorities).

Moral challenge

It follows that in discourses promoting equality among persons from a range of cultural traditions, a high degree of relativism must be fostered (that is, one system of truths, morals and values cannot be assumed superior if equal provision for another set is to be created and maintained). Tests of such relativism in the name of multiculturalism have surrounding issues such as polygamy, ritual practices, aspects of family law, female circumcision and other less drastic treatment of women (Parekh 1994).

Reactions against this dimension of multiculturalism arose in the early to mid-1980s with the 'Honeyford affair', in which an outspoken headmaster, Ray Honeyford, publicly denounced central tenets of multicultural education, especially the harbouring in Britain of what he saw as depraved customs from Pakistan and elsewhere (Halstead 1988). By the late 1980s, the 'Rushdie affair' became the *cause célèbre* for people (on the left as well as the right) who felt that 'unacceptable behaviour is being tolerated under the cloak of multiculturalism' (Alibhai 1989: 12). Tolerance toward minorities, many began to say, had gone too far. 'Fundamentalist leaderships have been the main beneficiaries of the adoption of multiculturalist norms', suggested Nira Yuval-Davis (1992: 284). The implications of multiculturalism for basic democratic premises of free speech, pluralism and social integration were reviewed in both the popular media (Appignanesi and Maitland 1989) and semi-official circles (see, for instance, CRE 1989, 1990a, 1990b).

New political struggles

The increasingly effective political mobilisation of groups based around ascribed characteristics or shared values involves another discourse in which 'multiculturalism' is a key notion. In such mobilisation or campaigning, there is an assertion of (or calls for) collective rights, as well as lobbying for meaningful forms of political inclusion for groups according to their own preferred modes of expression and representation. In recent years, these activities have been deemed the 'politics of recognition', 'politics of identity', or 'politics of difference' (see for instance, Gutman 1992; Kymlicka 1995b; Young 1990). Such a politics – and by extension, this particular discourse of multiculturalism – includes groups based on criteria of gender, sexuality, disability and poverty in addition to those based on ethnicity or 'race'.

In the USA, many observers have described how the movement for the political recognition of 'difference' has sometimes developed into calls for ethnic enclavisation. For example, 'This has turned', says Australian journalist Robert Hughes (1993: 83), 'what ought to be a generous recognition of cultural diversity into a worthless symbolic program, clogged with lumpen-radical jargon. The offshoot is the rhetoric of cultural separatism'. Subsequently, prominent intellectuals like Arthur Schlesinger (1991) and Thomas Sowell (1991) have taken examples of the most extreme advocates of ethnic separatism to pose a generalised 'multiculturalism' as a force endangering US identity and national integration.

In a similar manner, the debates around 'political correctness' and 'the struggle for the canon' have reduced and trivialised what some proponents have argued to be a profoundly political aspect of multiculturalism (see, for instance, Gates 1992; Giroux 1993; Goldberg 1994b). Following what can be deemed a 'cultural studies approach', this discourse points to the ways in which social groups 'give expressive form to their social and material life-experience' (Kobayashi 1993: 207). Images and texts, as well as institutions, then, are considered 'sites of struggle' with the reigning (white, male, 'Eurocentrist') hegemony which historically has sought to erase, marginalise or control subordinated peoples via manipulating forms of representation. The political agenda, consequently, is informed by the need to engage in 'acts of cultural recovery' (Hall 1991a: 10), to reappropriate an historically subjugated self-image and 'de-centre' the oppressor.

A feature of postmodernism

Further, the discourse of multiculturalism as struggle or social movement, as framed by certain views from within cultural studies, is largely located within a postmodernist paradigm. Together, these orientations are posed against what are considered the traits of modernism, as Henry Giroux (1993: 63–4) explains:

Instead of recognising multiple, collective agents capable of both challenging existing configurations of power and offering new visions of the future, modernism constructed a politics of identity within the narrow parameters of an individualism that was fixed, unburdened by history, and free from the constraints of multiple forms of domination. . . . Modernism's second basic assumption was grounded in the attempt to construct cultural differences within a discourse that was simultaneously ethnocentric, colonialist, and anti-democratic.

The task of multiculturalism, then, is to overturn modernism's straitjacketing of minority groups. Poststructuralism, postcolonialism and (post)feminist theory are called into play as intellectual tools for doing so (Giroux 1992). As with postmodernism generally, multiculturalism comes to stand for new relativism, the endorsement of different truths, alternate ways of knowing and being, fractured realities, challenges to 'grand narratives' (particularly of the Triumph of the West), polycentrism (in contrast to 'Eurocentrism') and the recognition of multiple, non-essentialised, situated selves.

In this way, political discourses of multiculturalism have led to broader discourses of multiplicity. Iris Marion Young (1990) is one advocate of a renewed pluralist approach along these lines. Despite constitutional and electoral frameworks purporting to safeguard a degree of equality and justice for all, Young points to all sorts of conditions reproducing exclusion, disadvantage, oppression and injustice. Therefore, she broadly questions the whole idea of 'the common good'. In place of the traditional political structures, which aim to create a homogeneous public, Young sees the need for a participatory democracy based on the idea of 'a heterogeneous public' much in line with other, earlier discourses of multiculturalism. 'Instead of a fictional contract, we require participatory structures in which actual people, with their geographical, ethnic, gender and occupational differences, assert their perspectives on social issues within institutions that encourage the representation of their distinct voices' (Young 1990: 116).

Yet, unlike many earlier discourses, Young does not wish for wholly 'group' differentiated representation, for 'in complex, highly differentiated societies like our own, all persons have multiple group identifications' (Young 1990: 48). '[I]ndividual persons', she observes, 'as constituted partly by their group affinities and relations, cannot be unified, [they] themselves are heterogeneous and not necessarily constant'.

This perspective is shared by Stuart Hall (1991b: 57) in his call for 'the politics of living identity through difference'. 'It is the politics of recognising that all of us are composed of multiple social identities, not one', he says, 'That we are all complexly constructed through different categories, of different antagonisms, and these may have the effect of locating us socially in multiple positions of marginality and subordination, but which do not operate on us in exactly the same way'.

In these ways, discourses invoking multiculturalism have shifted profoundly in a rather short period of time, from posing relatively simplistic matters of acknowledging the condition of ethnic pluralism and praising 'tolerance', through the critical task of reshaping public structures to ensure equality and assist cultural maintenance, to asking deeply probing questions about the limits of accommodating contrasting moralities, the political power of images, and the creation of new modes of political pluralism.

Implications

While each discourse of multiculturalism has wrought important sociopolitical advances, there have been drawbacks as well. Features of almost every one of the above-mentioned discourses and institutions surrounding multiculturalism have been subject to criticism (Ålund and Schierup 1991; Bonnett 1993; Kobayashi 1993; Radtke 1994; Vertovec 1996c). Some of the most significant critiques include the following.

- Almost all discourses of multiculturalism entail 'ethnisation', a process Carl-Ulrik Schierup (1992: 10) says, 'blocks the conscious formulation of those common interests that transgress ethnic–cultural divisions. It hampers the generation of trans-ethnic forms of organisation and of the immigrants' development into genuine political subjects in their own right'.
- Political representation or consultation under multiculturalism amounts to internal neocolonialism based on undemocratic forms of leadership. In this way, Ulf Björklund (1986: 302) writes, by 'co-opting ethnic leaders into councils, commissions and offices within state-run programmes, and by incorporating ethnic associations into existing systems of state-sponsored organisations, the political centre shows its goodwill, and, at the same time, makes ethnic leaders co-responsible for the administration of state policies.'
- Another view of the kind of ethnic minority representation that ensues from these discourses is that it is at best partial, at worst, false. Anthony Messina (1989: 71–2) points to one such problem here, that of the local state freezing a specific kind of relationship with highly institutionalised minority groups:

[F]irst, by concentrating on groups and not individual affiliates CRCs are reaching only the already organised; non-whites outside this group world and specifically, those outside the political arena remain unorganised. This practice has the obvious advantage, for local authorities, of decreasing the chances that a hitherto unpoliticised segment of the ethnic-minority community will become politically active as a consequence of their affiliation with the local committees. Second, the group affiliation structure has the effect, perhaps intended, of making CRCs less democratic and, hence, less open to groups challenging their conservative orientation.

- In yet other ways, the well-meaning multiculturalist policies local government authorities initiated in the 1980s may work to the disadvantage of minorities by creating conditions of dependency and rivalry. Marian Fitzgerald (1984: 63) writes:

  The immediate gains of funding and the political influence which comes through consultation and co-optation may depend on the patronage of one party. If that party loses power, groups may be left high and dry and those most closely identified with it may be those regarded with greatest suspicion by its successor. Moreover, competition for this patronage may divert groups from their primary purpose and collectively weaken them by intensifying the forces of division between them.

- Another form of rivalry or divisiveness has been observed in relation to the funding of expressive cultural activity. Floya Anthias and Nira Yuval-Davis (1992: 173) observed that 'spokespersons from the African-Caribbean groups often resented Asian religious groups getting funds from the council; they felt at a disadvantage in speaking on behalf of their own smaller and less cohesive group. They considered Asians to be getting more of the available resources precisely because they had so many different religious and cultural practices'.

- Too much attention to cultural identity diverts attention from other issues of inequality surrounding racism, sexism, class, housing, unemployment, the justice system. For instance, here Anthias and Yuval-Davis (1992: 182) recount that due to the tendency to fund non-politically 'safe' cultural activities, 'Asian religious groups or a scheme set up to promote, for example, African drumming, would have a stronger chance of survival than, say, a group concerned with the treatment of young West Indians in police detention'.

- In these ways the many policies and institutions surrounding multiculturalism come to involve differential access to the public domain, raising serious questions concerning the actual exercise of power (Asad 1990).

- The inability to affect power, it is reasoned, means that multicultural discourses merely represent ways of maintaining a status quo. Schierup (1992: 7–8) concludes that 'The incorporation of various broker institutions, like immigrant associations, family counsellors and local immigrant advisory bodies, into the instrumental forms of bureaucratic organisation has been used to control the range of what is acceptable.'

- This has even backfired on ethnic minority populations, who have been effectively put in cultural conservation areas like endangered species. In the name of a vague relativism and non-interference with tradition, culturally-defined no-go areas have been created among social workers, healthcare practitioners, police and other workers in the public realm who 'feel a paralysing inability to act because they think it is racist to interfere with "ethnic cultures"' (*Guardian*, 6 October 1993).

- With regard to the call to recognise multiple identities in forms of political representation, Gregor McLennan (1995) warns of the danger that 'The principle of difference of multiplicity turns into just another ontological or methodological "absolute", a new all-purpose privileged abstraction' whereby everything is necessarily assumed to be multiple, separate, and different. It becomes impossible to get a 'fix' on anything. 'A descriptive vastness ensues', he says, 'a bland and thin egalitarianism of concerns, in which myriad micro situations have a rightful claim to full representation in the sociocultural matrix' (Vertovec 1996b).

Many of the diverse uses of 'multiculturalism' are comparable or overlapping by way of certain shared, implicit understandings of 'culture' (Ålund and Schierup 1991; Dirlik 1990; Vertovec 1996c). In this set of understandings, 'culture' is a kind of catalogue of collective behavioural-moral-aesthetic traits which are rather mysteriously transmitted between generations, best suited to particular geographical origins yet largely unaffected by history or a change of context, which instils a discrete quality into the values, practices, social relationships, predilections and intrinsic nature of all who 'belong to (a particular) it'. Entire population segments, it follows from these assumptions, can be categorised and catered to culturally. Stephen Feuchtwang (1990: 4) elaborates:

> The premise of sorting populations by ethnic origins according to presumed cultural essence is that a culture is a community of deep-seated values. For values one may also read social rules and meanings, or customs and traditions. But what makes cultural origin a category of population is the additional assumption that a culture is a community of original identity, to which individuals belong by birth. By the common sense of being and belonging which sets the tone of this cultural recog-

nition, all those born into a community absorb and ineradicably sediment within themselves its customary ways of thinking, feeling and being. Even if they do not so identify themselves, they are nevertheless properly identified with that community, whatever subsequent layers of other cultures they may have absorbed to cover over the original sediment.

'Culture', in this sense, is presumed to be something virtually burnt into the genes of people, forever distinguishing and separating them. A 'multicultural' society, in this reasoning, is therefore a pool of bounded uni-cultures, forever divided into we's and they's. This view is propounded in both overt and subtle ways through a variety of contemporary discourses describing culture, to which those of multiculturalism contribute. Through these there is a danger, Aleksandra Ålund and Carl-Ulrik Schierup (1991: 10) warn, that: 'The hidden logic of a new common-sense cultural racism (demarcating, in terms of a fixed cultural essence, "other cultures" as different from "our culture" and disturbing to the normal order) finds its way into the language and practices of public servants, professionals and into the everyday common-sense discourses of ordinary people.' Certain discourses of multiculturalism, then, may end up reinforcing the kinds of prejudice for which they arose to combat.

Conclusion: new and extended discourses

We are left, then, with a conundrum: basing participation, representation and public service delivery on ethnicity/'culture' can stigmatise people, thereby maintaining or exacerbating conditions of exclusion; yet ignoring ethnicity/'culture' – instead basing participation, representation and public service delivery on a generalised set of criteria only – can (a) neglect legitimate special needs (based on particular values and practices), and (b) perpetuate patterns of discrimination and inequality. Middle-path solutions are necessary, requiring further elaborations of discourse.

A long-asked question also remains: multiculturalism for whom (Lynch 1993)? Is it for the minorities, as a means of assisting in the reproduction of values and practices and for reaffirming their sense of worth? Or is it for the majority, as a means of education into the life ways of the minorities? Or is it for society in the abstract, as a way of fashioning new ways of belonging, participating, living together? Surely the latter, since, as Stuart Hall emphasises, 'diversity is, increasingly, the fate of the modern world. The capacity to *live with difference* is ... the coming question of the twenty-first century' (1993: 361, italics in original).

Important new discourses related to the umbrella of multiculturalism, which may lead us to the needed middle path, are emerging. One avenue has been to describe, criticise or advocate qualified versions: 'conservative' or 'corporate multiculturalism' (Goldberg 1994a), 'radical multiculturalism' or 'polycentric multiculturalism' (Shohat and Stam 1994), 'insurgent multiculturalism' (Giroux 1994), 'public space multiculturalism' (Vertovec 1996a), 'difference multiculturalism' (Turner 1993) and 'critical multiculturalism' (Turner 1993, Chicago Cultural Studies Group 1994). Another avenue involves extensions or rethinking of issues concerning ethnic pluralism by way of notions of cosmopolitanism (Waldron 1992), modes of incorporation (Goldberg 1994a, Vertovec 1996c), modes of citizenship ('transnational', Bauböck 1995; 'postnational', Soysal 1994; 'multicultural', Kymlicka 1995a), 'managing diversity' (Jackson et al. 1992) and 'managing cultural pluralism' (Dacyl 1995).

The diversity of discourses around multiculturalism is no bad thing (despite the confusions when interlocutors debate employing different meanings of the term). There is no need or desire to concede one 'real' meaning of the term, since it is but an umbrella for a range of issues surrounding fairness, equality and the plurality of identities, values and practices in contemporary societies. Instead, concepts, frameworks, programmes and initiatives within the discourses outlined above must be sharpened, expanded and related.

Note

1. Problems of meaning, of course, arise with regard to this generalisation since it begs basic questions regarding the meanings and usages surrounding 'ethnic' – and its conflated usages connoting 'race', culture, religion, identity, and nation – which lay beyond the scope of this chapter.

Multicultural society: the case of Flemish Brussels

Eugeen Roosens

To sketch a picture of the various cultures, their bearers and their relationships as they developed on Belgian soil is an impossible task. I therefore will focus on the Brussels ethnoscape only, adding some evidence from Antwerp. Being an anthropologist, I am first taking the terms 'multi' and 'cultural' seriously, highlighting how these notions are used in political and media discourse, and how they are distorting the realities they are deemed to signify. Drawing heavily on the existing literature, I then will sketch how the relationships between the Flemings and Francophones are setting a prestructured inter-ethnic stage on which immigration takes place. To limit the subject of this chapter, I will look at the phenomena from a Flemish point of view. Consequently, my picture will be unavoidably one-sided.

In the second part of this chapter, I will turn to the empirical research conducted on allochthonous groups by our Leuven team.[1] More specifically, I will use the ethnographic studies of the Brussels and Antwerp school systems to analyse the relationships between allochthons and the local majorities at the micro level. The school is the institution all children, immigrant and refugee descendants included, are expected to attend daily, from the ages of 6 to 18. What exactly the teaching staff is trying to transfer, and which interrelationships develop in the school context can be observed by participant observation. What parents from different cultural and ethno-national backgrounds think and do about school matters, their hopes and fears, can also be recorded in a reliable way. Observing the school in relation to the children's homes is a way of evaluating the respective positions of the various cultures and their bearers. Moreover, the school is one of the very important places where society is produced and reproduced.

The notions of 'culture' and 'multicultural society'

Culture, culture flow, and cultural inequality

In political discourse and in the media, the term 'culture' encompasses a wide variety of items. In daily speech, people frequently use the term 'culture' to refer to the groups or categories of people who are the 'bearers' of cultures. Culture is also currently used in the restrictive sense of 'fine arts' or 'high culture'. Moreover, now that keeping or restoring one's 'own culture' has become a right and a number of political fights are put up in the name of culture by sophisticated leaders of 'cultural minorities', learned and popular meanings are interfering continuously.

In my view, culture is a collection of interrelated schemes (D'Andrade 1992) providing meaning or a frame of reference towards the self, the other, the material and the supernatural world, at the cognitive, affective and evaluative level. These meanings are expressed and embodied in a material, outside world. 'Inside' and 'outside' evolve in a permanent dialectic relationship (Hannerz 1992): people pick up what is externalised by themselves and by others, use it, and, in one and the same move, con-firm, transform and reinterpret parts of themselves, as well as the schemes of meaning and what they stand for. These meanings can be rational, irrational or non-rational. Culture is intentional (Shweder 1992): it contains crystallised queries, and desires and passions of those who have produced and produce it. Moreover, no culture ever is a closed system: culture traits are borrowed from other cultures and are partially adapted to the prevailing configuration. Culture is never uniform, offering alter-natives for many issues, and is unequally spread over the population. Every culture ramifies in subcultures and individual cultural perspectives. Science, technology and techniques are important parts of culture that are very unevenly distributed, especially in industrialised and urbanised countries where they are highly developed. Numerically speaking, every specialist equals thousands of non-specialists (Hannerz 1992).

Moreover, in today's world in which tourism, numerous TV channels and the entertainment industry are reaching out worldwide, it is unthink-able to sort out what in a given culture is 'genuine', 'original' or 'authentic'. Every single culture always includes a vast and variable amount of cultural traits (food, music, ways of dressing, words, dances, religious ideas and values) borrowed from others through various com-munication channels. Even the 'European' notion of 'multicultural society' may stem from the USA. It has now made its way into Japan as well (as C. Pang indicated in a personal communication in 1996). It would be impossible to compile a list of 'pure' Flemish or 'pure' Walloon cultural traits and nobody can find out with precision which cultural traits offered by the media are selected and assimilated, or, on the contrary, rejected or simply ignored by their fluctuating audiences.

In this context, preserving one's 'cultural purity', as some nationalists are preaching, is an impossible mission. Exchange of cultural items and partial cultural systems is going on continuously all over the world, making people belonging to various ethnic groups more similar by the day, while internally diversifying these same social entities. There is overwhelming evidence that most Flemings, Walloons, Turks, Sicilians, Spaniards and Moroccans living in Brussels practice subcultures that contain 'recently imported' cultural elements. Participant observation among Sicilian, Spanish, Turkish and Moroccan youngsters over the years by members of our Leuven team has shown how many cultural traits these young people share with their Belgian peers: including body language, the Flemish dialect, French, Dutch, trendy clothing, styles of street behaviour, music, disco bar dancing, and an interest in motorcycles and cars (Cammaert 1985; Foblets 1994; Hermans 1992; Joris 1991; Leman 1987; Timmerman 1996). Huge quantities of objectifiable cultural items or schemes are not regarded as 'culture' in the subjective sense of the term by the actors because they are not used as ethnic or ethno-national markers in the inter-ethnic context.

This continuous culture flow notwithstanding, cultures do have some objectifiable, internal consistency and continuity. One field of culture that can be neatly defined and even kept under control is written and (to a lesser degree) spoken language. The Joint Language Committee of the Netherlands and Flanders recently published a revised official lexicon listing the 'correct words' in the right spelling. Mistakes are punished by examination systems as well as by selection and appointment committees. The far reaching consequences of ignoring the rules, for example, missing a professional appointment or promotion, confers considerable power on this cultural institution.

Language use is another exact given. Which language is used and when and where it is written or spoken can be observed with precision. It is no coincidence that both language form and language use are the main tools of cultural policy in bilingual Brussels. They constitute the rare cultural fields on which political authorities have a grip because they can be objectively controlled and, hence, legally sanctioned. Although it is perfectly possible to wear American shoes, an Italian jacket, a French shirt, to relish Chinese and Thai cuisine, to adore Pavarotti or Michael Jackson, to read Proust, to drive a Swedish car and to watch American soap operas on a Japanese television set and still be a leading Flemish intellectual, speaking French on too many occasions will jeopardise your Flemish identity. Not everything cultural is flowing in a postmodern fashion.

In addition to recognising and maintaining language differences, all ethno-national groups agree about what material objects (houses, cars, furniture, TV and hi-fi sets, and numerous other goods) are desirable and what professional occupations enhance social status. The means of production of these goods, including higher education, the sciences and the applied sciences and technology, are originally a product of the West. It is a matter of fact that among all the ethnic or national groups who coexist in Belgium, those who command these means of production are also the ones who have the means to stick to cultural practices they deem fit, and to the use of their language while at the same time enjoying high social status. On top of this, they generally have the opportunity to educate their children in their own language and, to a certain extent, in their own cultural style. Under prevailing conditions, only the well-to-do natives and residents hailing from rich countries are in a position to enjoy these privileges. Only this kind of immigrant or expatriate and their children can relate to people from different cultural and ethno-national backgrounds without feeling threatened by the use of other languages or other cultural traits. They, and they alone, can really enjoy additive acculturation (Roosens 1995), or the benefits of 'multicultural society' in the strict sense of the term. The children of immigrant workers, on the other hand, are forced to drop a considerable amount of their parents' culture and language if they want to make a living. Their acculturation is clearly subtractive.

This situation is not merely due to oppression, exploitation, discrimination or coincidence. The cultures of the two coexisting camps, the rich and the poor, are as a matter of fact unequal in some respects, deplore it or not. First, by its sheer structure, the non-man-made material world demands highly efficient techniques if a competitive quality:price ratio is to be reached. Not all cultures are equally good at this (Hannerz 1992). Second, the way in which the quasi-totality of human beings crave a maximum of enviable goods (and the material security and status they provide) are another powerful reality. That is precisely why the migrants from the south came to the north. It is also why, on the one hand, many natives want the 'profiteering' migrants to return to their country of origin, and, why, on the other, the migrants refuse to do so. Considered from this point of view, the deepest cause of ethnic tension and opposition in Belgium, as in many other countries, is not cultural difference in the first place, but cultural and human similarity: what all people have in common, making them want the same things that are available only in limited quantities. The climate of 'global economic competition' and fanatic striving towards 'excellence' or 'being the best', or at least 'better' than most others whatever the costs in the other spheres of life, is at the heart of inter-ethnic or 'intercultural' relations (Roosens 1989). New racism (Taguieff 1988) and European cultural fundamentalism (Stolcke 1995) – 'Get out and keep out the profiteering, "incompatible" strangers!' – are immediately related to this climate.

Culture and ethno-national relations

Although cultural content on one hand and ethnic or ethno-national identity on the other are functionally independent (Hutnik 1991), a limited number of cultural traits in the strict sense of the term are seamlessly interwoven with ethnic matters. Every single ethnic or ethno-national category or group we have studied over the years (Roosens 1989 and 1995) always constitutes its ethno-national figure in an almost identical fashion. On the one hand, solidarity, belonging and being like a big family are founded in a common origin, a cultural tradition (frequently language and/or religion) originating in a mythical past and grounded in folk biology: members of one 'people' are of the same blood (Roosens 1994). On the other hand, ethnic or ethno-national social boundaries are constituted and maintained in an interactive way with other similar groups. A limited number of selected phenotypical and/or cultural traits are used as the content of these boundaries. Mostly these cultural elements are taken from daily life, like current beliefs, emblems and practices. Sometimes, they are created or invented.

There is ample evidence that the overwhelming majority of allochthons, as well as those who are naturalised, while continuously changing culturally are ethno-nationally staying what they are. They stick to what they feel as a continuity with the past (keep their 'identity' staying the same through time), going back to their roots through their parents and grandparents to end up with their nation or people. Ethno-national identity is predominant everywhere, be it in various degrees of intensity at various times, whatever the cultural flux described above. It is exactly this reality, called 'ethnic' or 'inter-ethnic' for decades in the professional literature (Barth 1969), that is most often designated by the vulgarised notion of 'multicultural society'. In Brussels, the autochthons (Flemings, Walloons and Germanophones) and also the residents hailing from other European countries, and from Turkey, Morocco, Ghana, Zaire and other parts of the world all maintain their own ethno-national identities. Allochthons coming from more than 100 different countries and constituting about 30 per cent of the one million inhabitants coexist with Belgian citizens in the same city. In one of the 19 Brussels townships, the alien population amounts to even more than 50 per cent (van der Haegen et al. 1996). While objectifiable cultures are overlapping in many fields of life, ethnic identities are not. What is at stake, then, in 'multicultural society' is not as multi- or as cultural as suggested; it is overwhelmingly ethnic.

Nevertheless, political leaders and policymakers seem to prefer the expression 'multicultural society' to that of 'multi-ethnic society', although it is the latter about which they are talking. When used by Belgian policymakers, 'multicultural society' can best be considered a euphemism or diplomatic expression. It dodges the question of the cohabitation of the autochthonous majorities with diverse ethnic groups of newcomers who refuse to be assimilated or naturalised, while enjoying equal social rights and claiming franchise, thus tending towards a 'post-national citizenship' (Soysal 1994). This undesirable 'anomaly' is somewhat covered up by using the term 'multicultural' in a hazy manner. As the term 'multicultural' can signify folklore, fine arts, cuisine, music and dress, it does not necessarily sound divisive. People can take part in a lot of cultural events and happenings, stemming from several heritages, without losing their own ethno-national identity or putting their own subjective culture at risk. The word 'multi-ethnic', on the contrary, does not allow for this overlap and vagueness, for it divides the population into clear-cut categories and groups. Moreover, in many countries of Europe, especially in France and the southern Mediterranean, the words 'ethnic' and 'ethno-national' remind one too much of 'blood', Nazism and racial issues. Used in its politicised sense, 'multicultural society' confuses culture as it can be studied by an observer (objectifiable culture) and culture as seen by the various actors as 'their' (subjective culture) and, besides, is mixing up both of these notions with an ethnic or ethno-national group or category. Moreover, in some reconciliatory contexts, 'multicultural society' suggests that all cultures and their respective bearers are equal. In that sense, it comes close to what scholars such as Charles Taylor (1994) would call 'multicultural society' in the strict sense of the term: a set of cultures officially recognised by the state as being of equal value.

Although the historical background is different, the expression 'multicultural society' as used in Belgium comes close to its US counterpart. On both continents the word suggests equality, and in both cases, the various 'cultures' and their respective bearers are far from equal (Hollinger 1995; Patterson 1978; Portes and Rumbaut 1990; Schlesinger 1991).

The native ethno-cultural setting

As already stipulated above, the use of 'correct language' seems one of the most robust and resilient cultural contents and markers, symbolising and embodying the different cultures involved in multi-ethnic settings like Brussels. It is exactly in this domain that quite a number of political fights between the Flemings and the Francophones or 'Walloons' have been taking place for decades. Even today, the 'language struggle' could flare up at any moment. For politically conscious or 'proud' Flemings or Francophones, to speak the language of the other is felt as a form of bowing or giving in. In these very concrete interpersonal, micro social confrontations, the question of being socially superior, inferior or equal emerges in full force. As many Flemings are able to make themselves understood in French and quite a number of them are really fluent in their second language while most Francophones are unable to reciprocate in Dutch, exchanges between members of the Belgian sub-nations generally do not lead to 'mutual cultural enrichment'. Quite the contrary, they create an atmosphere of uncertainty and uneasiness.

Almost since the foundation of Belgium in 1830, Flemish leaders have been putting up linguistic battles, claiming recognition of Flemish (or Dutch) as an official language. The dialect speaking Flemings of the nineteenth century were considered as belonging to the lower layers of Belgian society, while the upper strata were composed of French speakers who occupied the main positions in the administration, the army, the universities and in all the spheres of public life. This even applied in the hierarchy of the Catholic Church. Moreover, quite a number of Flemings seeking socio-economic promotion had been 'passing' into the French ranks. Descendants of these French speaking 'ethnic Flemings' are still to be found in Brussels, as well as in Flemish cities like Brugge, Ghent and Antwerp. Over the years, militant Flemings have taken advantage of their higher demographic expansion, the general franchise and (later, after the Second World War) the economic boom in Flanders to overcome their minority position. Language and language use have been concrete and highly efficient tools in this strife: *De taal is gans het volk!* (the language is the people). As a result of this battle, Dutch (or 'general Flemish') was declared a second official language and soon afterwards language use became linked to territory. This tendency became so pronounced that in the 1960s lecturing in French in the Francophone division of the University of Louvain in Leuven, on Flemish soil, was no longer acceptable. *Walen buiten! Eet meer Walen!* (Walloons out! Eat more Walloons!) were popular slogans at Flemish student meetings. The venerable Catholic University of Leuven, founded in 1425, had to split. The French speaking division of the university moved, partly to Brussels and partly to Ottignies in Wallonia, where the new campus city of Louvain-La-Neuve was built.

The older generation of Flemings see and still remember the equal (or slightly dominant) Flemish position of today as a victory won after a long battle. Moreover, the struggle for Flemish recognition has a history of disruptive internal divisions and deeply embedded emotions. While the overwhelming majority of Flemings closed ranks with the Francophone Belgians against the German oppressors in both world wars, a limited number of Flemish separatists collaborated with the Germans. Some of them even became part of the SS. At least some of the collaborators seem to have been naïve idealists who expected a better future for the Flemings once the Flemish people were united with their fellow 'Germanic' nations. Also, the unification of Flanders with the Netherlands (Groot-Nederland) had been and still is a dream in some Flemish nationalist circles (Wils 1995).

After the wars, repression against the collaborators followed. Some were executed as war criminals or traitors; other lost their civil rights. Quite a number of their families are still, in 1996, pressing for an amnesty, even a post-mortem, but find the radical refusal of the patriots in their way. In June 1996, the president of the extremist nationalist party, the Vlaams Blok, openly declared in his farewell speech that his party should remain, first and foremost, the party of the 'victims' of the repression and their grandchildren.

All these past events have left wounds and have caused internal divisions among the Flemings, making ethnic confrontations with their Francophone counterparts still more sensitive. Again and again in the years following the Second World War, Flemings who had nothing to do with the collaboration and had even fought the German enemy, have been scolded for being 'blacks' (collaborators) by Francophone citizens when, for example, they claimed their linguistic rights in a predominantly French-speaking Brussels. With the wartime population ageing and dying out, these practices are decreasing but have not yet entirely disappeared.

Autochthons and allochthons

It is against this background that the overwhelming presence of alloch-thons and the use of various languages in Brussels, capital of Europe, is perceived by the militant Flemish leaders and their organisations (Verlinden 1991). There is the fear that, again, the Flemings, especially the young, will give in too easily because they are fluent in several languages. As fluency in various languages is frequently absent on the other side – native English speakers mostly stay monolingual – it is feared that the languages of the 'domineering' segments of society will prevail. After winning the battle against the Francophones, the Flemings seem well on their way to losing to the wealthy Eurocrats and other 'international' residents. It is probable, so it is argued, that the over-whelming majority of shops, hotels, restaurants and other businesses will try to address their patrons in their respective languages, and, if not able to do so, will turn to English or French. From their side, the overwhelm-ing majority of 'poor' immigrants from North Africa use French as their second language. Thus, the Flemings are bound to be sandwiched between the rich and the poor aliens on their own soil.

These fears are not without foundation. There are clear indications that hardly any allochthons are learning Dutch (Viaene 1996). If they decide to learn or speak a 'native tongue' it is French. Under these conditions, the use of Dutch will decrease. Militant Flemings who consider Brussels as the capital not only of Belgium but also of the sub-state of Flanders, or even as a Flemish city located on Flemish soil (Brussels is surrounded by Flemish territory), see these developments as a disaster for the Flemish people. Although it would be wrong to attribute this view to the majority of the Flemings, the feeling of being linguistically dominated is certainly widespread.

From this perspective, it is difficult to sell the idea that various com-munities living together with different cultures and languages leads to cultural enrichment. The very fact that, after decades of struggle, Belgium very recently became a federal state, with each sub-nation or cultural community linked to its own territory, seems to indicate that the opposite is true. Physical, legal and social boundaries seem to be necessary to make mutual tolerance possible (Finkielkraut 1994).

According to the extreme right-wing political party, Vlaams Blok, the co-presence of several ethnic groups on the same territory unavoidably leads to conflict and to the degrading of all the cultures involved (Tastenhoye 1993). That more than 27 per cent of the electorate in the 'cosmopolitan' city of Antwerp and 10 per cent throughout Flanders voted for the Vlaams Blok in the local elections two years ago, clearly shows that, whatever their other motives (disappointment with politics or anti-corruption sentiments), numerous voters were prepared to back a political party that used slogans attacking non-EU migrants as its main weapon (Swyngedouw 1991).

A more restrained Flemish agency, the *Comité Stop Euro-Brussel* (Stop Euro-Brussels Committee), is less opposed to the presence of the so-called migrants *par excellence*, the Moroccans and Turks, who are mainly unskilled immigrant workers with, according to the agency, no cultural or linguistic powers or attraction whatsoever. Influential mem-bers of the committee ironically state that they have never heard of Flemings becoming Turkish or Berber speakers. In their eyes, wealthy high-status 'international' people pose the true danger: the British,

Swedes, Americans, Japanese and French use their money and power to impose their language and way of life. These aliens resist acculturation by putting their 7000 or more children into elite private schools where they are taught in their own language. They organise church services in their own language and they create their own associations. In other words, they organise themselves into distinct cultural and ethno-national networks or groupings.

On top of all this, according to the same leading Flemings, the Francophone people from Brussels, who constitute more than a 50 per cent majority, would have no objections to this 'multicultural' presence. Quite the contrary. As the majority speak a domineering major language, French, the Walloons would feel strengthened by the presence of an increasing number of immigrants using French, or bound to do so one day. The Walloons would not even see any socio-technical problem, for, according to the old Francophone recipe, they sincerely believe that allochthons will eventually assimilate. Whatever the merit of these Flemish interpretations, Francophone experts have shown that Flemish and Walloon perceptions, feelings and attitudes about the presence of aliens on Belgian territory differ markedly (Martiniello 1994).

Ironically, while many Belgian natives spend their vacations abroad in countries like Spain, Italy, France, Turkey and Morocco, from where the migrants come, they do not mingle with the allochthons in Brussels. There is no general mood in favour of diversity *per se* prevailing in the capital of Europe. In the minds of many natives, the integration of aliens, meaning their absorption or quasi total assimilation, is seen as the only true solution. While allochthonous Muslims hail leftist intellectuals who strive for a society that will accommodate genuine, recognised and established diversity as a new order, the majority dismisses them as nonsensical utopianists.

Even the most visible and prestigious authority fighting for the coming about of a 'multicultural society', the former royal commissioner of migration, Ms Paula D'Hondt, meant by this term a society in which citizens are allowed to remember that their ancestors were living on another continent and that they have some of their own cultural traditions, including religion, left. But D'Hondt expects assimilation as well. In her vision, all immigrants must conform to all Belgian laws, and must respect the basic principles of Belgian society, like, for example, the separation of religion and the state, or the equality of men and women. She also demands the willingness to learn, speak and write the local language and imposes automatic naturalisation from the third generation on. In other words, D'Hondt clearly tells the immigrants that she wants them to assimilate in various fields of culture (Tastenhoye 1993). These mitigated

‚attitudes notwithstanding, Paula D'Hondt has received hundreds of scolding and menacing letters written by furious Belgian natives, and has been physically threatened several times, even within her private home. Although moderate by most standards, her ideas on multiculturalism have been violently attacked and ridiculed in the right-wing press and in television debates.

Communication between the various cultural communities, then, is not easy. Most allochthons are not looking for 'intercultural' contact with the local population. Wealthy Eurocrats and other well-to-do expatriates live in their own rather closed circles. This is even more true of the Japanese. At their side, first generation immigrant workers from southern Europe, Morocco and Turkey stay oriented to their region of origin and do not consider Belgium their country. Many of them, though not all, plan to return and do so after retirement. Alternatively, they go back at their explicit request after their death to be buried in the soil of their ancestors.

Moreover, a recent, important inflow of undocumented immigrants from Latin America, Poland and Nigeria, in addition to the already existing illegal immigration from North Africa, is further complicating the picture (Leman 1995). Illegal work by undocumented migrants and a rise of criminality in some parts of the city negatively reflect on migrant labourers in general. High unemployment and job insecurity make exclusion and repatriation of 'profiteering' aliens ethically acceptable to quite a number of natives (Roosens 1995; Suarez-Orozco 1995).

Looking somewhat from afar then, as an outsider, one could wonder how under the present conditions, the coexistence of these various categories and groups could possibly make believe that 'multicultural society' offers a new, enriching perspective, a mind-opener for the future. The maximum one can hope for, so it seems, is absence of violence and coexistence in juxtaposition. This could well be the predominant form of living for a long time to come. As the US experience has demonstrated, ethnic categories or ethnic groups can stay juxtaposed over very long periods of time without constituting a melting pot in the true sense of the term, even when the overwhelming majority are immigrants without autochthonous roots (Glazer and Moynihan 1993; Portes and Rumbaut 1990). The same situation has developed in the colonies, where decades and even centuries of living on the same soil has failed to fuse the colonisers and colonised. This also applies to the native Belgians: Flemings and Walloons born and raised in the same city do not play down their subnational origins and differences. One could even say that their daily contacts make both groups more assertive. This confirms Fredrik Barth's well-known remark (1969) that direct contact between ethnic groups does not reduce their profiles, but, on the contrary, tends to increase social differentiation and boundary maintenance, even while exchange of culture traits and an objective reduction of cultural differences occur.

The relations between the different ethno-national groups or categories and their respective cultures as they function at the micro level can be readily grasped from the educational system, as we will show in the second part of this chapter.

Increasing and depleting acculturation in schools

The European schools

The prototype multicultural setting in the strict sense of the term may well be the European school. Nine European schools have been operating in recent years, of which three are on Belgian soil. About 15,000 pupils between the ages of 6 and 18 attend the courses taught by more than 1000 teachers. European schools have been in existence for more than 43 years. They were created in a spirit of reconciliation in 1953, in the aftermath of the Second World War, by the founding fathers of a United Europe and their collaborators (Anon 1993).

Instead of creating several schools for the various nationalities of expatriate functionaries' children, it was decided to establish one single school with different sections where youngsters from a range of national backgrounds would meet on a daily basis and sit together on a number of courses.

The European school system may have its own setbacks and shortcomings, as some who call it a 'caste school' suggest, but it does at least respect the first language (L1) and culture (C1) of each of its pupils on an equal basis. L2 starts at the age of 6 and L3 by the age of 13. A fourth language is optional at the age of 16. Every student is entitled to attend lessons in the subjects that are considered the most important, such as science and mathematics, in L1 throughout the curriculum. Less demanding subjects, such as economics and geography, and optional courses are taught in the student's second language. L2 is used as a 'vehicular' language. This means that students from different national backgrounds sit together for L2 courses and for courses taught in L2. Only the teachers are native speakers. The students hear expositions on a number of topics concerning the country of origin of their parents from the mouth of an outsider who uses his or her own language.

Moreover, continuity is maintained between the home milieu and the school setting. L1 and C1 are given dominance and the students' national or ethno-national identities are taken seriously. At the same time, pupils are in continuous touch with peers from other backgrounds. This allows for conversations in several languages, cultural exchanges in a practical and functional manner and a long-term experience of intercultural inter-action. The advantages and disadvantages of a multicultural social environ-ment become apparent in daily life. The pupils are given the chance to explore other languages and cultures in a non-menacing setting in which their own language and culture is guaranteed.

Moreover, the subcultures of the European functionaries' elite families are in harmony with an international culture of individual competition attempting to reach the highest level in terms of income and status. This includes education of the highest quality, requiring maximal school per-formances. Most life projects of the adolescent children of European functionaries educated in European schools meet these norms, goals and means. The school system explicitly confirms these values and intentions: it is explicitly stated that the school stands for excellence and delivers the European baccalaureate giving access to major European and US univer-sities.

The objectifiable culture of origin, as found in the families, is inte-grated in the school situation. Both the parents and the children experience their own subculture, and more especially their language, as being taken seriously, preserved and promoted by the school. Moreover, national, ethno-national or ethnic identity as developed in the family circle are confirmed by the school, both *de jure* and *de facto*. This mutual confirmation by the family and the school of the child's culture and (ethno-)national identity, creates a safe atmosphere in which to study foreign languages and aspects of foreign cultures without feeling threatened.

This is a micro version of a multicultural society in the strict sense of the term, generating increased, not reduced, acculturation.

Educating immigrant children

Six researchers at the University of Leuven's Centre for Interculturalism and Migration Research (CIMO) have, in projects involving three to six years of field research (1988–93), followed 240 immigrant youngsters through the transition between the last year of secondary school and higher education, or between school and the Brussels and Antwerp labour markets. The research focused on school and family contexts as loci of preparation for adult life in terms of culture and ethnicity. The young people belonged to the Moroccan, Turkish, and Spanish immigrant com-munities in Brussels, Ghent and Antwerp (Roosens 1992). According to official sources, 79,399 Moroccans, 19,310 Turks, 25,710 Spaniards and 717,339 Belgians resided in Brussels in 1990 (Leman 1993). Three female researchers worked with three groups of 40 young female students; three male researchers with three male groups. Each group was composed of at least 20 young people who achieved the highest grades in the best schools and 20 youngsters who, by educational standards, failed in the worst fashion in the worst 'concentration schools' (schools with a student population of more than 50 per cent immigrant ethnic minority youngsters). In addition, three researchers of the same team, after working with the students, spent eight months of fieldwork among a selection of their teachers (Roosens et al. 1993).

Looking at the results of this field research, one notices a striking difference between the opportunities the children of European employees are given and what happens to the sons and daughters of immigrant workers coming from the southern parts of Europe, Morocco and Turkey.

Youngsters with a Spanish background

Most Spanish parents can look for help from their parents' associations and manage to select schools with high academic standards. Although they themselves received poor schooling and often did not even finish primary school, they are absolutely convinced that school is the best road to socio-economic promotion. Most of the Spanish parents select Catholic schools, not primarily for religious motives but because Catholic schools have the best academic reputation. A second important criterion of selection is that there must be as few 'foreigners' (Moroccan or Turkish) children in the school as possible. Spanish parents are convinced that 'foreign' children tend to bring down the quality and reputation of the school and hinder the performance of the other children.

A number of Spanish children attend the complementary Spanish schools, where they can improve their Spanish and knowledge of Spanish culture and history, which enhances their opportunities if they ever return to Spain.

Spanish parents generally disregard the advice of the psycho-medical centres, which try to direct children finishing primary school either into general (high level), technical (medium level), or vocational (low level) secondary education. Most parents ignore the advice of the psycho-medical centres, which they regard as xenophobic and racist, and direct their children into general secondary education. Although a number of pupils learn by trial and error what they can achieve and what they cannot, most youngsters obtain a maximum of opportunity in the system thanks to the strategy followed by their parents.

Though some young Spaniards have problems with local languages, they perform quite well in Belgian schools. Their level of achievement is almost identical to that of Belgians of comparable socio-economic strata. It was striking that neither teachers nor psycho-medical personnel ever spontaneously mentioned Spanish cases as problematic. Quite the contrary, Spanish youngsters were seen as well behaved, cooperative and hard working, even more so than many of their Belgian peers.

At the end of secondary school, we were able to observe at least four different types of cultural orientation in our Antwerp sample, which we studied closely with respect to this particular topic. About 50 per cent of our subjects felt culturally very close to their Belgian peers, much closer than to the Spanish counterparts they met while on holiday in Spain. The remaining 50 per cent were almost equally divided between three other types of orientation. One category of youngsters felt very Spanish culturally. They attended every possible conference, course and seminar about Spain and were extremely well-informed about the country of origin of their parents. They also strongly identified, ethno-nationally, as 'Spaniards', be it Spaniards from a specific region, and were preparing for their return to Spain in a realistic fashion. It is striking that these youngsters were to be found among the high achievers at school as well as among the less successful. Another category of youngsters felt quite insecure and rootless, culturally speaking. There was no doubt in their minds that they were Spaniards and felt Spanish, but they were unhappy about having to live with two different cultural systems and did not quite know how to handle this situation. A fourth group of young people felt excited by their bicultural position and experienced it as an asset. They enjoyed playing the two systems and adapted in a few days to the local situation in Spain during annual holidays.

It should be stressed that nobody reported problems with ethno-national identification. It was only the content of their culture and their cultural identity that were not reflected by the school.

Spanish immigrant parents took it for granted that remaining a Catalan, Basque or Galician and, vis-à-vis the Belgians, remaining a 'Spaniard', did not present any problem for their children. They never raised the issue. They themselves remained strongly oriented toward Spain, even after 30 years. They had formed Spanish ethno-regional networks in Belgium, lived in their own circles and encouraged the use of Spanish as a family language. The presence of Spaniards in Belgium is no longer seen as problematic, not even by extreme nationalists. Their situation improved dramatically once the idea of a strongly unified Europe was propagated in the 1980s and once Spain became an integral part of the European Community, now the European Union.

Spanish parents, although very isolated and almost completely separated from the autochthonous population, managed to find their way via their own networks in the Belgian system of education.

It struck the two researchers, that all the parents, both in Brussels and

Antwerp, had exceedingly high expectations for the careers of both their sons and daughters. To become a wealthy lawyer, medical doctor or well-to-do professional was considered the apex. Parents had no knowledge of the content of the school programmes or curricula or of how secondary school and university might influence and transform their children. They were not even aware of what the difference between general secondary education and technical secondary education was, but they did know that the 'general' was better than the 'technical', and chose the best.

The parents were not particularly concerned whether their children studied in Flemish or French and did not see this switch of languages as threatening their ethno-national identity. The issue at stake was school success as a tool for socio-economic promotion.

Although the sons and daughters of Spanish immigrant workers did not have the opportunity of their EU personnel counterparts to study most curriculum subjects in their first language or to become accustomed to living and sharing their experiences with youngsters from other nationalities in an attuned and well-balanced setting, they managed to find their way in the Belgian school system and to establish quite a number of relationships with their Belgian peers.

Both the Spanish and the Dutch of most of the youngsters is deficient. Spanish youngsters who 'move back' to Spain experience difficulties in obtaining employment. The content of their own culture has been left uncontrolled, and no educational efforts have been made to integrate this important aspect of their lives into their educational package.

As we will see, the situation of the Moroccan and Turkish immigrant workers and their children and grandchildren in Belgium, and more specifically in Brussels, is strikingly different from the situation of the Spanish communities and constitutes almost the antipode of that of the EU personnel.

Young people of Moroccan and Turkish origin

The Moroccans' image in the media, in political life and among the public in general has deteriorated over the last few years. Twenty or even ten years ago the category of 'aliens', 'foreigners, 'guestworkers' or 'migrants' contained Greeks, Italians and Spaniards as well as North Africans, Turks and others, and opposition between Belgians and non-Europeans was somewhat mediated by the south European foreigners, who have dropped out of the picture in recent years. Although EU allochthons remain physically present, do not assimilate ethno-nationally with the native mainstream and are still homeland oriented, they are no longer termed 'migrants' or 'immigrants' by the media or in daily life (Billiet, Carton and Huys 1990). This almost unbelievable turn-around happened in just a few years. Although it is impossible to prove this, I am convinced that this dramatic change was brought about by the widely publicised and loudly proclaimed unification of Europe in the magic year of 1993. All of a sudden, in a certain sense all Europeans became natives all over Europe. Aliens of this type are no longer mentioned as migrants or immigrants, not even by extreme nationalist action groups or political parties. Extremists stress that they are opting for a 'white' Europe, which includes the inhabitants of the southern European countries.

In Belgium, this powerful logic of inclusion and exclusion at the macro level left the Moroccans and the Turks alone as the undesired and undesirable outsiders who constitute the real problem. In Brussels, the Moroccans are the first to come to mind when the terms migrants or immigrants are mentioned. The struggle against illegal immigration and economic refugees, and the obsession that northwestern Europe is being overrun by all sorts of poor devils from Africa, Asia and the former eastern bloc aggravates their uncomfortable position.

The spectacular rise over the last few years of the Vlaams Blok in Antwerp (where it did so well in recent elections) and the upsurge of other extreme nationalist parties in the French-speaking parts of Belgium, have pushed the ruling and other important political parties and form-ations to the right. While a local franchise for non-EU residents was on the government's agenda in the 1980s, it is no longer considered oppor-tune to discuss the topic. Common actions by migrant associations were demanding voting rights in the spring of 1996. In a meeting in May 1996, Muslims argued that 'migration' terminology and discourse belong to the past, 'to the Belgium of grandpa', and that Islam is the second important religion in Belgium today.

Political parties like the Vlaams Blok have turned to what is tech-nically called 'new racism', using unbridgeable cultural differences as their main tool (Taguieff 1988). Although in public discourse, race or physical features are not mentioned, it is stressed that Islam and the asso-ciated Moroccan and Turkish cultures of the Muslim immigrants are irreconcilable with the Christian and European tradition and, more specifically, with Flemish culture. These Flemish nationalists stress loudly that the Muslim immigrants are fully entitled to retain their religion, ethnic identity, and culture and are even under an obligation to do so, but not on Flemish soil. They belong in their country of origin and must be strongly encouraged to go home.

The opportunities offered (or not offered) Moroccan immigrants can-not be separated from their position and image in wider society. More-over, their socio-economic position puts them on the bottom line if not on the fringes of society. Moroccans are mostly unskilled labourers, practically illiterate, and profess popular variants of Islam, lower status for women and 'all the medieval superstition and fanaticism that goes with it'. They live mostly in the dilapidated quarters of Brussels. On top of all this, many of them are unemployed; their sons and daughters are failing *en masse* in the school system and stay unemployed, making some parts of Brussels unsafe. In others words, socio-economically, they are the antipodes of the EU personnel and their families.

Nevertheless, Moroccan parents harbour the same dreams about their sons' (if not their daughters') futures as the European elite. They hope that their children will be successful at school, are disappointed when they are not, and wish that those who seem to have opportunities and to make their way to university or higher education will become highly successful in the professions or business. Almost all parents in our sample tell their children, and continue to do so, that studies are a very important means of socio-economic advancement.

A limited number of parents are very conscientious in that they supervise their children's homework and force them to study before allowing them to leave the house, something that goes against the grain of Moroccan tradition, where male adolescents can move about freely.

Although nobody has yet been able to show in a fully convincing way what factors make for success or failure at school, it is highly probable that parents' care and attention, and their unstinting support of their children are important elements, transculturally, although not the only relevant factors. It seems right, then, to accept that a number of lifestyle elements hamper good school results, such as giving priority to family visits over study at examination time, not providing a quiet place to study and not giving the child a chance to participate in examinations because holidays must be spent with the family in the home country, and not returning in time to give the children a chance to participate in the second examination session (Hermans 1992).

The other side of the coin, the school system, may be more important. Most Moroccan parents lack the resources needed to find out which are the good schools for their sons. If they do find out, the chances are high that they will be turned away with the excuse that enrolment has already stopped because of the large numbers of candidates or that only youngsters with exceptionally strong primary school results are accepted. It is a fact that elite middle schools avoid enrolling Moroccan pupils.

In the present situation, it is no overstatement to say that the enrolment of Moroccan or other North African or central-African students can mean a disaster for the school. Once a certain number of Moroccan pupils are enrolled, the chances are very high that Belgian and other parents will withdraw their children from the school. This mechanism has been in full operation for years at the primary school level. A large number of these schools have become what are called 'concentration schools', schools in which more than 50 per cent of the children are from non-EU 'migrant' backgrounds. In recent years, the Flemish Minister of Education has been encouraging the spreading of migrant children to avoid concentration schools.

Once 'the migrants' have taken over the school, projects or programmes or even experiments of intercultural education become totally impracticable. There are no partners from the other side left, and it would sound like a joke if the teacher demanded mutual respect for different cultures and different lifestyles.

As I mentioned earlier, three of our researchers have been working with teachers in French community schools, the type of school in which almost all Moroccan youngsters enrol. They met very few idealistic fighters doing their utmost to understand their pupils or visit their homes. The overwhelming majority, at all levels of the school system, were bitterly disappointed and discouraged. Teachers felt abandoned and unprepared. They were even openly stigmatised by their colleagues in better schools where no migrant children were enrolled. One of the schools we visited, although fully entitled to receive subsidies from the government as it was educating a good number of disadvantaged migrant children, refused to collect the money for fear of being labelled a concentration school (Roosens et al. 1993).

Although they had been working with migrant youngsters for years, most teachers had never been in touch with the children's families or visited their homes. They therefore lived with a number of totally misleading stereotypes, for example that Moroccan parents did not care at all about their children's school results, that they were lazy and that the children simply imitated what they saw.

Teaching of the mother tongue (*langue maternelle*) and the culture of origin is left entirely in the hands of teachers sent by the respective countries of origin and controlled only by the consulates or embassies in question. These courses, in which only 22 per cent of the primary school children participate at present (there are no figures for secondary education), are not compulsory: they are neither part of the regular curriculum nor taken into account in the calculation of school results. The only link to the school is the building in which they are taught. In an overwhelming number of cases, the teachers sent by the countries of origin are ill prepared, do not know the language of the receiving school, are unaware of what is going on in the local immigrant community and do not function as members of the school team. There are clear indications that at least some of these teachers are selected by their government with 'political' aims in mind (Ministère de l'Education de la Communauté française 1992).

Thus, the maternal language or L1 and the culture of origin (C1) are associated with low status and unimportant curriculum topics (not compulsory and not relevant for school results). In a number of schools, Belgian teachers even flatly refuse to collaborate with the foreign teachers and oppose any expansion of the matters of origin. Although some aspects of the system parallel the European school model of L1 and C1 taught by teachers sent by the home country, the system turns into a caricature and is rejected by a good number of the youngsters involved. Without providing figures, the official report states that the young people themselves reject the courses and ask for additional, 'useful' English and Flemish language courses.

The official *Rapport communautaire* mentions that the Belgian authorities who signed the conventions with the sending countries always took care to mention in the text that the L1 courses are not about teaching or learning a language as such but are offered only for psychological reasons and are meant to facilitate integration into the local, receiving society. In other words, the L1 and C1 courses must provide a feeling of continuity but are not to be taken seriously as far as their content is concerned. If the organising authorities start with this aim in mind and mention this openly in an official report, what 'respecting the right of immigrants to receive instruction in and about their own language and culture' as stipulated by the European authorities, really means, becomes clear. All the (very recent) experiments and positive intentions mentioned in the official report become extremely suspect, if not in bad faith, in the light of these facts.

This 'classic' setting is miles away from the European school, where teachers are carefully selected, extremely well paid, and given the means to elicit mutual respect and even admiration of one's neighbour' s culture.

What those Moroccan youngsters want is to be able to get a job, so that they can marry, have children, buy a car and lead a normal life. When there is no hope of these elementary conditions being fulfilled, the other facets of life become unimportant. One may ask what an underpaid teacher who has never been given a decent training in educating allochthonous youngsters would possibly be able to do to prepare young people to live in a multi-ethnic or so-called 'multicultural' society.

The two hours a week the Flemish educational system provides in *Onderwijs in Eigen Taal en Cultuur* (OETC) – educating children in their own language and culture – is in poor shape (internal information from official sources, May 1996).

Formal education is even bleaker for Moroccan girls. Their parents do not care much about the quality of the school, but consider physical and 'moral' safety to be of critical importance. If they can find a primary and, later on, a secondary school located close to home so that their daughters can be kept under maximum surveillance, they will pick that school. As migrant housing is almost always located in the poorer quarters of the city, the chances are high that the school they select and where their children are accepted for enrolment will be of a lower level as well.

One of the researchers traced as many Berber (Moroccan) young women as possible who had made it to a university or other institution of higher education, or at least graduated from secondary school, and collected their detailed biographies. Of the 27 women she was able to meet, only four complained about racism or discrimination in schools. Their main remarks were about their own families and more specifically about the elder men in their own migrant communities who tried, over the years, to stop the development of their careers by restricting their freedom to move, by stating that higher studies are unimportant for young women who must, first of all, be mothers and spouses, and by trying to impose arranged marriages. All 27 young women stated and stressed that their greatest problem was making their success acceptable within their families and their own immigrant community.

Our research among young Turkish men and women led to similar results. Our female researcher working among Turkish young women came across several concentration classes where the teachers were just about the only people who did not speak Turkish and where the young women cocooned themselves in a 'traditional Turkish' world of their own making, having a good time while being away from their homes, dreaming and talking about their future marriages and married lives. This type of education, of course, inhibits intercultural contact and later employment. Moreover, these segregated young women will probably educate their own children in a segregated way, making them unfit to live in harmony with the other members of the 'multi-ethnic society'.

Again, a few Turkish girls have made it to the elite schools. Unlike the youngsters of the concentration schools, these young women, who were often the only alien students in their classes, achieved good results and caused no problems. These youngsters were culturally very similar to their classmates. Most of them had been growing away from the immigrant milieu, though they kept their ethnic identity, feeling proudly Turkish. Most of these girls dreamed of marrying a modern Turkish intellectual in Turkey and of spending their lives in a sophisticated and urbanised Turkish environment, far from the rural area from which their parents had come. Here again, these young women have been neglected culturally, and, without disappearing ethnically, have been culturally assimilated in most domains of life.

The situation I have been describing is not entirely new. It has been developing over the years and numerous agencies have been trying to remedy it. The most promising experiment in attempting to deal with this situation is the Bicultural and Trilingual Education Project based on the Foyer model. It was started in 1981 and has now been extended to nine schools in the Brussels area. This formula is presently only applied to kindergarten and primary education, but is a striking way of preparing youngsters for secondary education and could be continued throughout secondary school if funding were available (Byram and Leman 1990).

From this, we can conclude that there is virtually no equality between cultures (Taylor 1994). Cultures are graded according to their members' socio-economic status and ethno-national background.

Conclusions

By way of conclusion, I would like to draw attention to the following twelve points.

First, the monolithic and reified notion of culture, as often used in political and media discourse, distorts the phenomena by overstating intercultural differences, while grossly underestimating similarities and intracultural diversity.

Second, the term 'multicultural society' confuses objectifiable culture, subjective culture and ethnic category or group.

Third, in Brussels and Belgium at large, immigrants or alien residents are entering an ethnically prestructured field: what has been happening and is going on among the Flemings and Francophones is influencing how newcomers are perceived. Moreover, their arrival and presence are differently evaluated by the various Flemish and Francophone subgroups. People who are deeply convinced that Brussels is 'by nature' a Flemish city and should stay that way because it is surrounded by Flemish land, will act and react differently from the Flemings who see Brussels as the capital of Europe, bringing wealth and fame. Nationalists who see the congruence of nation and territory as a condition for survival will experience the massive presence of newcomers as an invasion. To them, the role Francophone-minded aliens could play when given franchise looks menacing.

Fourth, as far as we can see (and we grant that our look is limited) the predominant mode of coexistence in Brussels seems to be juxtaposition. 'Intercultural' contact is limited. Relations between individual members of the different ethno-national groups certainly do exist, and small groups in the various camps do organise 'multicultural' happenings and meetings. However, I think it is safe to say that the overwhelming majority of residents, both natives and aliens, are not interculturally involved. Immigrants prefer their own circles, and Belgians choose to travel abroad to meet 'other cultures' (Tastenhoye 1993).

Fifth, I use the term juxtaposition metaphorically to designate a juxtaposition on a hillside: not all groups are located at the same level – some live higher, some lower. There is a clear-cut difference between the socioeconomic well-to-do and the 'poor' ethno-national categories or groups. Non-EU immigrant workers, their descendants and all kinds of illegal immigrants are clearly classified as being in a 'lower' position, even by those who organise positive action on their behalf. Official policy tends to classify many of them with the native unequal opportunity people, the *kansarmen* who have fewer chances of success in life. Those so classified are aware of their inferior position and consider low status to be overcome by social promotion defined, at least in part, in terms of the dominant majorities.

Sixth, the overwhelming majority of immigrant workers enhance their social status and self-esteem by comparing what they have achieved socio-economically with those who stayed behind in the country of origin, using the community of origin as a yardstick. Quite a number of immigrants consider their moral and religious standards, especially concerning the control of female sexual behaviour, as markedly higher than the anomie and lack of respect and shame they notice in the surrounding majorities.

Seventh, the juxtaposition is first and foremost a juxtaposition of ethno-national groups. Cultures overlap. Each category or group uses cultural traits or markers to trace social boundaries, cultural traits that are auto- and/or hetero- attributed. Language may be the most pervasive marker for all the categories and groups involved, immediately followed by religious membership and emblems of religious belonging for the Muslims.

Eighth, cultures, as conceived in folk discourse, receive a rating that is almost congruent with the socio-economic position of their bearers. There are higher cultures and lower cultures.

Ninth, in part, this hierarchy is in part based upon a socio-economic and physical reality: wealthy material culture requires technology and science plus competitiveness at the international level; all this presupposes advanced schooling and training. Not all the cultures are equally good at manipulating the 'natural'; non-man-made world.

Tenth, it is logical also, that the well-to-do are the ones able to educate their children in L1 and C1 if they wish to do so. When the families of Turkish or Moroccan, or even Italian or Spanish, unskilled workers want their children to reach high levels of promotion, they have to accept drastic cultural changes, which they mostly do.

Eleventh, under present conditions, instead of a 'multicultural society', Belgium is better termed a *jurally* non-ranked (Horowitz 1985) multi-ethno-national society offering a huge diversity of cultural schemes hailing from various backgrounds, but tending towards a shared cultural pool of meanings, while maintaining powerful and durable cultural markers used as ethnic boundaries by the various ethno-national categories and groups, which are stratified in daily praxis.

Finally, meeting the 'other' in a sphere of mutual cultural enrichment – increased acculturation – without feelings of inferiority and without feeling threatened, seems to be a privilege of the wealthy.

Note

1. In the Netherlands and Flanders, the adjective allochthonous and the noun allochthon refer to second and third-generation migrants or, to be more precise, people in the Netherlands or Belgium whose parents or grandparents are migrants.

Nationalism, multiculturalism and women

Nira Yuval-Davies

Trin T. Min-ha (1989: 89–90) has commented that there are two kinds of social and cultural differences: those that threaten and those that don't. Multiculturalism is aimed at nourishing and perpetuating the kind of differences that do not. As Andrew Jakubowicz concluded in relation to the Australian policies of multiculturalism, 'Multiculturalism gives the ethnic communities the task to retain and cultivate with government help their different cultures, but does not concern itself with struggles against discriminatory policies as they affect individuals or classes of people' (Jakubowicz 1981: 42). Carl Schierup (1995) has claimed that multiculturalism is an ideological base for transatlantic alignment for the transformation of the welfare state which aspires for the position of the hegemonic credo in postmodern modernity. He argues, however, that the paradoxes and dilemmas of existing multiculturalisms presents its ideological framework with similar problems to the ones 'real socialisms' present to 'socialism'.

Multiculturalism has been developed in Britain as a major form of accommodation to the settlement of immigrants and refugees from the ex-colonial countries, and broadly followed forms of legislation and political projects that were developed for this purpose in the USA as well as other ex-imperial settler societies such as Canada and Australia. In all these states there is a continuous debate about multiculturalism, between those who want a continuous construction of the national collectivity as homogenous and assimilatory, and those who have been calling for the institutionalisation of ethnic pluralism and the preservation of the cultures of origins of the ethnic minorities as legitimate parts of the national project.

A controversial related question is the extent to which the conservation of collective identities and cultures are important in themselves or only as a result of collective will, and whether projects aimed at conservation of cultures can avoid the reification and essentialisation of these cultures. As Floya Anthias (1993: 9) put it, 'Debates on cultural diversity confuse culture and ethnicity. ... Is it the boundaries that should be kept or the cultural artefacts that act as their barbed wire? However, the question is not just about homogeneity, but also about western cultural hegemony.'

In Australia, for instance, the call of those who have objected to multiculturalism has been for an 'Anglomorphic society' even if the members of the Australian national collectivity would not be of Anglo-Celtic origin, as the quote by Knopfelmacher (1984; see also Yuval-Davis 1991a: 14) could demonstrate: 'With Anglomorphy firmly established in Australia and stable as a rock, the "British" character of the country is independent of the "race" of the immigrants.'

In the USA, the ideological target has been the American 'melting pot', but those who have been objecting to multiculturalism in the US context have emphasised the primacy of the European culture in it. 'Would anyone seriously argue that teachers should conceal the European origins of American civilisation?' (Schlesinger 1991: 122). Collective cultural identity rather than ethnic origin and colour of the collectivity members seems to be the crucial factor in these constructions.

However, it would be a mistake to suppose that those who support multiculturalism assume a civil and political society in which all cultural identities would have the same legitimacy. In Australia, for instance, the government's document on multiculturalism emphasises 'the limits of multiculturalism' (Office of Multicultural Affairs 1988) and in all states in which multiculturalism is an official policy there are cultural customs (such as polygamy or using drugs) that are considered illegal as well as illegitimate, giving priority to cultural traditions of the hegemonic majority. Moreover, in multiculturalist policies, the naturalisation of the western hegemonic culture continues while the minority cultures become reified and differentiated from 'normal' human behaviour.

John Rex (1995: 31) describes multiculturalism as an enhanced form of the welfare state in which 'the recognition of cultural diversity actually enriches and strengthen democracy'. There are three basic reasons for this – the values of specific cultures might have important values in their own right that might enrich the overall society; the social organisation of the minority communities provides them with emotional support; and it also provides them with more effective means of getting more resources and defending their collective rights. Over the nature of these collective rights, however, the question arises of what notions of 'culture' are behind various state policies and what specific provisions the state needs to make towards individuals and collectivities in its heterogeneous population. Jayasuriya (1990: 23) has pointed out that two separate issues are involved here, 'One is the centrality of needs in the collective provision of welfare and the other is the difficult question of boundaries of need in claiming for one's right.'

The most problematic aspects of these questions become apparent when the provision relates not to differential treatment in terms of access to employment or welfare but to what has been defined as the different cultural needs of different ethnicities. These can vary from the provision of interpreters to the provision of funds to religious organisations. In the most extreme cases, as in the debates around Aboriginals on the one hand and Muslim minorities around the Rushdie affair on the other hand, there have been claims for enabling the minorities to operate according to their own customary and religious legal systems. While the counter arguments have ranged from the fact that this would imply a *de facto* apartheid system to arguments about social unity and political hegemony, those who support these claims have seen it as a natural extrapolation of the minorities' social and political rights. This raises the question of how one defines the boundaries of citizens' rights. Jayasuriya (1990), distinguishes between needs, which are essential and which therefore require satisfaction by the state, and wants, which fall outside the public sector and are to be satisfied within the private domain in a voluntary way.

The differentiation between the public and private domain plays a central role in delineating boundaries of citizenship in the literature, though not enough attention is being given to the fact that the public domain contains both the state domain and the civil society domain. Turner (1990), for instance, has anchored his typology of citizenship on the extent to which the state enters or abstains from entering the private domain. However, as the examples above show, the dichotomous construction of private/public spheres are culturally specific, as well as gender specific in themselves (Yuval-Davis 1991b; 1996/7). The whole debate on multiculturalism stumbles on the fact that the boundaries of cultural difference, as well as the boundaries of social rights, are determined by specific hegemonic, maybe universalistic, but definitely not universal, discourses. Universalist discourses that do not take into account the differential positioning of those participating in it, often cover up racist (and I would add sexist, classist, agist and disablist) constructions.

Cultural discourses often more closely resemble a battleground of meaning than a shared point of departure. Cultural homogeneity, therefore, would be a result of hegemonisation, and would always be limited and more noticeable at the centre than on the social margins, being affected by the social positioning of its carriers. As Gill Bottomley (1993: 312) claims, '"Culture", in the sense of ideas, beliefs and practices that delineate particular ways of being in the world, also generate conscious and unconscious forms of resistance – to homogenization, to devaluation, to marginalising by those who fear difference.' As Friedman (1994: 76) points out, cultures are not just an arbitrary collection of values, artefacts and modes of behaviour. They acquire, to a lesser or greater extent, 'stabilising properties', which are inherent in the practices of their social reproduction. These processes of social reproduction are not just processes of cloning, but of social interaction in which motivation and desire play their part. As a result, cultural models become resonant with subjective experience. They become the ways individuals experience themselves, their collectivities and the world.

Because of the central importance of social reproduction to culture, gender relations often come to be seen as constituting the 'essence' of cultures as ways of life to be passed from generation to generation. The construction of 'home' is of particular importance here, including relations between adults and adults and children in the family, ways of cooking and eating, domestic labour, play and bedtime stories, out of which a whole world view, ethical and aesthetic, can become naturalised and reproduced. However, as Floya Anthias and I have pointed out (Yuval-Davis and Anthias 1989: 7–8), one can only hold on to the problematic notion of reproduction at all if processes of growth, decline and transformation are included in it.

Cultures operate within both social and spatial contexts that cannot be understood separately from the time dimension (Massey 1994). Different positionings, both socially and geographically, would affect the ways cultures are articulated and used, both inside and outside collectivities. Gerd Bauman (1994) has pointed out that, while dominant discourse assumes the congruence of culture and community, demotic (of the people) discourse tends to deny this. A clear example of such a 'demotic' discourse has been the slogan of Southall Black Sisters and Women against Fundamentalism when they chanted in anti-domestic violence demonstrations in Southall and in countering the Islamist anti-Rushdie demonstration: 'Our tradition – resistance, not submission!' (Sahgal and Yuval-Davis 1992).

Rather than a fixed and homogenous body of tradition and custom, 'cultural stuff' needs to be described as a rich resource, usually full of internal contradictions, which is used selectively by different social agents in various social projects within specific power relations and political discourse in and outside the collectivity. Gender, class, membership of a collectivity, stage of life and ability all affect the access and availability of these resources and the specific positionings from which they are being used. It is important to differentiate and avoid the conflation of cultural discourse, identity narratives and ethnic processes (Anthias and Yuval-Davis 1992; Yuval-Davis 1994). Ethnicity relates to the politics of collectivity boundaries which, by using identity narratives, divides the world into 'us' and 'them'. Ethnic projects are continuously engaged in processes of struggle and negotiation aimed, from specific positionings within the collectivities, at promoting the collectivity or perpetuating its advantages via access to state and civil society powers.

Ethnicity, according to this definition, is therefore primarily a political process that constructs the collectivity and 'its interest', not only as a result of the general positioning of the collectivity in relation to others in the society but also as a result of the specific relations of those engaged in 'ethnic politics' with others within that collectivity. Gender, class, political and other differences play central roles in the construction of specific ethnic politics and different ethnic projects of the same collectivity can be engaged in intense competitive struggles for hegemonic positions. Some of these projects can involve different constructions of the actual boundaries of the collectivity (as, for example, has been the case in the debate about the boundaries of the 'black' community in Britain (Brah 1991; Modood 1994). Ethnicity is not specific to oppressed and minority groupings. On the contrary, one of the measures of the success of hegemonic ethnicities is the extent to which they succeed in 'naturalising' their social and cultural constructions.

Ethnic projects mobilise all available relevant resources for their promotion. Some of these resources are political, others are economic and yet others are cultural – relating to customs, language, religion and other cultural artefacts and memories. Class, gender, political and personal differences mean that people positioned differently within the collectivity could, while pursuing specific ethnic projects, sometimes use the same cultural resources for promoting opposite political goals (for example using various Koran *surras* to justify pro- and anti- legal abortion politics, as was the case in Egypt, or using rock music to mobilise people pro- and anti- the extreme right in Britain). At other times, different cultural resources are used to legitimise competing ethnic projects of the collectivity – for example, Bundists used Yiddish as *the* Jewish language in an ethnic-national project with identity boundaries that were East European Jewish, and Zionists (re)invented modern Hebrew (till then used basically for religious purposes) in order to include in their project Jews all over the world. Similarly, the same people can be constructed in different ethnic-racist political projects in Britain to be 'Paki', 'black Asians', and 'Muslim fundamentalists'.

Given the above, it is clear why ethnicity cannot be reduced to culture, and why 'culture' cannot be seen as a fixed, essentialist category. As Aleksandra Ålund (1995) comments, 'the tendency to conflate ethnicity and culture leads to [an] inability to attend to the political dynamics of ethnic difference.' Moreover, defining and differentiating between culture, identity and ethnicity in this way pre-empts debates on the notion of 'authenticity'. Authenticity assumes fixed, essential and unitary constructs of cultures, identities and groupings. 'Authentic voices' are perceived as their 'true' representatives. In multiculturalist politics, 'authenticity' can become a political and economic resource in specific ethnic projects, but can also give rise to what Kubena Mercer (1988) has called 'the burden of representation' and Amrita Chhachhi (1992), in a somewhat different context, has called 'forced identities'.

Women especially are often required to carry this 'burden of representation', as they are constructed as the symbolic bearers of the collectivity's identity and honour, both personally and collectively. Claudia Koonz (1986: 196) quotes the different mottoes that were given to girls and boys in the Hitler youth movement. For girls the motto was – 'BE FAITHFUL; BE PURE; BE GERMAN'. For boys it was 'LIVE FAITHFULLY; FIGHT BRAVELY; DIE LAUGHING'. The national duties of the boys were to live and die for the nation; girls did not need to act – they had to become the national embodiment.

A figure of a woman, often a mother, symbolises in many cultures the spirit of the collectivity, whether it is Mother Russia, Mother Ireland or Mother India. The symbol of the French revolution was 'La Patrie', a figure of a woman giving birth to a baby, and in Cyprus, a crying woman refugee on roadside posters was the embodiment of the pain and anger of the Greek Cypriot collectivity after the Turkish invasion. In peasant societies, the dependence of the people on the fertility of 'Mother Earth' has no doubt contributed to this close association between collective territory, collective identity and womanhood. However, women symbolise the collectivity also in other ways. As Cynthia Enloe (1990) has pointed out, it is supposedly for the sake of the 'women and children' that men go to war. Women are associated in the collective imagination with children and therefore with the collective, as well as the familial, future. Recently, one of the participants in the riots that flared among Muslim youth in Bradford, clarified the motivation behind their actions to a newspaper reporter: 'It's not about prostitution or unemployment or about all that nonsense of the Chief Constable. It's about the way two police officers treated one of our women' (*Guardian*, 18 June 1995).

Women, in their 'proper' behaviour, their 'proper' clothing, embody the line that signifies the collectivity's boundaries. The 'burden of representation' on women of the collectivity's identity and future (destiny?) has also brought about the construction of women as the bearers of the collectivity's honour and many women are murdered every year in many different countries because they were constructed as having brought shame on their communities. The shaving of heads of women who were accused of befriending the occupying Nazi armies after the Second World War is just the tip of the iceberg. The other side of the coin has been the systematic raping of women of the other community during wartime, as encapsulated in the videos the Serbs made of their own rapes of Bosnian women. In international law, such as in the Geneva Convention, until very recently, rape in war was not defined as a mode of torture but as a 'crime against honour'. Whose honour? Definitely not only that of the woman involved.

Even when things do not reach these extremes, exceptional circumstances, cultural traditions and often the (re)invention of traditions (Hobsbawm and Ranger 1983) are frequently used as ways of legitimising the control and oppression of women. In situations in which individual men as well as whole collectivities feel threatened by 'others' this phenomenon may intensify. Verity Safullah Khan (1975) carried out a comparative study on women's purdah in Bradford in the UK and in Bangladesh in the villages from which the Bradford immigrants had come, and found the practice of purdah to be much more extreme and rigid in Bradford than in Bangladesh. These policies of restriction of women are often reinforced by multiculturalist essentialist notions of culture, which are assumed by multiculturalist social services.

Although multiculturalism is generally hailed by its promoters as a major antiracist strategy, it has been criticised from the left for ignoring questions of power relations, representations of minority members in positions of power and of being divisive by emphasising the differential cultures of members of the ethnic minorities rather than what unites them with other blacks (Bourne and Sivanandan 1980; Mullard 1984). Other critiques from the left have been directed against both the 'multiculturalist' and 'antiracist' positions (Rattanzi 1992; Sahgal and Yuval-Davis 1992). These critiques have pointed out that in both approaches there is the inherent assumption that all members of a specific cultural collectivity are equally committed to and engaged with that culture and in the same way. It tends to construct the members of minority collectivities as basically homogenous, speaking with a unified cultural or racial voice. These voices are constructed to be as distinguished as possible (within the boundaries of multiculturalism) from the majority culture in order to be able to be 'different'; thus, within multiculturalism, the more traditional and distanced from the majority culture the voice of the 'community representatives' is, the more 'authentic' it would be perceived to be within such a construction.

Within 'antiracism' such a perspective also prevailed. The voice of the 'black' (of the all-encompassing binary division of black/white) has often been constructed as that of the macho liberatory hero, rejecting all that might be associated with white Eurocentric culture.

Such constructions would not have space for internal power conflicts and interest differences within the minority collectivity, conflicts along the lines of class and gender as well as of politics and culture, for instance. Moreover, they would tend to assume collectivity boundaries that are fixed, static, ahistorical and essentialist, with no space for growth and change. When such a perspective becomes translated into social policy, 'authenticity' can become an important political resource with which economic and other resources can be claimed from the state as being the representative of 'the community' (Cain and Yuval-Davis 1990). As Yeatman (1992: 4) observes:

> It becomes clear that the liberal conception of the group requires the group to assume an authoritarian character: there has to be a headship of the group which represents its homogeneity of purpose by speaking with the one, authoritative voice. For this to occur, the politics of voice and representation latent within the heterogeneity of perspectives and interests must be suppressed.

This liberal construction of group voice, therefore, can collude with fundamentalist leaderships that claim to represent the true 'essence' of their collectivity's culture and religion and that have high on their agenda the control of women and their behaviour.

Multiculturalism, therefore, can often have very detrimental effects on women, as often 'different' cultural traditions are defined with specific gender relations and the control of women's behaviour (in which women themselves, especially older ones, also participate) is often used to reproduce ethnic boundaries. An example of such a collusion, for instance, is the case in which the judge refused an Iranian woman (who had escaped from Iran after refusing to be veiled) a request for asylum because 'this is their culture'. Another is the placement of a young Muslim girl (who had fled from her parents' home because of their restrictive control over her) in another even more pious Muslim home, against the wishes of the girl and the advocacy of the Asian Women's Refuge.

Jeannie Martin (1991) describes a contradictory multicultural practice in which the customs of 'ethnic families' are weighted against a 'good society' model – an unspecified Anglo family norm – 'on behalf of ethnic women', focusing on atavistic practices such as clitoridectomy and child marriages as the limits of multicultural diversity. Martin describes this approach as typical of the 'ethnicists' among the multiculturalist theorists in Australia and points out that this is not a real concern for women – because the ethnicists assume women's subordination to be part of the natural order of things in which the family is at the forefront. Rather, this is a devise of ranking among men according to the extent of their deviation from the Anglo model – constructed as the ideal positive model.

Homi Bhabha (1994a and b) has developed a dynamic model of cultural pluralism as an alternative to the multiculturalist ones. Abolishing the dichotomy of time/space and emphasising the constantly changing boundaries of the national 'imagined communities' and of the narratives that constitute their collective cultural discourses, Bhabha notes the emerging counter-narratives from the nation's margins – by those cultural 'hybrids' who have lived, because of migration or exile, in more than one culture. Those hybrids both evoke and erase the 'totalising boundaries' of the nation. Such counter-narratives do not have to come, of course, from immigrant minorities. The growing voice of indigenous people, for example, is an instance of a counter-narrative that is heard from within. And, of course, counter-narratives have disintegrated the former Yugoslav and Soviet nations. It is important to note in this context, however, that counter-narratives, even if radical in their form, do not necessarily have to be progressive in their message.

Another danger in Bhabha's approach might be in bringing back essentialism through the back door – in other words, the old 'multiculturalist' essentialist and homogenising constructions of collectivities would be attributed to the collectivities from which the hybrids have emerged, thus replacing the mythical image of society as a 'melting pot' with the mythical image of society as a 'mixed salad'. Characteristic of such a position, for example, is Tri Min Ha's description of herself, at a conference in Vienna on Racism and Feminism in October 1994, as standing 'on the margin, resisting both the majority culture and that of her own group'. It is against this construction of essentialist fixed construction of cultures and their boundaries and the reduction of ethnicity to culture that transversal politics have been developed.

Conclusion

The critique of multiculturalism in this chapter obviously does not call for the traditional alternative of so-called universalist assimilationist policies. What it does call for is a pluralist approach that would not assume discrete homogenous blocs of the 'other'. Transversal politics – to use a term originally used by Italian feminists (Yuval-Davis 1994) – differentiates between social categories, social identities and social values and does not collapse them together. This would avoid the danger of a backlash from poor members of the hegemonic majority who feel that policies of affirmative or even positive action, which are determined by people's identities rather than their class position, can disadvantage and exclude them. Such an approach might also avoid the space and resources multi-culturalist policies give to fundamentalist leaderships to grow and impose their authority on other people in their communities in ways that abuse their individual human rights.

People who are positioned differentially in terms of ethnicity, race, class and gender might want – and often need – to interpret their indi-vidual rights in different ways in which different cultural traditions might play smaller or larger roles (for example – they might choose to get married via a romantic involvement, via a familial arrangement or not to get married at all). However, this is very different from the discourse of 'collective rights' in which the boundaries of these collectivities necessarily have to be defined rigidly and a homogenous construction of membership has to be assumed.

The main obstacle to applying transversal social policies, however, is not so much the construction of the minorities by multiculturalist policies but the naturalisation of hegemonic cultural traditions by the state. A genuine antiracist commitment would not so much collectively import 'other' cultures into specific closures within the public domain as con-struct them in such a way as to become open for a variety of transversal policies that would be accepted as legitimate.

Part 2

Multicultural policies and the state in Britain and Belgium

Integration policies and the politics of integration in Belgium

Jan Blommaert

This chapter is aimed at refining a critical analytical approach to the political processes involving the positioning of ethnic minorities in Belgium. These processes, we argued elsewhere (Blommaert 1996; Blommaert and Verschueren 1994), can be captured under the label of the 'migrant debate': a political debate on the presence and nature of 'migrant' communities in Belgium.[1] This debate is complex and involves far more actors than those who are usually identified as 'politicians' (even more, politicians are a minority in the political migrant debate). They include intellectuals, professionals from the social welfare sector, executives of trade unions and other corporate organisations, artists, journalists, along with backbench MPs, local politicians, members of pressure groups and activists of all kinds. It is this wide and diverse group of actors who fill the columns of newspapers' opinion pages and letters to the editor, who appear on talk shows on radio and TV, who write leaflets, brochures and all kinds of publications on migrants and migration, who organise multicultural festivals or happenings, who organise petitions, protest marches, demonstrations. In short, this group shapes 'public opinion' on migrants in Belgium.

Critiques of migration policy in Belgium have, in the past, too often focused on the policies themselves: a set of texts produced by policy-makers and intended to sketch a coherent and detailed 'integration policy'. All sorts of theoretical, philosophical or ideological shortcomings and biases were discovered in those texts (Blommaert and Verschueren 1992; Martens 1993; Martiniello 1994; Rea 1993), and the central concepts of the integration policy, when put into practice, were observed to cover a very different reality (Jaspaert and Verlot 1992). Still, criticising the policy is criticising only one part of the political process. The policy texts themselves, as soon as they were launched, went on to live a life of their own. They were echoed, reformulated, copied, amended and sometimes even perverted in a process over which the original authors of the policy seemed to have lost control.

It is this process that I want to identify in this chapter: the politics of integration as opposed to the integration of policies. The policies are just one part of the politics, and it is the politics of integration – that is the whole complex of reformulations, echoes and so forth – that shapes the social and political realities in which migrants and Belgians find themselves and that is called (with another catchword) the 'migrant problem'. I will try to illustrate the structure of this process by highlighting how the central concept of migrant policies in Belgium, the concept of integration, has become a sort of semantic harmonica: a user-friendly concept, mobilisable for all kinds of purposes and insertable in all kinds of discourses from the left to the right of the political spectrum. Hence, a critique of the Belgian approach to migration issues should rather be directed at the totality of the politics of integration, rather than to just the integration policies.

Integration

Belgian integration policies took shape between 1989 and 1993 when a Royal Commission for Migrant Policies (henceforth KCM) headed by former Christian-Democrat Minister Mrs Paula D'Hondt and supervised by Prime Minister Wilfried Martens produced report upon report littered with scientific facts and analyses and invariably ending with dozens of policy proposals. The most crucial document defining integration policies is the first KCM report (KCM 1989): a monumental three-volume work in which the blueprint for what was to become the official Belgian approach to migrant affairs was sketched and in which a plethora of demographic, administrative, social-economic and other basic facts were presented.

The most crucial fragment of this important report is the definition of the 'concept of integration' (KCM 1989: 38–9). I will quote it at length, because it will serve as a yardstick for discussing the reformulations in the next sections:[2]

> The proposals (...) that will follow, will be inspired by a concept of integration, which simultaneously
>
> 1. Starts from the notion of 'insertion', using the following criteria:
>
> (a) assimilation where the public order so demands;

(b) a consistent promotion of an optimal insertion according to the guiding social principles that are the basis of the culture of the host country and that revolve around 'modernity', 'emancipation' and 'full-fledged pluralism' – in the sense given by a modern western state;

(c) unambiguous respect for cultural diversity as mutual enrichment in the other domains.

2. And which is accompanied by a promotion of the structural involvement of minorities in the activities and the objectives of the authorities.

For the purposes of this analysis, I will call this formulation the dogmatic version of the concept of integration. It was the KCM's central policy instrument and it has been adopted by various governments since 1989 as the basis of 'migrant policies'.[3] The concept was also used in a dogmatic way. It was repeated time and time again (although in various reformulations, as we shall see), and it did not change in crucial policy texts during the whole of the KCM mandate. The final KCM report simply repeats the original 1989 formulation (KCM 1993: 50), adding, moreover, that:

[I]n criticisms from the democratic opposition,[4] we never discovered fundamental contradictions with regard to the options proposed by the KCM. Thus, among other things, the KCM's concept of integration has been accepted by almost everyone – be it in different formulations.

(KCM 1993: 15)

After the end of the KCM mandate, some of its functions were adopted by a newly-established permanent government body, the Centre for Equal Opportunities and the Fight Against Racism (CGKR), headed by the former KCM Chief of Staff, Johan Leman. The CGKR works completely within the integration paradigm and describes its own role as one of implementing the basic lines of the policies developed by Paula D'Hondt's KCM. The real policy development work related to migrant issues has been disseminated over a large number of ministries and administrations, and obviously the productivity of the various policy agents fluctuates significantly.

What does 'integration' mean? In the eyes of its advocates, it means the rise to full group membership within Belgian society of members of ethnic minority groups, who at the same time enjoy full 'cultural rights', i.e. they can retain their 'cultural identity' in the context of a multicultural society. To its critics, it is a culturalist concept with minorising[5] effects, designed to perpetuate migrants' inferior socio-economic position and often bordering on racism. To the former, it is an expression of our society's greatest qualities: humanism, tolerance and pluralism. To the latter, it exposes a more grim and xenophobic face of our society because it conditions access to the fruits of an open democratic society by evidence of (cultural) 'integration'. Upon closer inspection, both sides in the debate defend at least a partially true position. Integration policies contain very sweet sounding statements about respect for cultural diversity as well as harsher and more repressive ones about degrees to which cultural expressions are deemed acceptable, most notably with respect to Islam. They are anchored in a textual tradition of humanism and pluriformity, as well as in a tradition of colonialism and superiority. The fact is that integration policies are intrinsically vague and ambiguous (which is probably a key characteristic of political texts in general) and contain everybody's truth at the same time. We must therefore step beyond the policies and take a look at the politics, which appropriates and explores this vagueness and takes integration in previously unintended or unforeseen directions.

Politics and formulations

Formulations are key objects of analysis. A lot of power can reside in small, often hardly noticeable reformulations of policy texts. The use of another term substituting an established one, a structural, syntactic or argumentative adjustment to a well-known statement, substituting an and for an or, inserting or changing a modal qualifier (could instead of should, perhaps instead of probably) are all textual instruments that may open up new or different possibilities for political practice. At the same time, the importance of formulations is often played down by politicians themselves. In the extract from the final KCM report quoted above, the authors claimed that the concept of integration had been accepted by almost everyone, 'be it in different formulations'. A suggestion is embedded in this statement: everyone accepted the gist, the crucial ingredients, or the spirit of the integration concept; the formulations are just a matter of words. In the next section, I will explore a series of such formulations, and inquire whether, indeed, the concept of integration was essentially accepted by everyone, and whether different wording patterns are just a surface phenomenon.

Formulations and reformulations

The concept of integration has been used thousands of times, sometimes fully and detailed, but more often elliptically, reduced to the use of the mere term 'integration' in relation to specific policy options or practices. In a number of cases, the term 'migrant policy' stands as a synonym for 'integration policy'. Similarly, the term itself has been provided with at least two synonyms in the debate: (a) insertion (*inpassing* in Dutch), a term used by the KCM itself, originally as a label for the first part of the dogmatic version of the concept (see above); (b) citizenisation (*inburgering* in Dutch), a term coined by the chairman of the Flemish Liberal opposition party, Guy Verhofstadt, and used as the label for an alternative migrant policy which, in fact, is nearly identical to the one proposed by the KCM (Verhofstadt 1992).

It is remarkable how widespread the use of 'integration' has become, and what a wide variety of approaches, ideological stances and practices it can cover. Integration has been used to justify decisions and actions that can hardly be associated with the original intentions of the architects of the Belgian integration policy. At the same time, however, small reformulations of the concept have been used to insert new or different connotations, policy preferences or ideological emphases in the discourse on migrants. The first set of phenomena can be called appropriation; the second I will call manipulation.

Appropriation

The right wing, including the Vlaams Blok, has been an avid consumer of the term 'integration'. In right-wing discourse, the term is loaded with one-sided references to cultural (or other forms of) adaptation, and thus becomes a formidably repressive weapon. Part of its power and effect is derived from the appropriation of the terminological repertoire of integration rhetoric: the right wing uses the same words, the same key terms and the same basic frame of reference (us–them, culture, traditions, the law, our social system). This has a disarming effect: people opposed to right-wing approaches find themselves confronted with (parts of) the powerful rhetoric of integration, to which they themselves feel strongly attached.

Example (1) is taken from the transcript of a TV talk show held in February 1994 on the Flemish public network. The interviewer invited the mayor of the town of Sint Truiden to clarify the decision of his social service council to reduce the social allowances to Sikhs living in Sint Truiden. The few hundred Sikhs in question were temporary residents employed in harvest work on the fruit plantations around the town. In the summer of 1993, there had been a Molotov cocktail attack against one of the Sikh houses, a sign of an intensely anti-Sikh racist climate among local people. The social service council of Sint Truiden had decided to reduce allowances to Sikhs on the grounds that Sikhs live with many in one house and don't eat meat; hence, they wouldn't need much money. The interviewer intends to challenge the mayor on this decision:

(1) *Interviewer:* I'd like to discuss the argument you used, that they live with so many in a house and need less...

> *Mayor*: THEY have to be able to integrate themselves like our people; when there are ten people living in a house [owned] by the local population then there is a regulation for asylum seekers, for the foreigners, they have to adapt to OUR culture, to our regulation and to our norms and not the other way round.

The mayor interrupts the challenge from the interviewer, and constructs a somewhat confused argument, which nevertheless contains enough effective apologetic strategies based on the appropriation of integration rhetoric. First, his response is neatly framed in a clear 'us–them' opposition (intonationally marked by a high pitch on THEY and OUR). In this opposition, the 'us' stands for order, rules and regulations; the 'them' stands for infringements of rules and regulations, on disobedience and disturbing behaviour. The bridge between the two is 'integration', here seen as a strictly one-way concept: 'they have to adapt to OUR culture, to our regulation [*sic*] and to our norms and not the other way round'. The mayor of Sint Truiden here selects one particular inter-pretation of the concept of 'integration': an interpretation focused on unilateral cultural and behavioural adaptation, refusal of which may lead to repression and the loss of basic rights (such as the right to a fair social allowance). It is a classic example of right-wing integration rhetoric: integration equals adaptation (or even assimilation), and is used as a social condition *sine qua non*, which, if need be, can be imposed by force.

In the second example, taken from the parliamentary records of the Flemish Parliament (17 February 1993), Vlaams Blok spokesman Filip Dewinter challenges a recent decision by the Minister of Education to allow Muslim girls to wear scarves in public schools:

(2)   Of course this matter touches on more than just wearing a scarf. The Flemish government with this new approach plays into the hands of the Islamic fundamentalists. This is an obstacle for the integration of second – and third – generation migrants. Even in certain North African countries, the scarf is only worn among very traditional groups of the population. Allowing the scarf impedes integration. By allowing the scarf, the Minister in fact admits that integration is an illusion. In that sense he comes close to the views of the Vlaams Blok. Only, we are much more consistent, and we conclude from this that only a policy of repatriation makes sense. The Vlaams Blok advocates the reintegration of foreigners in their own community. In view of this, we want to build a separate education system for them, which could prepare them for their repatriation.

The Vlaams Blok spokesperson, like the Christian-Democrat mayor of

Sint Truiden, constructs a clever piece of political rhetoric, built around a one-sided interpretation of integration. The line of argument runs as follows: 'the scarf is a symbol of Muslim oppression of women and of Muslim fundamentalism; fundamentalism is inconsistent with the aims of integration; therefore the minister's decision goes against the aims and goals of integration policy.' From that point onwards, the argument is reinforced with the basic tenets of Vlaams Blok ideology: the minister's incongruous decision is evidence that integration is impossible and that the only viable solution to the 'migrant problem' would be to have them return to their 'country of origin'.[6] As in the case of the mayor of Sint Truiden, this line of argument, one-sided though it may be, has a paralysing effect on Vlaams Blok's opponents. Many people would indeed agree with the propositions of the argument that wearing a scarf signifies sympathy for Muslim fundamentalism and that fundamentalism is incompatible with the idea of integration. In fact, people closer to the political centre, such as the Liberal chairman Verhofstadt, echoed the same theme: Doesn't [the Rushdie affair] show that Islam is essentially an intolerant and totalitarian ideology, which clashes with the cultural, moral and legal prescriptions valid in an open and democratic society?' (Verhofstadt 1992: 65).

Even the Royal Commissioner for Migrant Policy herself repeatedly expressed an aversion to radical forms of Islam. In a speech on youth work in Leuven on 23 October 1992, Paula D'Hondt said: 'But conversely, it is the case that a fundamentalist variant of Islam cannot be accepted, at least not here. An Islam that integrates [itself] can.' In other words, the Vlaams Blok anchors its argument in a textual tradition of anti-Islam rhetoric, which had some respectability. Just like the mayor of Sint Truiden, Dewinter does not formulate a controversial argument, he stays within a mainstream interpretational space of aspects of integration. In both examples, the use of integration is based on and vindicated by existing and respectable traditions of discourse.

The strategy of appropriation also emerges in connection with foreigner-related repressive policy decisions. A case in point is asylum policy, and the basic pattern of argumentation used by advocates of a more restrictive asylum regulation can be summarised as follows: 'The uncontrolled influx of asylum seekers and illegal aliens jeopardises integration policy, because the newcomers stimulate racist feelings and feelings of insecurity among the local population; furthermore, all efforts should be concentrated on the successful integration of those foreigners who legally reside in Belgium.' In other words, the extreme reduction of new immigration is motivated by reference to the integration of the people stemming from the old migration. Integration policy can only succeed if it goes hand in hand with a restrictive immigration policy. This argument is quite widespread. It can be found in the KCM's programme statement, where the 'humane control of immigration flows' is defined as one of the priorities. It can also be found both on the left and right of the political spectrum, sometimes even in almost identical versions, as in examples (3) and (4):

(3)   'And yet this group [illegal aliens] spoils the situation for the minority, who are indeed genuine refugees, and they jeopardise the whole of the migrant policy. The population does not make a lot of difference between a rejected applicant who disappears into illegality and an ordinary migrant.'

(Flemish Socialist Chairman then Minister of Interior Louis Tobback, interview, *Fuga*, October/November 1991: 20)

(4)   'An efficient repatriation policy is the first priority. As long as the population notices that the wave of asylum seekers grows in size, and that the rejected applicants go underground, one will get sharp reactions such as in Lint (where the population protested against the opening of a refugee centre). This also jeopardises the migrant policy.'

(Flemish Liberal MP and expert on migrant affairs Ward Beysen, interview, *Fuga*, October/November 1991: 16)

The reference to integration policy (here synonymous with integration policy) is cursory and appears almost as a side remark. Yet, politically, it is heavy artillery aimed at pacifying the protests of people who feel that Belgian asylum policy is too restrictive and too repressive. By referring to the aims of the integration policy, another set of legitimate and existing interpretative traditions is invoked: humanism, the desire to give multi-culturalism a fair chance, even the protection of resident migrants who already suffer from racism. A basically very hard policy is so motivated and neutralised by referring to a 'soft' tradition of integration discourse.

What we have noticed in the examples is how wide and diverse is the interpretational space of integration. The term can be legitimately used both in an oppressive, right-wing register focusing on law and order and unilateral adaptation (as in examples (1) and (2)), as well as in a soft, humanist left-wing register in which the values of minority protection and multiculturalism are invoked (as in examples (3) and (4)). Both directions of interpretation are linked – loosely sometimes – to aspects of the dogmatic version and its vulgate, in a discursive network of considerable complexity, full of quotations, echoes, amendments and so on. The vulgate will be discussed in the next subsection. Here, we can already indicate that, in terms of real power and effects on people's lives, diverging interpretations such as the ones discussed here are far more important than the dogmatic version of the concept of integration. Implementation programmes are shaped and measures are motivated on the basis of these secondary versions of the concept of integration, however far these interpretations may be removed from the original intentions and ambitions of the architects of the integration policy.

Manipulation

Apart from the dogmatic version of the concept of integration, central actors in the development of integration policies have reformulated the concept time and time again, thus shaping a degree of textual and conceptual vagueness in the domain of integration, and allowing for a number of secondary interpretations, such as the ones discussed above, that are sometimes very different from those of the original authors. The reformulations produced by KCM and CGKR officials are not all that innocent, though they may appear to be mere clarifications or vulgaris-ations. They may, in cases, steer the interpretation of the concept of integration into a 'soft' or 'hard' direction, depending on time, occasion and audience. Consider the following four examples. The first two are reformulations, made by Paula D'Hondt herself. Example (5) is taken from an opinion survey in a daily newspaper (*De Standaard*, 1–2 February 1992: 7); example (6) from the speech on youth work quoted above.

(5) 'Integration of migrants in our society has been defined as insertion by us. We have concretised this concept in four points. One can find these four points in our first report of November 1989: in the first two points, we demand things from migrants, in the other two, we are open to them.

- We demand assimilation where public order is concerned. That means migrants have to respect Belgian laws, with no exception, all of them, just like any Belgian.
- We demand that the fundamental social principles of our society be respected by everyone, so also by migrants: the emancipation of women, as we understand it; mutual tolerance; our language, and so forth.
- Apart from these two very important things that we demand from migrants – and more cannot be demanded from people in a law-abiding society, regardless of whether they are migrants or Belgians – we are open to what those people can contribute: in the artistic, culinary, linguistic, cultural and other domains. There, we assume

that mutual enrichment is not only possible but even desirable, a condition for progress.

- We also say that sufficiently competent people from migrant circles should be involved in the objectives and the activities of the authorities, because this is the only road to emancipation, just like it was for women.'

(6)   'Therefore, "insertion", for migrants, means:

- A complete assimilation to Belgian law. Belgian law is everybody's law on our territory, regardless of whether he [*sic*] is a migrant or a Belgian.
- A complete respect for the orienting, fundamental ideas of our western society. And that means that my [*sic*] concept of integration is not neutral! It includes, for instance, the knowledge of the regional language. Also, the separation between Church and State, as it has been shaped here, remains primordial. Also, the emancipation of women, as we understand it; and the reciprocity among people as we understand it. But it also means – and that is the proposed respect for minorities:
- that, once the two first conditions have been met, there will be openness, and even promotion, of mutual cultural enrichment;
- that there will be promotion for people from the minority groups who have complied in an exemplary manner with the first three criteria, in the sense that they would fulfil exemplary functions in important societal niches.'

The following two examples are taken from notes made during public debates on integration. In example (7), CGKR director Johan Leman comments retrospectively on the adventures of the original concept of integration (Antwerp, 14 June 1995). Example (8) is the definition of integration given by CGKR official Houssein Boukhriss (Roeselare, 23 September 1993).

(7)   'One has to read the concept of integration in the context of a policy document made in 1989. Today, we'd rather speak of a concept of emancipation. I don't care about the name; the point is: we had to obtain a parliamentary majority for our policy, and the concept proved to be a handy mobilising instrument. The original concept contained four parts. For as far as the "'orienting fundamental principles" goes, I myself was upset by the kind of referents given to this. And I wouldn't use a term such as "modernity" any more. In general, this element was too vaguely put.'

(8)
- 'Assimilation to the public order.
- Stimulate (not force) the acceptance of emancipation, pluralism etc., because these values generate social opportunities.
- Accept that others are different, including in the domain of religion (Islam).
- Participation to power.'

Examples (5) and (6) show 'harder' reformulations of the concept, for they stress the conditional nature of 'insertion' in the migrants' structural involvement in Belgian society. When compared with the dogmatic version of the concept of integration, two elements stand out:

- the fact that 'integration' has been totally eclipsed by 'insertion' – what Paula D'Hondt described was an *insertion* concept. Note that in the dogmatic version, 'insertion' only touched the 'demand side' of integration – those things that the Belgians demanded from migrants; and
- instead of the two-part organisation of the dogmatic version (in which part 1 was a three-part 'insertion' programme, and part 2 dealt with 'structural involvement'), D'Hondt uses a linear textual organisation divided into four points, in which 'structural involvement' is juxtaposed to and *conditioned* by the three 'insertion' elements. The bottom line, somewhat vulgarly put, is that migrants will only get decent jobs if they are 'well integrated' – an interpretation that falls into the same tradition as the one used by the mayor of Sint Truiden and Filip Dewinter, and far removed from the original spirit of the concept.

Examples (7) and (8), on the other hand, provide 'softer' readings of the concept. In example (7), Leman expresses his a posteriori surprise over the exuberant interpretations given to the 'cultural' part of the concept and admits that it was somewhat too vaguely put. In the same breath, he replaces 'integration' with 'emancipation', adding that the name itself does not matter much. However, it makes a world of difference whether one speaks of integration (with all its culturalist connotations) or of emancipation (with its distinct ring of economics and power, embedded as it is in the semantic history of the labour movement and feminism). Leman draws integration away from the swamps of cultural adaptation and into the domain of jobs, upward social mobility, prosperity and well-being – a definite left-wing interpretation of the concept. Similarly, Boukhriss, in example (8), plays down the adaptationist dimension of the concept, saying that migrant communities should be encouraged but not forced to accept 'Belgian values' for the utilitarian reason that it will enhance their socio-economic opportunities. Boukhriss also uses the term 'participation to power', a term that is almost taboo in current integration discourse but is well in line with left-wing demands and preferences. As an aside, one could also point to the inclusion of Islam in the domain of acceptance of diversity, a point about which, as we saw above, Paula D'Hondt was slightly more sensitive.

If we take these four final examples together, we notice how central actors in developing integration policy themselves put the interpretation of the concept on widely divergent tracks, and that they do so by means of seemingly innocuous reformulations. A small word here and there, downplayed as if it were a trivium, a reordering of the various parts of the original concept: they all trigger tremendously different interpretations, all of them vindicated by the fact that their authors are the main players in the field of integration policy. Part of the vagueness of the concept of integration, and hence part of what Leman complains about, has been created by the authors of the concept of integration themselves.[7]

Conclusion: vagueness and power

What we have witnessed in the previous section is the emergence of integration as a *space* within which various often conflicting interpretations float around. A wide variety of social actors use and shape the interpretations through a discursive process best described as a debate. It is in the debate on migrants that the politics of integration develops, and in which we see how the dogmatic version of the text – the policy itself – becomes subordinate to the secondary interpretations of social actors, including – amazingly – the policy's authors themselves. In a critique of Belgian migrant policies, therefore, it may be wise to shift the focus of attention away from the formal sphere of policies (strictly speaking) into the informal sphere of what happens to these policies after they have been launched. As noted above, these secondary interpretations have far more impact when it comes to assessing the real experiences and practices of the people involved in constructing or solving the 'migrant problem'.

Another necessary shift in attention is, I believe, the shift from texts to actors. There is little virtue in doctrinaire text exegesis when one wants to inquire into the intentions of policymakers. It may be more useful to follow the discursive practices of policymakers over a longer span of time, together with those of the people they react against, respond to or challenge in the debate. As seen above, policymakers sometimes move into the 'informal' domain of reformulations themselves. Just like other social actors, they indulge in shaping and exploring the interpretative space of the key concepts they have developed. This may sound incongruous and indeed it is when one takes a pristine, abstract view of politics. It is, however, totally coherent with a view of politics as the exercise of power. Creating vagueness and confusion in the interpretation of key political terms is a rewarding endeavour in a context where discrete alliances have to be made and a wide enough political consensus has to be reached on sensitive issues. In Noel Thompson's words (1996: 37): 'Over-arching concepts ... have their value both in determining the ground upon which political debate takes place and broadening the basis of support for the party which successfully employs them. There is considerable electoral virtue in a concept open to disparate interpretations and satisfying a variety of political tastes.' In short, blaming policy-makers for remaining vague about the precise meaning of key terms may be a futile exercise. The effectiveness of their policies rests to a considerable degree on keeping concepts open, on leaving them floating in the space of interpretation.

Important in all this is the role of wording. It was most remarkable to see at what level subtle policy preferences were articulated, and how. First, every actor in the field makes use of a seemingly stable lexical frame: they all use the key term 'integration' and elements from its associative lexical register ('culture', 'values', 'norms', 'traditions', 'us–them'). This is what keeps the debate together as a topical unit each time people talk about integration, using the right words. At the same time, differences reside in the general wording pattern, in the precise shape of formulations and reformulations. As a consequence, the different formulations mentioned by the KCM in its final report may indicate less of a consensus than meets the eye. It may indicate a tremendously divergent set of interpretations, held together by the joint use of the lexical frame and by agile manipulations of the interpretational space by the policymakers themselves. In that sense, what the KCM has accomplished is not consensus, but the kind of uncertainty that may enable successful power elaboration.

Notes

1. I use the term 'migrant' in its everyday sense, that is referring to groups of people who arrived and settled in Belgium as the result of migration. The term is, strictly speaking, semantically nonsensical, since the groups of people commonly denoted by this term do not migrate. They are permanent residents in Belgium.

2. All the examples used in this chapter were originally in Dutch. All translations are mine and I take full responsibility for possible translation errors. In quoting the KCM reports, I used the official Dutch version of texts. Other data used in this paper include transcripts from a TV talk show,

newspaper articles, the written version of a speech, and notes I made during debates in which I participated.

3. Note that the federalisation process has decentralised part of the migrant-related policies. The Flemish government now has its own migrant policies, and a comparison of doctrinaire texts would undoubtedly yield revealing results.

4. A distinction is presupposed between 'democratic' and 'undemocratic' opposition parties, the latter being a synonym for the extreme right-wing Vlaams Blok party.

5. I use the term 'minorisation' in the sense of Rath (1991): a series of explicit and implicit processes by means of which a group's status of 'minority' is institutionally anchored and expanded.

6. Which, in real terms, is Belgium for a majority of the people targeted by the Vlaams Blok.

7. At the same time, critics of the concept of integration are systematically countered by referring to the dogmatic version of the text, arguing that people misquote or misinterpret the text (Blommaert 1996).

Multicultural policies and the state: a British paradox

Malcolm Cross

Any evaluation of the British approach to the management of ethnic minority incorporation in the years after the Second World War has to start with emphasising something which it was not. Unlike most countries in the rest of western Europe, experiencing the same or similar imperatives for pliable, low-cost labour and (in some cases) the consequences of colonialism, the issues were never those of citizenship or – in a simple sense – of membership and belonging. Thus, while 5.5 per cent of the UK population has its origins in these postwar population flows, the vast majority were citizens of the Commonwealth and – at the time of entry – entitled to British citizenship. From the outset, the issues of policy have been issues of 'integration', albeit defined in a myriad of often conflicting ways.

In a fairly recent article, Stephen Castles points out that 'the British model (of integrating minorities) is currently a mixture of assimilationist and pluralist policies, without a clear overall objective' (Castles 1995: 301). His argument is that assimilation may well have been the original intent but that continued marginalisation and racial inequality have forced upon (reluctant) policymakers a greater degree of pluralism. Thus, pluralism is the radical option. As Castles writes elsewhere: 'The core of multiculturalism is the demand for full political, economic and social participation of all members of society' (Castles 1993: 33). In this sense, Britain has never pursued a multicultural policy. On the contrary, while never wholly consistent, the principal objective of intervention from central government has been assimilationist. Yet, the outcome is far from the US ideal of *e pluribus unum*: arguably, Britain today is more divided behind walls of defensive ethnicity than at any time in its history. In this chapter, I seek to explain how this has come about – the argument presented here is elaborated in a parallel paper (see Cross, forthcoming).

It is important to begin by stressing that *multiculturalism* and *pluralism* are not the same thing. The former is inherently a policy goal while the latter is sometimes used in this sense but is also a condition of society. The opposite to multiculturalism is *assimilationism*, while the opposite of pluralism is cultural and structural consensus and uniformity.[1] Thus, it is not contradictory to propose that pluralism can be an outcome of assimilationism. Indeed, that is essentially the resolution of the British paradox. The reassertion of specifically ethnic identities is one response to failed integration; that is the reassertion of difference in the face of apparent indifference, or the declaration of a quality of distinctiveness when confronted with apparently intractable inequality. It is true that this may produce different local agendas, so that it might be analytically useful to draw a distinction between *proactive multiculturalism* and *reactive multiculturalism*. *Proactive multiculturalism* is a characteristic of countries of immigration such as Canada or Australia that approach the issue of integration through the celebration of cultural difference. The panoply of measures this generates are foreign to the British experience. Britain has no 'office of multicultural affairs' or anything similar. *Reactive mutliculturalism* is the generation of divergence by failing to deliver a promise of convergent opportunity or by actively fomenting inequality. In fact, the story of British policy interventions shows both, as the discussion below will show.[2]

In drawing these distinctions, there is an obvious reference to one of the long-running debates in the literature on the sources of ethnic distinctiveness. Primordial theories are largely concerned with exploring the power of ethnic identity to shape and refract all – or most – others (Geertz 1963). Instrumental perspectives give greater weight to the situationally specific function of ethnicities to frame and project an interest (Hall 1992). Academic debate in the UK has evolved from a version of one to several versions of the other. In the 1950s and 1960s, the focus was largely on cultural baggage. Migrants were 'dark strangers', in Sheila Patterson's telling phrase, whose location in British society was generated by their cultural distinctiveness (Patterson 1965). Much more recently, under the influence of postmodernist discourse, ethnicity has become the symbolic representation of an ever-shifting fragmentation which is moulded by day-to-day encounters. The dangers of cultural determinism have been replaced by the perils of cultural relativism. The assumption that ethnicity can be considered as either a 'first moment' phenomenon or one that is shaped and moulded solely by street-level events is rejected here. The encounter between the British state and ethnic minorities shows that the imaginings of a shared past are neither non-contingent nor solely whisked together from a rational appraisal of interests. They become as forceful as they are precisely because they are a way of making the past live and serve the present (Cross 1994a). It is the interaction between the two that makes ethnicity such a powerful force. As Robert Park pointed out many years ago, the paradox of ethnicity is precisely its capacity to be sustained by its denial through attempted assimilation (Ballis Lal 1990: 96–7).

The proposition that state intervention can be divisive needs to be carefully framed. Not all state involvement has this effect. Moreover, this is rarely the intent and it is all too easy to reify what is denoted by the term 'the state' into something monolithic, unified and impenetrable by those who are affected by its actions. While the outcome may have been similar at different levels of state intervention, the motivation was clearly different. For this reason, it makes sense to draw a distinction in the British case between the central state, the local state and something in between, which might be termed the 'meso-state' level. As the following argument will attempt to show, the failure of the first was less of intent and more of implementation; the second did not fail at all but by articulating the priorities of different groups at a time of unprecedented state centralisation opened up ethnic fissures that might otherwise have remained bridged by interests held in common. The 'meso-level' refers to the role of agencies that are constrained and regulated by central government but which possess devolved responsibilities at a higher level than local municipalities. The system of criminal justice in Britain has had a major impact on the fortunes of ethnic minorities in Britain and is the example to which I shall refer.

Encounter with the central state

While there is no general theory to guide our understanding of the encounter between minorities and public policy, the central issue is 'social integration', by which I mean an equivalence of opportunity with the majority. A minority may be said to possess this equivalence when individual members are free of impediments to utilising opportunities which are, in turn, distributed in the same for all. In practice, public policy has tended to isolate three components parts:[3]

- the opportunity structure in which different groups are located (for example what chances of employment are available);
- the resources which groups possess (for example education); and

- the barriers affecting how resources can be utilised in accessing opportunities (for example attempts to control discrimination).

Thought of in terms of this model, the role of the central state can be seen in terms of demand management, policies affecting the quality of the labour supply and in terms of strategies for lowering barriers to accessing opportunities. While it would be folly to deny the salience of other central state functions, nonetheless what a government does to provide employment, to create opportunities for enhancing skills and educational qualifications and to ensure the control of both direct and indirect discrimination are certainly important in effecting the long-run integration of migrants and minorities. All three are evident in the British case. The first led to an inner cities regeneration programme; the second to the attempt to improve educational success through additional expenditure (Section 11 of the Local Government Act 1966) and the third to the 1976 Race Relations Act. After a comment on the brief period when an alternative policy of pluralism looked possible, I shall examine each area in turn.

The mid-1960s was the period in which Britain woke up to the realisation that action over integrating new citizens from the Caribbean and sub-continental Asia was essential and most of the key legislation has its roots in the first and second Labour governments first elected in 1964 (for earlier history see Fryer 1984; for descriptions of the politics of the period, see Jacobs 1986; Saggar 1992; Solomos 1993). The then Home Secretary, Roy Jenkins, declared in 1966 that the objective was threefold. The aim was for 'equality of opportunity, coupled with cultural diversity, in an atmosphere of mutual tolerance' (Jenkins 1967: 267). It is arguable that, for officials at least, this trinity became the agenda for the following decade. The second component was always the weakest. Insofar as it became embodied in anything it was in the Local Government (Ethnic Groups) Bill of 1978/9 which fell with the triumph of Margaret Thatcher and the Conservatives in May 1979. There had always been a tension between two concepts of 'ethnic needs', one which was assimilationist and one which was pluralist. The first assumed that what was 'special' about recent migrants or their descendants was their newness itself and that policy provision should focus on the acculturation of newcomers to their adopted surroundings. The second took the opposite line, arguing that 'special needs' were those that flowed from difference, particularly cultural forms. The changes that had to be made therefore were to the monocultural institutions of civic and public life. The Ethnic Groups Bill proposed numerous initiatives based on the concept of 'racial disadvantage' affecting particular ethnic communities. Its loss was the end of pluralist thinking from central government.

Regenerating cities?

Most commentators suggest that the origins of the Urban Programme lay with the famous speech in 1968 by Enoch Powell in which he foresaw the equivalent of the 'Tiber foaming with blood' unless action was taken to counter the build-up of large populations of visible minorities in British cities (Solomos 1993: 67–8). The Urban Programme Harold Wilson, the then prime minister, announced in 1968 offered an alternative objective to Powell's xenophobic tendencies and enthusiasm for repatriation. Further developments in the administration of race relations in the context of inner-city policy were to emerge during 1977, with the publication of the White Paper, 'Policy for the Inner Cities' (Home Office 1977).

The policy of inner-city regeneration has been pursued in one form or another ever since, achieving something of an apotheosis during Margaret Thatcher's premiership (Edwards and Batley 1978; Jacobs 1986). Since then the panoply of 'partnerships' between national and local government and the private sector have become concentrated into what has come to be called the Single Regeneration Grant (SRG). The problem is that all the independent evaluation studies point to the inadequacy of the results in countering the tendency of British cities to suffer relative decline in their economic fortunes . This decline has three main reasons. First, it is a result of macro-economic management over the 1980s, which led to relative growth in inequality and poverty in Britain when compared with her European partners. As I wrote elsewhere (Cross 1993a: 9):

> Although only nine countries are included, the UK again comes out at the top of the league in terms of the increase of households in poverty. The number rose from 2.8m in 1980 to 3.8m in 1988, a rise of 36 per cent. Of the countries included in the comparison, only Belgium comes close to this figure and here it must be remembered that Belgium's overall rate of poverty was much lower (7.5 per cent compared to 17.0 per cent). The UK contained a quarter (26 per cent) of the poor households among these nine nations in 1980 and a third (33 per cent) towards the end of the decade. Over the same period the numbers of poor persons contributed by the UK in this comparison rose from 24 per cent in 1980 to 28 per cent in 1987/90. The fact that since the late 1980s the recession has been considerably worse in the UK than elsewhere makes it very probable that these data under-estimate the contribution that Britain makes today to the ranks of the European poor.

In other words, it is now widely acknowledged that one cost of the economic reforms of the last decade and a half has been a significant widening of economic inequalities. Where poverty has clear patterns of a real concentration, this fact itself is of considerable significance. Indeed, there is an association between the two. For example, since 1993,

Liverpool has been identified as an 'Objective One' region for the purposes of regional aid. Merseyside as a whole has also been the region of greatest population decline, experiencing a 19 per cent drop between 1961 and 1991 (*The Economist*, 24 August 1996: 24).

The second reason was the attack on local government, which led to the greatest decline in local government fortunes ever experienced and a massive centralisation of state power. The local state in Britain has literally been shorn of functions which, for a century or more, were regarded as essential for local civic governance. The consequence of this has been that, even where additional expenditure has been sanctioned under inner-city regeneration programmes, it has been rare for this to have counteracted the decline in central state support for local government with the effect that policy overall has had a negative impact at the local level (Cross 1992a). Finally, while there is little doubt about the impetus for the Urban Programme, as it evolved it became less and less concentrated in areas in which British minority ethnic communities lived. It was transferred, for example, from the Home Office (which has always had responsibility for British 'race policy') to the Department of the Environment. As the Secretary of State for the Environment put it 1977: 'I do not think that . . . the Urban Programme has been in the past a black programme. If it has been, it has been extremely ill-directed because an extremely small part has gone to areas where black communities are strongly established' (*Hansard* 929, 6 April 1977, col 1235–6)

Indeed, John Rex has rightly pointed out that far from focusing on the ethnic minority population, the Urban Programme came to identify the existing population of inner areas as part of the problem (Rex 1988: 59, 111). The White Paper of 1977 (Home Office 1977), which preceded what became known as the Inner Areas Act, proposed the dispersal of inner-city populations rather than attempts to improve education and training provision. Aside from the implication that the inner urban unemployed were unemployable, this also suggested an official indifference to the salience of ethnic communities.

It is not simply the case that central government policy on inner cities has failed to stem the flow of resources elsewhere, it is also the case that one consequence has been the promotion of ethnic division. I have written elsewhere on the impact of this period on a city (Greater London) where these impacts have been mitigated by relative buoyancy in economic fortunes (Cross 1992b; 1993b; 1994b). The conclusion I came to was that, on the one hand, the 'black' population, and in particular that of Caribbean origin, had suffered terribly in economic terms, being ever more likely to be caught up in ghettoisation processes of relative and real decline. This is regardless of where they are located in the city.[4] South

Asian groups, by contrast, have generally fared better, particularly outside the inner areas of London. The well-known exception is in Inner London where the Bengalis of Tower Hamlets have unemployment and poverty levels that are among the highest in Britain. This is partly a result of spatial decline, but is also influenced by the age profile of the community itself. Outside the inner city, Islamic South Asian groups tend to fare rather better across a whole range of measures, although this pattern is often obscured by the relative decline in the fortunes of all groups (as in, for example, Bradford).

This economic divergence extends to self-employment and entrepreneurship. Some of this is well known, but what is seldom recognised is the importance of this activity for South Asians in particular. The 1991 census showed, for example, that nearly one in ten employed South Asians in Great Britain was also an employer of someone else. Moreover, 44 per cent of the self-employed South Asians had employees. Only one in three white self-employed workers was in the position and one in four from the 'black' groups identified in the census. This can no longer be seen as merely the activities of the 'enclave economy', since much of this entrepreneurial activity is now in the mainstream, and neither can it be argued that it is seldom associated with economic success (Lyon and West 1995; Rafiq 1992; Srinivasan 1992).

It is possible that this ethnic divergence in fortunes would have occurred in different economic circumstances but to a lesser degree. It is important, however, to recognise an 'ethnic dimension' to urban processes in the sense that, for a combination of cultural, economic and social reasons, some groups have withstood the onslaught of economic restructuring better than others. In so far as urban policy has clearly failed to deliver a boost in fortunes for all, it has tended to fragment populations, often along ethnic lines (Cross 1993b).

Boosting human capital?

The second element, that of boosting resources of human capital, was largely to be the responsibility of schools. Section 11 of the Local Government Act of 1966 was highly relevant here for the vast majority of the expenditure under this legislation came to be directed at attempting to increase school performance by offering additional facilities for language instruction in areas of high ethnic minority concentration. The assumptions underlying this legislative provision were assimilationist as the relevant clause itself (Section 11, Local Government Act 1966, Ch 42: 2) shows:

the Secretary of State may pay to Local Authorities who in his opinion are required to make special provision in the exercise of any of their functions in consequence of the presence within their areas of substantial numbers of immigrants from the Commonwealth whose language or customs differ from those of the community, grants of such amounts as he may with the consent of the Treasury determine.

In other words, the expenditure was designed from the centre to be overcoming the drag on the accumulation of human capital that was felt to follow from adherence to non-British culture. Expenditure under this section of the Act rose from £3.2 million in 1967/8 to more than £100 million in 1983/4. Since then, the total has fallen, particularly with the introduction of the Single Regeneration Grant. All Section 11 monies payable to 'inner cities' are now merged with the SRG and the remainder (approximately half of the total) is now only approximately £40 million. The Home Office finances 75 per cent of expenditure, the balance being provided by local government. Of the total expenditure, approximately three quarters goes on paying for additional staff in education while the vast majority of the remainder is used for social services.

If the 1976 Act incorporates an implicit theory of discrimination that locates its aetiology in classical racism and xenophobia, Section 11 of the Local Government Act is based on quite different assumptions. Insofar as it addresses 'racial disadvantage' at all, it does so by focusing on cultural difference. It calls for the provision of supplementary services at the local level to meet 'special needs'. 'Special needs' in this context can be of two types. They can aid assimilation (for example language teaching) or sustain pluralism (support cultural festivals). By and large, pressure from the centre has been applied to further the former while applications from community groups have been more interested in the latter.

Up to 1983/4, when the formula was abandoned, the pattern of expenditure under Section 11 shows a highly variable overall outcome, regardless of how well a council, borough or district fulfilled the minimum criteria for aid. For example, in 1982/3, when Manchester was receiving grants of £2.1 million, Liverpool was allocated only £2384. Similarly, in the same year, while Brent received a grant of £3.7 million, Lewisham was paid £23,963. These differences cannot be accounted for in terms of 'special needs' as identified under the Act.

The central question that arises as a result of this legislation does not so much concern its administration; rather it relates to how well it has served to boost the educational performance of Britain's ethnic minorities. In fact, the answer cannot be anything but negative because there is no discernible relationship between educational performance by ethnic minorities and expenditure on additional teachers financed through this means. What has occurred in general is another instance of divergence or pluralisation with South Asians tending to outperform the Caribbean-British population. Perhaps the most thorough analysis of the general picture is that by David Drew (1995). Table 6.1 is derived from his analysis and it shows the extent of the divergence even when social class is controlled.

Table 6.1   *Average examination scores by ethnic origin, gender and socio-economic group*

Social Class	Afro-Caribbean		Asian		White	
	Male	Female	Male	Female	Male	Female
Professional	27.1	24.9	30.7	27.8	30.4	32.3
Intermediate	21.1	18.1	27.2	25.9	23.7	25.0
Manual	14.3	15.6	23.3	22.5	17.6	20.0

Source: Drew (1995: 79)

Social class and gender are powerful correlates of school performance, but so is ethnicity. In particular, South Asians are not as disadvantaged to the same extent as others in terms of school success by their social class origins. In this they are similar to the Cuban and other Hispanic migrant groups studied by Alejandro Portes (1993). Afro-Caribbean young people, by contrast, appear to experience the constraints of minority status and social class additively. This correlates also with the exclusion of many Caribbean-descended youngsters from school itself as being beyond control.

The reasons for these patterns are generally recognised as very complex. The central point here is not to give an explanation for them; rather it is to stress that a reactive form of ethnic differentiation has flowed from the absence of pluralist policies. Assimilationist assumptions, even in education where 'multiculuralism' is sometimes said to be stronger than elsewhere, have produced a passivity in specific measures to ameliorate the under performance of particular groups.[5]

Countering discrimination?

The first two Race Relations Acts date from 1966 and 1968 and it was only the second of these that showed any awareness of what legal remedies for the absence of mutual tolerance might entail. The legal deficiencies of the 1968 legislation were remedied to some extent by the 1976 Race Relations Act, which added the concept of indirect discrimination and enshrined the principle of 'non-discrimination', unlike the Civil Rights Act with which it is often compared.

The 1976 Act operates with a restrictive concept of discrimination. Section 3, for example, defines the 'racial grounds' that qualify in outlawing discrimination as 'colour, race, nationality or ethnic or national origins' (Race Relations Act, c74, section 3). At first sight this suggests an acceptance that discrimination may occur in a wide range of settings, but in fact 'ethnic origin' is not a satisfactory synonym for 'ethnicity'. This is most obvious in its exclusion of religion as a ground for discrimination (Modood 1993). In practice, therefore, appeals against unequal treatment under the Act are likely to be most successful in cases where physical appearance is the basis for differential treatment. Most minorities can be affected in this way, so to this extent the Act is of potential benefit to them, but it is bound to be less relevant in circumstances where ethnic identity is founded upon a set of values that the Act fails to identify as grounds for differential treatment. Tariq Modood (1993), for example, has argued that this is particularly important in the case of British Muslims: 'By the usual socio-economic measures of disadvantage Muslims may be the worse-off groups, and yet, unlike religious groups such as Sikhs and Jews, they are not deemed to be an ethnic group and so are outside the terms of existing anti-discrimination legislation' (Modood 1993: 522).

One consequence of this is that British policy has seen court-based contests over which groups are to be considered as having an identifiable 'ethnic origin' and which not (Cashmore 1989).

It is well known that the British legislation makes provision for 'indirect' discrimination, or differential effects that are a consequence of decisions motivated by non-racial factors.[6] In fact, this part of the legislation has been largely counter-productive. In the first place it has proved very difficult to sustain a case under 'indirect' discrimination clauses, although this is not the main problem. It has also had the effect of individualising what are structural changes. For example, if a firm chooses to relocate its production from Bradford to Bournemouth, or move (more improbably) from clothing to computers, it will probably have a profound effect on Bradford's Muslim population. But it is inconceivable that the 1976 Act could be used to oppose these changes, not simply because they might be thought desirable or inevitable on economic grounds, but because the actions of the firm are thought to be so far from the 'individual treatment' model embodied in the Act. It is not even possible to extend an individual case to encompass others similarly affected. What in the United States are termed 'class actions' are specifically proscribed by the legislation.

The result has been that division has again occurred in this sphere. The Act has inadvertently served to support those with an individual complaint against those who believe that their group position is the critical issue. Thus, minorities who define themselves as 'ethnic communities' on the grounds of their separate and distinctive cultural or religious traditions have been unable to mobilise the Act very effectively because in some cases they may have experienced difficulty in being defined as an 'ethnic' group and, second, because ethnicity is a group phenomenon whereas the Act only identifies individual actions as falling within its remit.

The Commission for Racial Equality is, of course, the chief custodian of the Act and its existence is as potentially important for the elimination of discrimination as the provisions of the Act itself. This is because its first and second duties go well beyond the legislation and specify a promotional function of opposing discrimination and furthering equality of opportunity and 'good relations between persons of different racial groups generally'.

There is much that can and should be written about the role of the Commission in performing these duties and I would not wish to dissent now from an earlier judgement that more could have been achieved with a stronger lead from central government (Cross 1992a: 86). The point is that, in seeking to combine the two major functions of policing the legislation and 'promoting harmony', the Commission has been a prisoner of the legislation. It has vigorously opposed discrimination but never defined its role as the promotion of group rights. 'Harmony' has been defined in practice as the absence of individual acts of dis-crimination. In important fields, such as the implementation of the 1976 legislation to oppose discrimination in employment, the evidence is that – whatever individual victories there may have been in bringing cases to industrial tribunals – these have done little to promote the equalising of employment opportunities between different ethnic groups. The best study in this field was published in 1991. It concluded that 'there is little scope, as matters now stand, for tribunal proceedings in Britain directly to influence the behaviour, policy or practices of employers towards racial minorities' (McCrudden et al. 1991: 282). This may be accountable in part by problems of implementation but the fundamental problem is that reordering the social position of ethnic minorities was never the purpose of the legislation.

Encounter with the intermediate state

In positing the existence of what I have termed the 'intermediate state', I am clearly departing from the norms of political science. Yet there are important policy fields which fall between local and national levels. One such is the criminal justice system which is heavily influenced from above, not merely by legislative fiat but also by increasingly interventionist home secretaries. On the other hand, it is hard to see the administration of justice as simply an aspect of national state action. There are in England and Wales, for example, 43 police forces and only one of these (the Metropolitan Police) is directly controlled from the Home Office.

If one were to posit the suggestion that stereotypes of minorities tend to fall into those concerning behavioural myths and those based on images of clannish and unmergeable cultures, then the administration of British justice would give ample evidence to sustain this theory. In fact, in both official and in popular opinion we have built up a strong image that groups differ in terms of the likely conduct you can expect from them. Similarly, while variations in cultural standards are not regarded officially as overly threatening, in popular opinion such differences are difficult to accept.

An observer does not have to look very far to see these stereotypes at work. Some 15 years ago the Scarman Report into street-level disorder in Brixton in 1981 – in many ways a model of classical liberal thinking – separated the young black man from others with the following words: 'Without close parental support, with no job to go to, and with few recreational facilities available, the young black person makes his life on the streets ... [where] he meets criminals who appear to have no difficulty in obtaining the benefits of a materialistic society' (Scarman Report 1981: 11).

Young Asians, by contrast, are seldom seen as lacking parental support. They are rarely regarded as 'people of the streets'. Frequently, the image is entirely opposite; one of closed communities committed to educational endeavour and to entrepreneurial success.

It is important to stress that images such as this have some foundation in fact. Lord Scarman in the same report was doubtless reporting accurately when he wrote: 'If the principal complaint about the police I have heard from representatives of the West Indian community is one of alleged harassment, the chief complaint of Asian leaders appears to be that the police do not do sufficient to protect their community from alleged attacks by racist members of the white community' (Scarman Report 1981: 12).

The question of whether these stereotypes contain elements of truth is much less important than how agencies respond to them. It is the relationship between how people are and how agencies respond to them which is important, mainly because these are mutually reinforcing. The power of stereotypes is because they have a tendency to be self-fulfilling or producing a cycle of amplification.

The encounter between the police and some sections of the Caribbean-

British and African-British population has been one of deviance amplification. The official police perception 25 years ago of what was then most commonly referred to as the 'West Indian' population was that crime rates were about the same as for the population at large. Since then, the black population, particularly young males, has been over-represented in arrest rates, charge rates and imprisonment rates. The differences are now quite extreme as Figure 6.1 reveals. Even taking into account other factors (by removing the foreign-born population and controlling for age group, region of residence and social class) the differences remain.

Figure 6.1   *Ratio of actual to expected prison population by ethnic group (1993)*

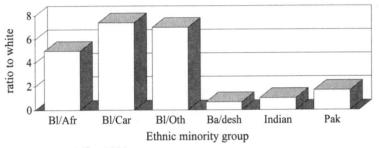

Source: Home Office 1994.

There is no doubt that this, combined with the perceived pattern of offending, has led to differential police attention. The figures from the British Crime Survey (BCS) show this to be so in relation to encounters on the street, such as 'stop and search'. In 1987/8, 19 per cent of Afro-Caribbean respondents had been stopped more than once in the preceding year, compared with 12 per cent of white people and 6 per cent of Asians. Other studies carried out by the Home Office reveal that the balance of types of police contact differs for different ethnic groups, and also that the perceived quality of the encounter varies too. Thus, in the 1988 survey, around two-thirds of young (16–24 year-old) Afro-Caribbeans felt that 'the police don't give blacks equal treatment', where only one in four South Asian young people felt this resentment.

A second type of cycle might be called 'amplifying community isolation'. It is quite clear why South Asian populations might be thought of as basically law-abiding. By the nature of the case, this is unlikely to be thought of as problematic by the police, except where what are perceived as cultural standards come into conflict with wider community norms. The position of young Asian girls, for example, is one often identified by the police themselves. Typically, the perception of cultural isolation makes it commensurably harder to gain access to such communities, with the result that a great deal of police energy may be taken up with locating 'community leaders' as the only available points of access.

The central point here is that under certain circumstances official agencies can generate ethnic differentiation even in the absence of multi-cultural policies. What has been termed here 'the intermediate state' level is a case in point. The British police are not bound by the 1976 Race Relations Act and it was only in 1991, with the passage of the Criminal Justice Act, that agencies in the criminal justice system as a whole were required to publish information that would show whether discrimination could be occurring.[7] Similarly, the most ambitious and thorough study of court procedures conducted in Britain showed, *inter alia*, a tendency for original differences in apprehensions between different ethnic minorities to be magnified by the courtroom procedures (Hood 1992).

If the actions of central government have tended to produce the paradoxical outcome of greater ethnic differentiation while seeking an individual remedy for discrimination and unfair treatment, the institutions at the level of the intermediate state have produced a similar outcome through the opposite process. Freed from the requirement until very recently to pursue policies of equal treatment, they have tended to reflect stereotypical images of group capabilities and behavioural patterns. From a general understanding in the early 1970s that all new citizens were closer than the general population to a law-abiding ideal, what has now evolved is a split perception in which one group is categorised as possessing a far greater potential for deviance than the other. The result is a process of amplification whereby policy and practice reflect these definitions of a divided reality.

Encounter with the local state

At the local state level there has been a very considerable variety of encounter. Overall, however, the local state has proved much more amenable to penetration by ethnic minority politicians if for no other reason than spatial concentrations of population (Geddes 1993). In this process the national system of representative democracy has become rather closer to a group participatory form; that is local government interest groups are more influential and sectional lobbies are commensurably more powerful. While it is important not to overstate this case, since ethnic minorities are still under-represented at the local government level, it is striking that Asian ethnic groups have been more successful than Afro-Caribbeans at using local government to gain a local voice. Andrew Geddes, for example, found that 70 per cent of the councillors in his national survey in 1992 were of Asian origin, whereas they constitute only a little over half of all ethnic minorities (Geddes 1993: 56).

In a study of the local authority of Brent in northwest London conducted in 1990, my colleagues and I showed how a borough with relatively high levels of ethnic minority representation (26 per cent in 1993) responded to local pressure this system operated (Cross 1992a). The politicians who saw themselves as representing the Afro-Caribbean population of the borough were keen to see the development of a non-discriminatory authority. Accordingly, they utilised Section 71 of the 1976 Race Relations Act, which allowed them to argue for a complex system of special units to police non-discriminatory practices.[8] This was quite effective in terms of recruitment strategy, although less so in relation to services. The Asian communities, on the other hand, were more concerned with service delivery, particularly in relation to meeting needs arising from the wish to retain cultural traditions.

The result was a battle which appeared on the outside to be fought along traditional political divisions, but which was in fact more a struggle over differing visions of ethnic minority incorporation. A policy of anti-discrimination was pursued on the one side, while the other tried to co-opt the financial support available under Section 11 of the Local Government Act 1996 to promote mother-tongue teaching, the maintenance of feast days and religious festivals and a less Eurocentric curriculum in schools. In other words, both sides were campaigning for equality of opportunity; one down an essentially assimilationist path and the other down a pluralist road. In this sense, the 1976 Race Relations Act and the legislation a decade earlier were mobilised in defence of contrasting visions of 'integration'. The local authority became transformed into warring factionalism and central government intervened on two important occasions to prevent the 1966 Local Government Act being used for pluralist ends and to water down the 'anti-racism' of the largely black faction (Cross 1991).

While it is perfectly true that local government continues to reflect national divisions of political ideology, nonetheless it has also provided a forum in which ethnic group interests can be pursued. In this way, it has served to articulate separate agendas. It is one consequence of ethnic diversity that where representative institutions are open to group pressure it will become institutionalised.

Conclusion

This chapter seeks to resolve a puzzle. To a Continental European eye, Britain appears almost an archetypal multicultural society. Yet the intention was very different. Each major initiative by central government – from both sides of the House of Commons – was assimilationist. For three major reasons what has evolved has indeed embedded ethnic differences so that a form of passive pluralism has been the outcome. First, assimilation requires the control of social inequality, at least to the extent that patterns of privilege do not correlate too closely with ethnic differences. That has not been the case, either because legislation has not delivered the promise it contained or because major areas of social life have been excluded from its remit. Second, the particular form that ethnic inequality has taken has tended to be divisive. In the vacuum created by the absence of a more positive stance, deep-seated stereotypes of community difference have flourished so that minority opposition to continued discrimination or the absence of opportunity for advancement has rarely managed to bridge what inevitably have been diverse agendas (James 1993). Finally, policies have themselves been divisive. For one section of British minorities, what appears to have been on offer was a pathway to equality of opportunity via the control of individual discrimination. To the other, there appeared to be the mirage of cultural recognition or the promise of pluralism. Unsurprisingly, where limited access to influence was possible – as in some local municipalities – these claims produced a further move apart. It is for these reasons, rather than for ideological difference or cultural preference, that Britain has become a land where ethnic boundaries rival even those of social class.

Notes

1. Clearly, both terms have a specialist usage in the study of ethnic group formation since neither refers to an empirical observable condition.
2. The argument that follows is an attempt to draw together some strands of thinking spanning a number of years and different research projects. In many cases, the evidence for the assertions this chapter contains can be read in the original work to which reference is made in the text.
3. It is not suggested that this is true of all state interventions; only that an analytical distinction can be usefully drawn.
4. In this sense evidence of a real dispersion among the Caribbean-descended population, recently reported for Greater London by Ceri Peach (1996), does not contradict this point.
5. It needs to be stressed that this failure to differentiate between different ethnic groups in their encounter with the school system has been, until recently, a hallmark of educational researchers. They have tended to assume that any form of differentiation undermines a critique of educational institutions and practices.
6. The Act states in Section 1 that a person discriminates against another if

   He applies to that other a requirement or condition which he applies or would apply equally to persons not of the same racial group as that other but:
   (i) which is such that the proportion of persons of the same racial group as

that other who can comply with it is considerably smaller than the proportion of persons not of that racial group who can comply with; and
(ii) which he cannot show to be justifiable irrespective of the colour, race, nationality or ethnic or national origins of the person to whom it is applied: and
(iii) which is to the detriment of that other because he cannot comply with it (Race Relations Act, Clause 74, Section 1).

7. Section 95(1) of the Criminal Justice Act 1991 states that 'The Secretary of State shall in each year publish such information as he considers expedient for the purposes of (b) facilitating the performance by (persons engaged in the administration of criminal justice) of their duty to avoid discriminating against any person on the grounds of race or sex or any other improper ground'.

8. Section 71 of the Race Relations Act 1976 states that: 'It shall be the duty of every local authority to make appropriate arrangements with a view to securing that their various functions are carried out with due regard to the need to eliminate unlawful racial discrimination and to promote equality of opportunity and good relations between persons of different racial groups.'

Part 3

Ethnic political mobilisation and cultural claims

Ethnic politicians in Belgium

Marco Martiniello

In Belgium, as in other European countries, post-Second World War immigration was seen exclusively as a temporary solution to manpower shortages in specific sectors of productive activity, such as the coal mining industry. Migrant workers were considered a cheap, docile and rotating additional labour force, to be sent back to the country of origin when no longer needed (Martens 1976). They were not supposed to settle, let alone become political actors and/or Belgian citizens.

Contrary to this view, labour migration inevitably led to an important settlement of migrants who started very soon to bring in their families. On 1 January 1996, the total foreign population in Belgium amounted to 909,769, composing about 9 per cent of the total population.[1] The profile of the so-called migrant population progressively changed in a dramatic manner. The first wave of migrant workers arrived from Italy in the second half of the 1940s.[2] This migrant group consisted of young male adults who were recruited directly in Italy on a temporary basis with contracts of usually five years. Most of them came from rural Italy. They were not well educated and were prepared to accept heavy and risky jobs for a low salary. They lived on their own in Belgium, where they were first housed in the barracks previously occupied by German war prisoners. Their social and economic statuses were determined by the Italian and Belgian governments within the framework of a bilateral agreement, in the negotiation of which both the unions and employers took part. As foreign citizens, these migrant workers were deprived of any political rights in Belgium. As guests, they were even expected not to interfere in the political life of the receiving country. Some 50 years later, the so-called migrant population includes men and women, families and single people, children and elderly people, and foreigners of various nationalities (such as Italians, Moroccans, Turks, French, Spaniards, Zairians); it is made up of Belgian citizens of migrant descent, of migrants and of Belgian-born people. As a matter of fact, a growing number of those who are still improperly called 'migrants' are actually born in Belgium and are legally full citizens of that country. Economically and socially, even though the majority of this population is still to be found among the popular classes, a process of stratification has occurred within groups of migrant origin. People of migrant origin are (under)represented in the professions, in business, in the arts and in sports. More recently, some of them have also found their way in to formal politics. As is sometimes said in the United States, migrants have become ethnics (Nelli 1983). Their presence in Belgium is definitive.

This dramatic change, as well as the global economic and political changes of the last 20 years, implied the progressive emergence of new issues in the field of migration. Contrary to the period just after the Second Word War, attempting to manage a rotating labour force politically was no longer sufficient. As immigration revealed its structural and permanent character, the question of the migrants' integration into Belgian society took on a greater salience, as did the issue, to be discussed in this chapter, of the population of migrant origin's political participation and active citizenship. (For a discussion of the distinction between active and passive citizenship, see Turner 1990.)

After a historical account and some general points on the political participation and active citizenship of the population of migrant origin in Belgium, the chapter will deal with an under-researched recent process, namely the emergence of politicians from this group. I will describe the gradual introduction of ethnic politicians into the Belgian political system at the European, federal, regional and local levels. The sociological profile of these politicians will then be sketched. The discussion will proceed with some observations about their strategies as well as their relations with 'autochtonous' politicians and political formations. Their difficult position of being caught between real or potential ethnic claims on the one hand, and the blind ethnic approaches often expected of them by their political party or more generally the Belgian polity on the other, will be examined. Finally, some conclusive points will be made to try to relate the present discussion to the literature on the politicisation of ethnicity and to the politics of presence (Phillips 1995).

The political participation of the population of immigrant origin in Belgium in historical perspective

Despite the dominant *economistic* approach to migration, the issue of social and political participation of migrants was raised very early on in Belgium. Labour unions, an important social and political force until not so long ago, quickly understood the necessity of incorporating migrant workers in the class struggle and in workers' organisations. By allowing the double exploitation of an underprivileged migrant section of the working class, the status of the local working class would have eventually been endangered too. Migrant workers, on their part, realised that it was to their advantage to get involved in union politics in order to defend their interests and rights as workers. As about 90 per cent of the local labour force was unionised, staying away from unions would have led to the marginalisation of migrant workers, which would have added to their social and cultural isolation. In a way, unionism played the role of a political school for emerging migrant political leaders. Even today, many unionists of foreign origin, mainly Italians and Spaniards, are to be found both at the grass roots level of factories and plants and at the intermediate and higher level of the union structure in the two main federations of unions, the socialist *Fédération Générale du Travail de Belgique* (FGTB) and the Christian *Confédération des Syndicats Chrétiens* (CSC).

It was in the unions that the question of political participation and voting rights for foreigners was first discussed in the early 1960s. In terms of the political incorporation of migrants, Belgium was at that time at the forefront in Europe. Local unionists were often key actors in formulating claims for migrants, which were then voiced by emerging migrant leaders. Historically, unions were the cradle of migrant politics and of politicians of foreign origin in Belgium.[3]

The other important institution that needs to be considered in order to make sense of migrant politics and the emergence of ethnic politicians are the local consultative councils for immigrants,[4] which started to be created in about 35 Belgian cities in the late 1960s under pressure from the unions. These specific local councils for migrants were supposed to establish a dialogue between local governments and migrants. The former were supposed to consult the immigrants' council when decisions about migration and integration were to be taken at the city level. In the official rhetoric, these advisory bodies were presented as a school of democracy for migrants, who were seen to be ignorant of the practice of citizenship and democracy. Consequently, the creation of these institutions was presented as a step towards granting local voting rights to foreigners legally settled in Belgium.

These proclaimed official aims were discussed and criticised at length both in academic and associative literature. As regards political incorporation of migrants, the experience was certainly far from being a full success. Contrary to the Netherlands and Sweden for example, foreign migrants have not yet been enfranchised either at the local level or at any other level of power in Belgium. Only European Union citizens living in Belgium have been granted local voting and eligibility rights as well as the right to vote and to be elected in the elections of the European Parliament in the framework of the Citizenship of the European Union included in the Maastricht Treaty (Martiniello 1995a). In terms of political incorporation, there is now a legal distinction between European Union citizens and the citizens of other countries living in Belgium.

Experience on local consultative councils for immigrants was nonetheless helpful to emergent immigrant ethnic politicians. In some cities, the local government first selected immigrant councillors for appointment by the mayor from among migrant unionists or the leaders of migrant associations. It was a sort of co-optation and a kind of official recognition granted to 'would-be' migrant political leaders. In other cities, immigrant councillors were elected by the migrant population legally established in the city. Candidates were then obliged to campaign to mobilise support and gather votes. In the Walloon industrial city of Liège, for example, the first elections of the local immigrants' council took place in 1973. Seats were distributed according to the relative importance of each nationality in the population of the city prior to the elections. Italians, being the largest migrant group, not only in the city but also in the region and country, were allowed 18 of the 41 seats. Only national lists could register to take part in the elections. It was implicitly assumed by many local government officials that migrants would logically vote for a candidate of their own nationality anyway. Furthermore, it was assumed that the political programme and general political issues would not, and should not, play a role in the elections. Contrary to this view, each national group of migrants was divided along political lines, often corresponding to the political divides of the country of origin. An Italian communist voter would certainly have preferred to vote for a Spanish communist candidate than for an Italian Christian democrat. Official encouragement of an ethnic vote was a way of trying to depoliticise the immigrants' council even before its creation, while simultaneously creating the illusion that migrants were being incorporated into local politics.

In the third elections held in 1984, multinational political lists were allowed and a socialist-communist majority came out of the vote led by Italians, who were often members of the *Partito Communista Italiano* (PCI) and increasingly of the *Partito Socialista Italiano* (PSI). Progressively, immigrant councillors were also establishing contacts with the Belgian corresponding party, which led in various cases to double membership. For example, members of the PSI would also become close to, or members of, the *Parti socialiste* (PS).

I have argued elsewhere (Martiniello 1992) that local consultative councils for immigrants were powerless bodies located at the margins of the local Belgian polity. In terms of the collective political empowerment of the migrant population, they have produced very minor results. In fact, they have helped reproduce the collective political powerlessness of ethnic migrant minorities. Nevertheless, they have played an important role (positive and negative) in the individual careers of 'would-be' ethnic politicians. On the positive side, they provided emerging politicians of migrant origin with a political arena; they were one of the few avenues open to migrants who wanted to get involved in politics. Joining these bodies could be part of a positioning strategy. On the negative side, as the younger generation of 'would-be ethnic leaders' understood, playing the councils' card is not necessarily a good investment for a political career because of the structural powerlessness of these institutions and their location on the margins of the political system. Therefore, they used it as a sort of stepping stone towards a career in Belgian politics. Clearly, migrants' perceptions of these councils varied according to their experiences of migration. Whereas they represented the height of political involvement for some of the earlier migrant leaders, their descendants (who were born and raised in Belgium) would more likely regard them as useless gadgets because, by virtue of their Belgian citizenship, they could claim, at least theoretically, more direct incorporation in the political system. Furthermore, the experience also demonstrated that the idea that migrants and their descendants were ignorant of politics was prejudiced and that many migrants had been involved in politics in their country of origin and were keen to pursue their activity in Belgium too.

As stated earlier, the so-called migrant population has changed dramatically over the years and an increasing fraction of it is being born in Belgium. According to Belgian nationality law, as revised successively in 1984, 1991 and 1995, so-called second- and third-generation migrants are automatically (or almost automatically) granted full citizenship. These 'new Belgians',[5] upon reaching the legal age, can theoretically vote and be elected at all levels of power in Belgium. Contrary to France, no registration procedure on electors' lists exists. When elections are planned and the date is decided, all electors automatically receive their convocation to take part.[6] Objectively and subjectively, specific advisory councils for migrants seem to make little sense to the 'new Belgians', for in theory they have other means of defending their interests and are not really considered to be migrants. Furthermore, even though naturalisation rates among adult migrants have never been very high in Belgium, it has always been possible to become naturalised and thus acquire full political citizenship. These *naturalised* persons of the first generation often saw no need to support the immigrants' councils.

The emergence of politicians of ethnic origin

These changes of nationality and the automatic or quasi-automatic access to Belgian nationality for second- and third-generation migrants, explain that, among the Belgian electorate, there are now several tens of thousands of voters who were either not Belgian citizens at birth or whose parents were migrants or migrants' children. However, since the Belgian census does not enquire into a person's ethnic origins and there are no official records or statistics available, it is not easy to estimate the size of this component of the electorate. Therefore, to avoid ambiguities, the question will not be dealt with here and no figure will be advanced. In any case, the mere fact that data are so difficult to obtain may be interpreted in at least two ways – proof of total assimilation or an indication of the political sensitivity of the issue. The latter seems more likely.

These Belgians (with a recent foreign or migrant background) came to the attention of the public during the first 'ethnic disturbances' in Brussels in the summer of 1991 (Martiniello 1991). Many of the youngsters fighting with the police in the streets of Brussels were able to show their Belgian identity card, yet they tended to be perceived of as Arabs, Moroccans, Muslims or migrants. Public opinion began to realise that these youngsters, who felt and largely were rejected by the national communities[7] and by a growing part of the Belgian population, were full Belgian citizens with the same rights and duties as any other Belgian citizen. They were also voters. Because of their high geographical concentration in specific inner-city neighbourhoods and their demographic expansion, they began to be considered as a potential electoral force, at least in some districts of cities such as Brussels. They thus started to interest political parties, which always try to expand and consolidate the electoral bases on which their power rests.

Apart from urban disturbances, which are quite exceptional in Belgium, 'new Belgians' have developed a set of associations active in the fields of culture, sport, social work, education, intercultural relations and so forth, which function alongside the network of traditional migrant associations dominated by the 'first' generation. Though, unlike the *Mouvement des Beurs* in France in the 1980s (Bouamama 1994; Feldblum 1993), they never engaged in large-scale collective action, their associations provide an arena in which leaders can emerge, get known and then move into formal politics. This is happening increasingly because many associations derive some financial support from the authorities' integration policies. This brings association leaders into contact with administrative staff and local politicians with whom they develop a professional relationship. In other words, from among the leaders of these associations political parties select potential 'ethnic' candidates to stand for election as communal councillors at the local level, provincial councillors at the provincial level, members of regional parliaments or community councils at the regional and community levels or, to a lesser degree, MPs or members of senate at the national level, and Euro MPs at the European level. The slow emergence of ethnic politicians is the result of both a process of co-optation and of community mobilisation among ethnic communities. Through their involvement in ethnic associations, social work, cultural activities and so forth, local ethnic leaders emerge and acquire a certain visibility within the larger society's formal institutions, for example state agencies dealing with issues linked to the integration of migrants, as well as within political parties. The most politically reliable of them are then approached by these parties to stand in elections and possibly to draw the 'ethnic vote'. The foregoing is certainly an oversimplification, but it nevertheless helps us to understand better the process of incorporation of ethnic politicians.

Because no official or public statistics record ethnic origin or ethnic identity, it is almost as difficult to estimate the number of ethnic politicians in the Belgian political system as it is the number of voters of foreign origin. The Belgian law protecting private life is very strict on issues of race, ethnicity, religion and political attitudes. While this is not the place to discuss the moral and ethical dilemmas these issues raise, let us emphasise that the methodological obstacles are not easy to overcome. Some indicators can be used and combined, such as name and place of birth, as well as the official naturalisation data. But these data do not lead to any homogeneity of the figures produced. Another dimension to be taken into account is that in some cases research deals only with Belgians with a non-European background, mainly Turkish and Moroccan (Lambert 1996), whereas other research, such as my own, includes Belgians with a European background, mainly Italian and Spanish. For all these reasons, the figures presented below only serve to illustrate the process of slow emergence of ethnic politicians in Belgium and should be taken as mere approximations.

In the 1994 elections for the European Parliament, about 30 ethnic candidates ran for office on about 15 different lists, ranging from the extreme left-wing party PTB (*Parti du travail de Belgique*) to the extreme right-wing FN (*Front national*).[8] None was elected, though some got encouraging personal scores in terms of preference votes.

In the legislative elections of 1995, no ethnic candidate was elected to the Chamber of Representatives, but two – both of Italian origin – were elected to the Senate. One of them, the Francophone socialist Elio Di Rupo, had had a long political career despite his relatively young age. He had previously been a member of the Belgian Parliament, a minister and a member of the European Parliament. After the 1995 elections, this son of an Italian mineworker who came to Belgium after the Second World War became one of the vice-prime ministers in the Jean-Luc Dehane government. Due to the share of power between Flemings and Walloons and the various parties in the coalition governments in the Belgian pluralist political system, this is the most powerful position a Francophone can attain at the federal level. Incidentally, for the last 20 years the prime minister has been a Flemish Catholic. Elio Di Rupo is therefore not to be underestimated, even though his success is highly unusual and is linked to various factors other than his own exceptional abilities and the favourable opportunity structure within the PS (*Parti socialiste*).[9] The other member of the federal Senate of Italian origin, Alberto Borin, is also a socialist. He was elected in the Charleroi area, a traditional immigration subregion of Wallonia.

The results of the regional parliamentary elections were equally disappointing for immigrant ethnic community politicians. No such politician was elected to either the Walloon or Flemish Parliament. In Brussels, however, four of the 39 candidates with a non-European background were elected to the 75-seat regional parliament – three socialists and one ecologist. Three of these successful candidates have a Moroccan background and the fourth is of Tunisian origin. Only one is a woman.

It is undoubtedly at the city level that the penetration of ethnic politicians is most visible. In Brussels, about 20 ethnic local councillors were elected in the 19 autonomous districts of the city: six are socialists, six are ecologists, two were elected on the lists of the Francophones' party, the *Front des Francophones* (FDF) allied to the liberal party. Two candidates with a European background (one Italian and one Spaniard) were also elected on the list of the extreme right-wing party, the *Front National* in the district of Saint-Gilles. Ethnic candidates were less successful in other big cities, even in traditional immigration areas. In Liège, for example, no candidate of immigrant origin gained a seat. Only one did in Charleroi and three in La Louvière. It should also be added that two mayors of Italian origin were appointed in small cities in Wallonia (Anthisnes and Farciennes).

These partial and superficial figures suggest that, contrary to what the over-exposure of the phenomenon in the media has led some to believe after the recent elections, the appearance of ethnic officials in public life in Belgium has been quite recent and rather slow. By and large, there is still a strong statistical under-representation of elected officials of ethnic origin: whereas the ethnic origin population makes up about 10 per cent of the total population of the country, ethnic elected politicians are in proportion far less numerous. Nevertheless, the meaning of this under-representation should be seriously questioned. Is it the result of processes of exclusion or does it reflect alternative incorporation strategies chosen by immigrant ethnics, such as business or the professions? It is too early to answer this question. The point to underline is that statistical under-representation does not necessarily mean – but of course can mean – discrimination and exclusion processes suffered by ethnic communities.

Another point to be made is that once they have made their way onto the list, ethnic politicians are not always less likely to be elected than their non-ethnic counterparts. In the Belgian electoral system, the position of the candidate on the list is of crucial importance, especially for unknown politicians. As a matter of fact, two main ways of voting are possible. One can either vote for the list of a particular party – in which case the voter accepts the order of the list of candidates as officially proposed – or one can give preference to one candidate on the list. Candidates can only move up to the top of the list to be elected if they get a high enough number of preference votes. Obviously, only well-known and popular candidates can hope to get a high number of preference votes. For the others – and this is the case for most ethnic politicians – it is crucial to be put in an 'eligible position' on the list. In each district, the parties try to predict the number of seats they can hope to win. If, for example, a party expects to win five seats, a candidate's chances of being elected are generally higher if she or he is placed among the first five candidates on the list. The candidate could then simply hope to take advantage of the global score of the list without having to rely on an exceptionally good personal score.

The position of the candidates on the list is discussed within each political party. Internal elections are usually organised to give the list its final shape. In other words, candidates must first convince the members of their party taking part in the internal polls that not only they should be placed on the list, but also that they should be given an eligible position on it. This is not an easy task for ethnic politicians whose involvement in the party is in many cases quite recent. Whereas most parties have recently opened up to the idea of presenting ethnic candidates in the various elections, granting them eligible positions remains a matter for internal discussion and sometimes dispute. Having ethnic candidates is increasingly seen as politically correct. It allows parties to refute any accusations of discriminating against minorities. It is also supposed to give credit to their anti-racist stands. And, finally, as I said before, it is seen as a means of getting the 'new Belgian' vote. Therefore, even though the idea of having ethnic candidates can meet with internal resistance, enough of a consensus often emerges for it to be accepted in principle and implemented. The issues of the number of ethnic candidates and their position on the list are far more problematic in most parties. It is often feared that ethnics will get more representation and power than that to which they are fairly entitled. In this case, parties fear losing some of their traditional support by giving too much space to ethnic politicians. The earlier-mentioned figures should be interpreted by keeping in mind that most successful ethnic candidates, through negotiations with their party, managed to obtain a reasonably good position on the list prior to the elections. In other words, an important key to their success is to be found in their relations with the party.

A further point deals with the political preferences of ethnic candidates. In the past, it was often feared that if immigrants were given the franchise, they would collectively support a particular party because of their ethnicity. For example, Italians were supposed to be either Catholics or communists and is was therefore assumed that they would support either the *Parti communiste* (PC) or the *Parti social chrétien* (PSC). Clearly, a link – which remains largely unproved – was made between ethnicity and political preferences. The same link was assumed in the case of ethnic politicians. It was for example feared that ethnic or religious – clearly, Islamic parties are seen as the threat – formations would be created and led by ethnic candidates. The available figures show that this has not been the case so far. Foreign origin politicians run for office on the lists of most mainstream parties and some of them do so on the lists of smaller extremist parties, either on the left or marginally on the right, as seen in the case of Saint-Gilles presented above. Judging by the number of ethnic candidates presented, the PS and the two ecology parties (the Francophone *Ecolo* and the Flemish *Agalev*) seem to be the most welcoming to ethnic candidates along with some extreme left-wing parties such as PTB or *Gauches unies*. But other parties also put forward ethnic origin candidates.

No Islamic party has so far been created, whereas the only experience of an ethnically based political organisation failed in the local elections in Brussels in 1994. A group of Belgians with a Maghrebian background launched MERCI (*Mouvement européen pour la Reconnaissance des Citoyens, en ce compris ceux issus de l'Immigration*). MERCI stood in four of the 19 districts of Brussels and in none of those did it manage to obtain more than 0.8 per cent of the vote. The Belgo-Maghrebian electorate in these four districts of Brussels were clearly not seduced by Belgo-Maghrebian candidates. Sharing ethnic origins was obviously not a main determining factor in explaining their voting behaviour. Immigrant origin populations, just like 'non-ethnic Belgians', are split along political lines. The assumption that their political behaviour, either voting patterns or political involvement, would have been ethnically motivated in a major way, compared with other Belgians, reflects an ethnic prejudice that seems widespread in Belgian society.

The figures suggest that the relative success of ethnic politicians is far more visible at the local level than at any other level of political power. Furthermore, the emergence of ethnic politicians is particularly significant in Brussels, where for the last 15 years migration issues have been hotly contested and politicised. When discussing problems of immigration and integration, many observers have Brussels in mind. Some would even go so far as to say that, compared with Brussels, most other Belgian cities have far fewer immigration and integration problems. The data on ethnic political success may thus seem surprising: in an immigration city like Liège, which is known for its openness and relatively unproblematic assimilation of immigrants into the local population, ethnic politicians are not very successful on the local political scene, whereas in Brussels, which is often singled out for its bad record in integrating migrants, ethnic politicians have begun to penetrate the local political power bases. It would be too simplistic to explain this difference by claiming that it is precisely because they are well integrated and have no special interests to defend or claims to make that immigrants in Liège do not feel the need to get involved actively in politics. A notion of successful integration that failed to consider political participation would be very partial. Part of the explanation could be found in the specific sociological profile of ethnic candidates in Brussels, who seem to have access to more mobilisable resources than most people of immigrant origin in Liège.

A sociological profile of ethnic politicians and their political strategies

Again, the available data on this point are far from being complete. The following developments should therefore be read as mere indications or hypotheses for elaboration in future research. Nevertheless, there seem to be important differences between the sociological profiles of ethnic politicians in Brussels and in other parts of the country, especially Wallonia.

The hypothesis can be made that ethnic politicians in Brussels have a predominantly North African background, whereas those in Wallonia are mainly European, especially Italian, in origin. There is a demographic explanation for this difference: in Wallonia, Italians constitute the largest ethnic immigrant group, whereas in Brussels it is North Africans, particularly Moroccans. It is thus logical that this difference should also be reflected among ethnic politicians. Because of their demographic power and complex political organisation (Martiniello 1992), Italians have traditionally assumed the leadership role in the immigrant politics of Wallonia. North Africans tend to adopt the same strategy in Brussels. Not only are they the most important group in the city, but they are also one of the most stigmatised, and this encourages a rich associative life. Therefore, Italians in Wallonia and North Africans in Brussels claim some sort of monopoly over the legitimate representation of the interests of all migrants and try to encourage the emergence of political leadership in their ranks first, sometimes at the expense of would-be leaders from other immigrant groups.

Another difference between ethnic politicians in Brussels and in other parts of the country concerns their migration experience. In Wallonia, ethnic politicians are predominantly recruited from among the offspring of migrant workers who arrived in Belgium after the Second World War. They are often improperly called second- or third-generation migrants, even though most of them actually did not migrate at all. They were born and educated in Belgium. These ethnic politicians have a working-class background. Their parents or grandparents, as noted above, were used as an additional labour force in heavy industry. While some of these migrant workers' descendants reproduce the class position of their ancestors, others have achieved some social mobility through the acquisition of educational and social resources. In Brussels, a significant number of ethnic leaders are not personally connected with this traditional migration pattern. Some come from the middle-class of their country of origin and arrived in Belgium as university students. They were supposed to leave the country after having obtained their degree. Some of course did, but some settled. Others arrived in Belgium as political refugees, being involved in opposition politics in their country. This subgroup is characterised either by a working-class background or by a middle-class one. Beyond the possible divergence in their social origin, these two subgroups of educated foreign students or political refugees share a relatively high level of education compared with the offspring of migrant workers. It is easier for them to understand and manipulate the symbolic codes of the local political society (language, for example) so that they can engage less problematically in a dialogue. They thus often appeared to be closer to the local institutions than the 'mass' of migrants. Some of them were therefore tempted to try to mobilise their educational resources in order either to try to assume a leadership role within immigrants' groups or to play an intermediary role between host society institutions and migrants' associations. The specificity of their migration history is not only a resource though. They are sometimes contested within immigrants' groups for not being 'real migrants' and for having played the immigrant for their own interest.

We could expect ethnic politicians to adopt different political strategies depending on their sociological profiles, and this may well be the case. However, to understand their strategies, we first need to understand the motives of the political parties confronted by this 'new' question of ethnic politicians. The Belgian political institutions in which parties play a central role largely determine the range of political opportunities open to them. As mentioned above, mainstream political parties are keen to have ethnic politicians on their side, not only because it has become politically correct to do so, but also because they want to try and attract 'the ethnic vote', the existence of which, at least potentially, they seem to assume more or less explicitly. Consequently, some political career opportunities are undeniably open to ethnic politicians. Obviously, these opportunities are not unlimited and ethnic candidates compete in trying to convince the parties that they are the appropriate person to achieve the party's goals. On the other hand, even though they can almost never rely on 'the ethnic vote' to be elected, ethnic politicians are bound to act as if they were trying to get it, if not for themselves personally, then at least for the party on the list of which they stand. As noted above, being 'ethnic' is not enough to get 'the ethnic vote'. Ethnic politicians often need to gain it by pretending to play a leadership role on behalf of their 'ethnic communities' and to voice and defend ethnically-framed political claims that may contradict their party's platform.

In other words, ethnic politicians are caught between two sets of constraints. On the one hand, the party may just want them there (tokenism) to attract the ethnic vote without questioning the party's view on immigration and ethnicity. On the other hand, to secure the support of their own ethnic group, they may be asked to act as community leaders, which sometimes translates into pressure from the ethnic community to act against their party's policy, for example in the field of migration and ethnicity. Their delicate position sometimes leads to a sort of political schizophrenia, since there can be inconsistencies between what they are expected to do either by their party or by the ethnic community, not to mention the non-ethnic electorate they also need to seduce. Those of them who actually want to act as ethnic community leaders may be forced by the party not to do so. Those who do not want to act as ethnic community leaders may to a certain extent be forced to do so by the ethnic electorate.

In attempting to manage their difficult position and to reconcile conflicting expectations, ethnic politicians often manipulate different discourses and practices according to their audience. When talking or acting within the party, they adopt a universalistic discourse. They avoid making any radical statement in favour of ethnic communities that might shed suspicion on their hidden agenda and give them the reputation of being troublesome ethnic leaders. When talking and acting within the ethnic community, they adopt a particularist discourse. They try not to defend their party's interests openly or those of the wider Belgian institutions. In any case, their fragile political position significantly reduces their margin of political autonomy; it imposes on them the highest caution and forces them to react immediately to any change in the political environment.

Conclusion

At the end of this brief examination of the process whereby ethnic politicians emerge, what can one conclude about its meaning and impact on political integration in Belgium? What difference does it make, if any, to have public officials from an ethnic background? Is Belgian political society more integrated? Are ethnic communities better off? Do they have more of a voice in Belgian politics? Is it because Elio Di Rupo has become a vice-prime minister in the federal government that the Italian community, which I pretend elsewhere does not exist (Martiniello 1992), has become politically powerful? Are Moroccans less discriminated against because Sfia Bouarfa is an MP for the region of Brussels?

Before answering these questions, it is important to emphasise that, at least for the time being, the presence of ethnic politicians results much more from the process of individual political integration than from the political mobilisation of immigrant ethnicities in the Belgian political and institutional sphere. Successful ethnic politicians are personally engaged in a process of social mobility through politics. They first mobilise the educational resources and only secondarily the ethnic resources, especially the ethnic networks. The presence of ethnic politicians does not mean that immigrant ethnic communities have been collectively incorporated into the Belgian political system.

In other words, the presence of ethnic politicians does not seem to mark a new step in the politicisation of ethnicity in the Belgian political system. Nonetheless, it reveals an important paradox in the latter. The Belgian political system is based on linguistic, cultural, religious and ideological pluralism, yet these divisions have led to an ethnicisation of politics in which only 'original national groups' (such as Flemings and Walloons) are considered legitimate. For example, all the political parties are either ethnic or religious, or both. With the one exception of the *Parti communiste*, all the other parties are split, not into a Flemish and Walloon branch, but into Flemish and Walloon autonomous parties (such as PS– SP; PSC–CVP; PRL–VLB). There seems to be an implicit consensus to limit the politicisation of ethnicity to the 'original national groups' only and not to accept its extension to immigrant ethnic communities: whereas Flemish and Walloon parties are generally considered normal, the creation of a Moroccan party would entail the resistance of both Flemings and Walloons; whereas the existence of two Christian parties is not seen as a problem, the creation of a Muslim party would be rejected in principle as an attempt to 'balkanise' politics. Clearly, in Belgian politics there are legitimate ethnicities and illegitimate ones.

The hypothesis can be made that the emergence of individual ethnic politicians is actually part of a strategy promoted by the legitimate ethnic actors in order to try to avoid any attempt to mobilise illegitimate ethnicities in Belgian politics. In other words, the inclusion of individual ethnic politicians could be seen as a means of avoiding the collective inclusion of immigrant ethnic communities into Belgian politics and their public recognition as legitimate actors in ethnic politics. Ethnic politicians are thus standing right in the middle of this paradox. On the other hand, they are supposed to bring the alleged 'ethnic vote' to the traditional parties and, at the same time, they are supposed to act as a barrier to the creation of ethno-religious parties within immigrant ethnic communities. In other words, they are supposed both to ethnicise the new Belgians' vote and to impede their autonomous political mobilisation. Their presence therefore seems to help the reproduction of the political powerlessness of immigrant ethnic communities.

Nevertheless, the political presence of ethnic politicians could have positive symbolic effects in the medium and long term. By being there, by being visible, they could be considered as living proofs that immigrant ethnic communities do not constitute any threat to Belgium, that most immigrants and their descendants, like any other Belgians, just want to enjoy a decent life and simply be recognised as members of the society, as citizens. In this respect, the symbolic importance of the politics of presence should not be neglected.

Notes

1. These official figures (Institut national de Statistique 1996) do not include Belgian citizens with an ethnic immigrant background.

2. The first bilateral immigration agreement was signed by the Italian and the Belgian governments in June 1946.
3. Migrant workers also developed a community and associative life. Several hundred migrant associations were created, but had no significant or direct impact on the Belgian political process (Martiniello 1992).
4. In French, les Conseils consultatifs communaux des Immigrés.
5. The media have used the expression *nouveaux Belges* when writing or talking about ethnic politicians in the recent elections for example. It is not a scientific concept.
6. Note that the vote is a duty and not a right in Belgium: it is compulsory.
7. The issue of a single Belgian national community has been discussed at length in Belgium. The new Constitution recognises three communities: the Flemish community, the French-speaking community and the German-speaking community (Martiniello 1995b).
8. Unless indicated otherwise, the data come from our own research in progress.
9. Elio Di Rupo was officially suspected of paedophile behaviour in 1996, but these false allegations did not mark the end of his brilliant political career.

Ethnic minority political mobilisation in Britain: competing claims and agendas

Shamit Saggar

In the mid to late 1990s it is commonplace to hear suggestions that ethnic minority[1] political participation, whatever the advances of recent years, still lags behind the standards expected of a mature industrial democracy. This suggestion is routinely illustrated by a willingness shared by all major political parties to encourage greater ethnic minority voter participation and occupation of elective office. It is further entrenched by a range of party and extra-party efforts to build democratic institutions that are social microcosms of British society. At one and the same time, it is also not uncommon to witness sharply contrasting claims made by political activists and party managers alike concerning the nature and behaviour of ethnic minorities in the democratic process. Some 20 years after the first party-based attempts to capture the so-called 'ethnic vote', conceptual understanding of that term remains as muddled as ever. The search has been on for the essence of ethnic minority political identity but, in truth, few breakthroughs have been worth reporting.

This chapter explores some of the ways in which the British political tradition has conceptualised ethnic minority political participation. It is primarily interested in the central race/voting nexus. The discussion is set within a wider conceptual framework that begins by highlighting the kinds of conceptual and conceptually-related difficulties that are thrown up in the study of race and ethnicity and electoral behaviour. The chapter then assesses the ways in which party strategy has developed to take account of ethnicity and ethnic minorities. Finally, returning to minority voters, it considers a major recurring controversy in both academic research and practical politics, namely the existence and character of a distinctive ethnic minority political agenda.

Conceptual uncertainties

The importance attached to race and ethnicity in shaping voting choice has been the subject of considerable academic and non-academic journalistic interest. It has, however, been a topic associated with muddled thinking. A large element of this fascination has been understandable. For one thing, the significance of ethnicity as a variable has been highlighted in the sense that it is associated with, and has been said to have yielded, a powerful influence upon party choice. That is to say, ethnicity has amounted to an amalgam of contributory factors shaping voting, selectively symbolising and uniting aspects of shared experience and common outlook. However, it should be stressed that few theorists of electoral behaviour have made much headway in explaining what it is about, or what is embodied within the concept of ethnicity that has counted in shaping political outlook and action. (Notable exceptions to this generalisation might include the work of Nie et al. 1976: 104–5; and Verba and Nie 1972, Chapter 10.) This central job of mapping out the terms and scope of such an ethnically-related form of thinking and acting politically is something that is considered more fully later in this chapter, when the focus is placed on the question of the degree to which a discrete 'ethnic agenda' exists in determining minority voting choice.

Ethnicity, in itself, does not mean very much for the job of predicting voting behaviour, other than to measure group membership sizes and proportions. Moreover, confusion results once ethnicity is described as a scientific variable when, in fact, empirical studies seldom treat it as something that actually varies. Academic studies usually go no further than treating it as a nominal variable, distinguishing, say, between patterns of non-white and white political behaviour. The only variance that does show up in such studies is that which distinguishes membership from one ethnic group to another. The old argument that a variable must vary is thus especially relevant here. Furthermore, no attempt is made in empirical research to link either 'lower' or 'higher' degrees of ethnicity or ethnic identity with political behaviour. It is not in that sense a particularly useful or adaptable variable, let alone one that counts greatly or can be measured meaningfully. One reason for this may be that ethnicity tends to work well enough as a scientific variable for the narrow purposes of survey research while lacking sufficient coherence in content as an analytical concept. This approach to identifying its meaning, while radically different from the comments made just previously, nevertheless draws attention to the task of interpreting correctly the relatively limited 'hard' data that exist on race/ethnicity and voting in Britain. Both approaches nevertheless point to the same kind of question.

These questions aside, ethnicity remains a concept that clearly matters for the purposes of moulding electoral choice. What is less clear is whether it is a metaphor for underlying causal relationships or indeed something that has a direct bearing on political orientation and activity. Additionally, accepting that it matters is not the same thing as holding the view that it matters alone. It is the latter view that has tended to pervade into the calculations of party strategists and managers who, over a period of more than twenty years, have become bogged down in an 'ethnicity counts' assumption that has bordered on a fetish. As this chapter makes clear, there can be good political reasons for this assumption despite the absence of strong analytical evidence.

If ethnicity is to be treated as an analytical category in British electoral behaviour, it can only apply to a small segment of the electorate (Heath et al. 1991: 99). As such, it is the ethnicity of ethnic minorities that analysts are concerned with, something which in Britain is therefore incapable of having a large impact across the electorate as a whole. For that reason, we have become used to thinking that ethnic minorities do not influence overall election outcomes. These voters are too few in number and concentrated away from the seats that matter, so the argument goes, for them to matter greatly on the wider political landscape (Crewe 1983). Yet, despite this stark message, there have been numerous claims regarding their great potential in: (a) delivering electoral victory (for example the much embellished 'ethnic bloc' voting argument); (b) in avoiding electoral oblivion (for example the Labour Party's reliance on 'ethnic safe seats' in its rout during the 1980s); or (c) even in swinging the outcome of general elections (for example the 'ethnic marginals' thesis applied to the second 1974 election).

The complicating twist is that many commentators have been driven by the vague and mythologised belief that, for ethnic minority voters, ethnicity alone counts. If true, this view begs the question: in what sense does it count? Is it a coincidental feature of their ethnic identity, or is it the product of a distinctive agenda of issue and policy concerns? This problem seems to lie at the heart of most of the conceptual muddle in the literature and is explored towards the end of the chapter.

Race and ethnicity and party strategy

At the heart of contemporary British party competition there is an assumption which implies that ethnic minority voters ought to be courted in ethnically-specific ways. The assumption is broadly shared by the three major political parties and generally receives the endorsement of party leaderships keen not to overlook innovative and unconventional approaches to electoral advantage.

Significantly, even the Conservatives, who have attempted to project an ostensibly 'colour-blind' self-image – for example the pointed 'TORIES SAY HE'S BRITISH, LABOUR SAYS HE'S BLACK' campaign pitch of 1983 – nevertheless have made concessions to ethnic politics. The party's Anglo-Asian and Anglo-West Indian Conservative Societies, though wound up in the mid-1980s, clearly signalled the acceptance by party managers to address these groups of voters – and donors! – using mechanisms that reflected these electors' ethnic distinctiveness.[2] Its successor, the Conservative One Nation Forum, continues in a broadly similar vein. While it may be debatable whether ethnicity counts so centrally for ethnic minority voters as a whole, Conservative Party strategy has been moved by the possibility that it might. The landmark Community Relations Commission report on the 1974 elections played a big part in shifting Tory strategy, appealing, as it did, to a narrowly-defeated party that had historically shown minimal interest in this section of the electorate (CRC 1975). Perversely, the acceptance that ethnicity might count for something among this group of voters has largely failed to shape Conservative Party strategy at any grand level and the party has strenuously avoided making any commitments on racial or ethnic lines that could spill over into its broad appeal to voters, white and non-white, at large.

Ironically, for most of the past ten to fifteen years, this willingness, possibly insistence, to see such voters through an ethnic prism of sorts seems to have gone hand-in-hand with a widely held desire to leave race themes on the backburner of party competition. Race and ethnicity in that sense do not seem to command any great significance in British politics generally – arguably since at least early in the 1983 parliament; and yet these concepts count as much as any when it comes to parties' attempts to gather non-white support. Furthermore, despite considerable evidence of confusion and muddle over the nature of the issues that are thought to motivate these voters (see following section), party leaders and strategists remain convinced that a specific race agenda exists and can be exploited for party gain.

Several points require elaboration. First, what have been the origins and reasoning behind this assumption? Second, are parties and non-white voters well-served or hampered by this central assumption? Finally, are electoral politics conducted in these terms capable of delivering beneficial change for ethnic minorities? We shall also consider how this assumption is influenced by underlying views of ethnic minority electoral motivation.

The origins of 'ethnic politics'

The background to this assumption can be traced back more than 20 years and, in particular, to the conscious decision by the Labour and Conservative parties to pay more attention to wooing the non-white electorate. A key element in this strategic calculation was the myth perpetuated following the October 1974 general election suggesting that (a) the Conservatives' second defeat was attributable to neglect of ethnic minority voters in crucial seats, and (b) these voters were an example of a floating vote that could be solicited on ethnic or racial lines (CRC 1975). Neither assertion was supported by much evidence; nonetheless, they proved a powerful force behind the parties' discovery of the 'ethnic vote'. On the first claim, the CRC study sought to highlight so-called 'ethnic marginals', where, it was believed, the size of the non-white electorate exceeded the size of the winning majority. This claim was methodologically flawed by the use of 1971 Census estimates of the size of the New Commonwealth and Pakistani (NCWP) origin population in these constituencies, making no allowance for calculations of age disqualification (the under-18s), rate of registration and propensity to turn out. On the second charge, the CRC report made no attempt to substantiate its claim that the support of ethnic minority voters – whether located in marginal seats or not – was dependent upon the major parties' policies and attitudes towards race and immigration issues. A final nail in the coffin of the CRC's argument was that, despite showing the degree of electoral volatility that had occurred in these marginal seats from the first 1974 election to the second, it could not produce any evidence to show that a non-white differential switch had produced the outcome of seats changing hands. Indeed, it was just as possible to argue the opposite on the basis of the evidence used: that non-white voters had largely stayed put, while white voters had changed sides in sufficient numbers to deliver Tory marginals to the Labour Party!

A further factor relating to non-white leadership fuelled this tendency. An established ethnic minority political leadership received growing media attention from 1976 onwards which, by standing for self-described immigrant interests, gave parties further reason to think about, and do business with, ethnic minorities in ethnic-specific ways. The logic of ethnic minority leadership meeting with a mainstream party system with virtually no experience of handling or aggregating ethnicity, meant that fertile ground was cultivated by proponents of the new ethnic politics. None of this, of course, particularly helps explain whether such a strategy has been empirically well-founded or successful. It says even less about whether the strategy delivered its anticipated results.

Assessing the dividend

Are British political parties rational or wise to approach ethnic minorities in this manner? The answer would seem to suggest that parties do a poor and patchy job by relying on such a strategy. Two arguments lie at the heart of this response, one that examines the historical-structural context, another based on the outlook of non-white and white voters themselves.

To start with, it should be remembered that there are real limitations to the 'ethnicity counts' assumption. Generally speaking, British parties are not in the universal business of trying to attract ethnic minority voters on all fronts and at all times. In truth, some parties have flirted from time to time with the notion of seeking the support of this constituency, while others have been content to let the matter lie undisturbed. The distinction, moreover, is even further underlined when examining the approach taken by different individual politicians. Thus, while Roy Hattersley regularly embraced the ethnic minority electorate at both constituency and national levels, his colleague Denis Healey, although equally sympathetic, remained distant to this task. Intra-party variance on this question reveals that the ethnicity of ethnic minorities can often be shunned and embraced at one and the same time.

However, one principle has tended to prevail across the parties. For the most part, political parties have worked fully within the understanding that ethnic minority voters are both attitudinally and geographically among the safest constituencies of the Labour Party. As Table 8.1 below makes clear, long-term backing for Labour from ethnic minorities remains strong and remarkably stable. In any other context, this group of voters would be described as a poor and unpromising opportunity for Labour's rivals. Recognising both Labour's reliance on non-white voters and these voters' strong orientation towards Labour, it has become increasingly apparent that few spoils are on offer to parties competing on this territory. Indeed, with the scale of this imbalance in mind, Labour's posture toward its ethnic minority supporters has been described in terms of neglect, if not arrogance (FitzGerald 1988). None of this has particularly discouraged those who continue to be determined to perpetuate still further the all too hollow 'ethnic marginals' thesis (CRE 1994).

In any case, it is appropriate to keep a sense of perspective. Whatever efforts have been made across the political parties to marshal ethnic minority support have been rather unique and unprecedented in the sense that, historically, ethnicity has long counted for little in British traditions of politics and party competition. Britain certainly has virtually no modern tradition of religious definition or determination of party labels and loyalties comparable with many continental European political systems. Equally, the ethno-linguistic character of politics in places such as Belgium, parts of Iberia, and further afield in Canada, appear largely alien in the British system. The extent to which the ethnicity of ethnic minorities receives attention in British politics is thus novel and far-removed from the familiar class basis of modern political mobilisation (FitzGerald 1985: 1).

Table 8.1 *Levels of Labour and Conservative support among ethnic minorities (per cent)*

	1974*	1979	1983**	1987	1992**
Labour	81	86	83	72	81
Conservative	9	8	7	18	10

Notes: * October 1974 general election; ** figures represent recalculated average of Asian and Afro-Caribbean support levels.
Sources: adapted from Ali and Percival (1993); BBC/Harris (1987); CRC (1975); CRE (1980)

Serving ethnic minority interests

In fact, it is not so much the ethnic identity of ethnic minorities that is the subject of attention but, rather, the presumption of politicians that racism and race relations are what count for non-white participants above all else. As we have already seen, this presumption is rather ill-considered since, according to existing though patchy survey research, ethnic minorities do not as a rule prioritise a race agenda over other concerns.

The upshot of this is that it has become increasingly difficult for ethnic minorities to participate in local and national politics without reference to (a) their ethnic identity, and (b) the wider meaning given to their ethnicity in British politics and society. Some might go further and say, somewhat regrettably, that these twin themes underline ethnic minority political participation in virtually every setting. Such critics of this state of affairs would claim that ethnicity has thus become institutionalised and been co-opted into mainstream political thinking. This scenario undoubtedly presents several opportunities for ethnic minority political leaders and sympathetic white politicians to push ahead and secure tangible gains on behalf of the non-white population. Indeed, much of this kind of advance-ment has already taken place, especially at the local level, enabling Asian and Afro-Caribbean Britons to achieve important breakthroughs in, for instance, accessing public service delivery processes and decision-making (Gyford 1985; le Lohe 1996; Nanton 1989).

On the deficit side, however, there has been something of a steady tightening of the ethnicity straitjacket that shapes major party strategic thinking towards ethnic minority participation. This may not necessarily strike all observers as a drawback since it successfully tackles the older-standing complaint that naïve colour-blindness characterised party thinking. The deficiencies are more apparent when it is asked to what extent ethnic minorities define their interests in solely ethnic-specific terms. Evidently, there is some ambiguity here (see also following section). Much hangs on the reading of the data though, in general, it is reasonably clear that ethnic minorities are not exclusively fixated on such an agenda. Whether these voters interpret ethnic-based channels of political action and policy influence as an opportunity or as patronising and burdensome is a debatable question. It is also a question which, in the view of the author, is sorely in need of extended empirical research in the future.

Benefits in kind?

Leaving aside this debate for the moment, there are some important conceptual implications that stem from the argument that valuable benefits accrue to ethnic minorities through (a) the present conduct of electoral politics and (b) affiliation with the Labour Party. The most significant of these implications is to ask what kind of benefits proponents of this argument have in mind? A frequent response has been to restate the view that ethnic minority interests are best served by policy commitments that target unemployment, educational attainment, housing provision, urban renewal, and so on. The reasoning offered in support of this view has been that the ethnic minority population is disproportionately afflicted by a lack of jobs, poorly resourced schools, bad housing, and so forth. Many of these policy commitments tend to overlap with traditional Labour and centre-left ideological territory, thereby encouraging the view that the Labour Party specifically is best placed to advance non-white interests.

However, once more, the complication arises from the distinction between race and race-related policy concerns on one hand and various superficially non-racial, mainstream policy concerns on the other. One reading would be to insist that ethnic minorities, by virtue of their socio-economic and geographic location, are likely beneficiaries of a range of public policy commitments that are aimed at improving conditions and opportunities for disadvantaged, less prosperous, urban population groups. Black people are thus not so much the targets of Labour or centre-left policies but, rather, the indirect and disproportionate 'winners' from such a policy agenda and its inherent priorities. This interpretation, if widely shared and expounded in Labour thinking and self-image, can serve as a powerful rationale for the party to continue presenting its policies towards ethnic minorities in such a generalised way. To be sure, if it can be argued that Labour's priorities will serve to benefit ethnic minorities indirectly, it becomes increasingly possible – and attractive – to defend a strategy of avoiding making any direct appeals to this group of voters. This defence can, in turn, appear seductive within a wider electoral landscape that additionally perceives – and fears – the power of a white 'backlash' (Saggar 1993).

There is one important caveat to this argument, however. A portrayal of ethnic minorities as potential beneficiaries of Labour's non-racial policies alone tends to stretch the true picture. Indeed, it is quite mis-leading to claim that these voters are not courted in race-specific terms. Clearly, they are wooed in such terms by both parties in general, and in particular by Labour's well-rehearsed display of overt policy commit-ments to further non-whites' collective interests. Labour, in particular, has come to be regarded by non-white and white electors as the 'ethnic minority-friendly party', though, as we shall note below, its record in office casts severe doubts on the party's right to deserve such a reputation (Layton-Henry 1992). In any case, Labour's putatively closer association with non-white interests makes it difficult for the party to continue to insist that the non-ethnic bond between party and group is all that matters. In many urban constituencies, Labour's long track record of involvement in various internal ethnic minority concerns demonstrates that its appeal for their votes is not solely a question of its indirect appeal on traditional employment and social welfare issues.

Furthermore, almost as if to ignore Labour's structural head start, other parties have periodically made efforts to attract ethnic minority voters using strategies that both recognise the ethnicity of this electorate and also make play of various unrelated factors. Tory and Liberal Democrat strategies are therefore similar in character to Labour's but differ only in degree.

Labour's reputation

Ethnic and racial considerations come into focus even more sharply when we examine the particular appeal that the Labour Party has attempted to project toward ethnic minorities. Despite numerous misgivings within the hierarchy of the national party over any overt, high profile association with non-white voters, it is nevertheless clear that the party has amassed a variety of policy commitments aimed at maintaining the loyalty of its non-white supporters. The strategic thinking behind this posture must, presumably, be that race issues matter and matter significantly to this constituency of supporters. For example, the party has gone on record to promise that it would introduce new legislation to promote race equality measures and to expand the legal basis of indirect discrimination. Labour has also indicated that it would take on many of the proposals from the Commission for Racial Equality to expand its powers (Layton-Henry 1992: 119). Elsewhere, it is also committed to scrapping the 1981 Nationality Act though, to an extent, its future plans for immigration policy remain sensitive to the electoral charge that it is a fundamentally weak party on immigration (Saggar 1993; Seyd et al. 1992). Even these plans must be seen in the context of the party's main pledge, which has been to remove the discriminatory aspects of the 1981 legislation, as a partial prelude to the possibility of wholesale immigration reform. As a party-of-government then, few voters, least of all ethnic minority voters, can have much doubt that Labour persists in its long-standing stance of backing non-whites' interests in ways that are not just universal and geared to general socio-economic change. Labour is, at one and the same time, squarely behind these interests using policy promises that are ethnically and racially-defined and thus of primary concern to non-white voters.

Does this then mean that the Labour Party qualifies for the reputation of best promoter designate of ethnic minority interests? Arguably not, since far too much is taken for granted in terms of conceptual and theoretical understanding of such interests. For one thing, this perspective necessarily reduces the question of race as a political issue to its barest essentials, relying instead on the idea that formal claims to eradicate discrimination are the same thing as substantive change. In the minds of many ethnic minorities, this simplistic equation commands nominal respect but, equally, among others, it does not. A prime reason for a possible disjuncture is that some ethnic minorities may, wisely or not, distinguish between rhetoric and reality when it comes to questions of race and politics. They may indeed be correct to do so, given the experience of vacillation and tough talk over race and immigration politics in the past 30 years.

Another equally important reason may be that they do not think that these kinds of interventionist policies are best suited to addressing British race relations. Instead, by viewing the conflicts thrown up by ethnic and racial pluralism in somewhat different terms, it is not hard to imagine that an element of the non-white electorate might hold some scepticism about the efficacy of legislative and public policy 'solutions'. These ethnic minority 'doubters' would not necessarily need to be described as neo-conservatives to conclude that alternative strategies, perhaps based on emphasising cross-cultural education and compromise, might be the best way forward.

Yet another reason is that Labour's arguably stronger, more activist approach to tackling race relations may be met with indifference and disinterest by yet other ethnic minorities. Thus, what for Labour – and indeed progressives in other major parties – may be seen as a priority, may not be accepted as such by elements of the target constituency. For some, the evidence for this sobering claim may be unwelcome and therefore resisted. In other words, it is increasingly apparent that it is hard, perhaps impossible, to make grand generalisations about the stance of ethnic minorities as a whole toward race relations questions. (Indeed, in the following section we shall review some perhaps unexpected evidence on ethnic minorities' attitudes to liberal race relations policies.) If this is hard enough, it is even less meaningful to try to draw out a strong correlation between Labour's policies on race on one hand and opinion on race among ethnic minorities on the other. The biggest hurdle would appear to be that there is only limited evidence to show that ethnic minorities attach special – let alone overwhelming – priority to the kinds of policy concerns that Labour's race-specific strategy is based upon (CRE 1994).

Imitation among Labour's rivals

More generally, as other parties attempt to make overtures to ethnic minority voters, many cannot avoid pitching their appeal in ways that mimic elements of Labour's strategy. Conservative and Liberal Democrat thinking may remain steadfast in their determination to avoid Labour-style racialisation of political discourse. However, it is noticeable that both of these parties have been prepared to utilise reasonably explicit strategies that assume that ethnic minority voters are chiefly interested in race and race-related issues. Both parties for instance make great play of the notion that they are committed to rooting out racial discrimination in their own ranks and that anti-discrimination laws have a proper and legitimate role in society (BBC 'East', 1996). Each of them has also been through recent public rows over the persistence of racism among party members and in high profile campaigns (for example the Conservatives' tussle over John Taylor's candidacy in Cheltenham in 1992 and the Liberal Democrats' squabbles in Tower Hamlets in 1993/4). These episodes both demonstrated that neither party can afford to maintain silence in the face of very serious complaints about racism. A part of their response has, presumably, been shaped by the need at least to recognise that potential ethnic minority supporters hold legitimate worries that are directly related to race. Equally, both have accepted, and even made some play of, the argument that ethnic minority voters are not the only ones concerned about racial discrimination; indeed, white, liberal sentiment on the theme is arguably of some considerable influence in shaping thinking in both parties.

Meanwhile, the Conservatives have made capital over the alleged separatist demands of Black Sections supporters in the Labour Party. However, with the constitutional blocking of such a proposal in the Labour Party, it is worth remembering that the Conservatives' own One Nation Forum exists chiefly in order to marshal ethnic minority votes and money by an appeal on both racial and non-racial grounds. Equally, the Liberal Democrats have been keen to condemn Labour-style codification of race, especially in local government. However, they too retain a formal and informal apparatus to rally ethnic minority supporters, chiefly through aggressive self-promotion of the party's long-standing pro-gressive stance on race and immigration.

Having rightly drawn attention to the remarkable degree of shared thinking toward race and electoral campaigning across the major parties, it is of course only fair to acknowledge that there is one area in which Labour's boast is founded on irrefutable evidence. The opportunities that have been carved out for ethnic minority political candidates over the past ten years serve to mark the party out as being especially sensitive to its non-white constituency. Geddes (1993) reports that a colossal 85 per cent of all ethnic minority local government councillors belonged to Labour's ranks. All but one of the six non-white faces in the House of Commons at the time of writing (June 1996) is a Labour representative. The remaining ethnic minority 'also-rans' in 1992 contained a much greater number of Labour candidates who were within reach of victory (though the absolute number of Labour candidates roughly matched the Conservative field). Underlying this track record, Labour has undoubtedly built up a much deeper seam of ethnic minority activists, officials and would-be candi-dates. It is from this seam that future numbers of successful candidates will emerge at both national and local levels, and we can expect the current picture of party imbalance among non-white representatives to perpetuate in future elections (Norris and Lovenduski 1995: 237–48).

The Labour Party therefore is in a curious and rather difficult position. It both receives the overwhelming bulk of non-white votes cast and also champions the rights of Britain's ethnic minorities. However, this posi-tion also means that it is under an obligation to present the ethnic minor-ity electorate with policy commitments that are designed to benefit this group of voters. The choice of commitments tends to vary but at heart it means that the party has to supplement its broad-based policies aimed at its general constituency of supporters and potential supporters. This supplementation, in effect, means that, however limited and superficial, Labour must offer a race-specific package of commitments that target non-white voters. The irony is that it is unclear whether the party needs to go to any great effort to massage what is, after all, among one of its safest constituencies; and, if it does, it is debatable whether a racial equality-led package of policies is most likely to sway its wavering non-white supporters back into line. Furthermore, Labour's need to show sensitivity towards racial and ethnic concerns is founded on very loose evidence that such issues are the key to retaining non-white support in general.

Such sensitivity is by no means confined to Labour's ranks and, to some degree, is shared by political parties in general. The willingness of parties to operate in these terms is, of course, partly a consequence of features within ethnic minority community-based politics. Nevertheless, British political parties are unlikely to rid themselves entirely of this style of strategic mobilisation and all regard the ethnic minority electorate in some way or another as an important component of electoral competition for the pursuit or retention of office.

The distinctiveness of a 'race agenda'

In this chapter so far we have noted that British political parties have shared a tendency to utilise racial and ethnic messages in their attempts to attract non-white support. Additionally, it has been the Labour Party that has extended itself farthest in this direction, while also maintaining a broad non-racial appeal to this electoral group. However, one element in this calculation remains elusive, namely in what sense and to what degree does ethnicity influence ethnic minority voters and political leaders? Rival responses to this question can be easily grouped together to reveal that empirical evidence is subject to interpretation. As the following section shows, much hangs on the way in which analysts and commentators conceptualise so-called 'racial' or 'ethnic' issues.

A central feature of the research literature has been an underlying debate, perhaps confusion, over the distinctiveness of non-white political outlook and action alike. At one end of the spectrum there have been strong cases made in favour of the idea that ethnic minorities are united under a common banner of shared political interests and persuasions (Werbner 1991). A theoretical variant of this line has been an insistence that an ethnically-related way of thinking and behaving politically is at work. At the other end of the spectrum, robust denials of such claims have been made, concluding that the basis of common behaviour has been a response to shared class and racial experiences, without any real sense of collective consciousness (FitzGerald 1987; Studlar 1983).

Understanding of non-white political outlook and behaviour is probably advanced if we think of ethnic minority political attitudes and action
as several overlapping and interrelated characterisations. Some appear to
be highly distinctive, while others attempt to disaggregate the data to
reveal a complex reality beneath.

Evidence for a 'race agenda' or 'race dimension'

It has been claimed that ethnic minorities collectively may vote in line
with a fully separate and discrete set of issues not shared by their white
counterparts. For instance, ethnic minority voters may base their discrete
agenda on a sense that racial discrimination and exclusion are both
widespread and endemic in British society. By constructing a political
view of the world that is centred on racialisation as a fundamental feature
of society, this is probably what is meant by the term 'race dimension'.
There is considerable reason to think, for example, that this kind of
dimension has been at the heart of radical black political activists' efforts
to promote Black Sections in the Labour Party (Shukra 1990). By the
same token, the common experience of racism in British politics – and
society generally – has undoubtedly contributed to the development of
something of a 'race dimension' for ethnic minority voters and political
elites across all parties.

Before turning to the evidence, it is important for the analyst to assess
the degree to which ethnic minorities' political outlook is based
exclusively on racial divisions. If the evidence suggests a strong degree
of such exclusivity, it is possible to speak of a 'race agenda' in the sense
that race and race-related issues are the prism through which the world is
politically understood.

For the most part, empirical evidence tends not to affirm this claim in
the strictest sense. For example, in a 1991 NOP survey, fully four in
every five Afro-Caribbeans agreed with the proposition that Britain was a
'very or fairly racist society' (Kellner and Cohen 1991). (Meanwhile, the
comparable figures for whites and Asians in the survey were 67 and 56
per cent respectively.) This kind and level of feeling might be described
as the building blocks of a wider 'race agenda' world view. In some
instances, a strong sense of counter-hostility toward 'white society', combined with reactive ethnic pride, have been highlighted by researchers
interested in the so-called 'culture of resistance' of black youth (Miles
1978; Troyna 1979). That said, the NOP survey data – in common with
other similar survey findings – had little to say about the depth of feeling
over race, and it is this depth that matters for assessments of a 'race
agenda'. These data may indeed conceal another hidden face whereby the
relevant ethnic minorities' views are highly skewed in one direction but

are views that are not held terribly strongly. Indeed, numerous commentators observing the broad canvas of race relations in Britain make the common assumption that these groups of voters are intensely motivated by racial considerations and that shared assessments about racism in society are the strongest motivators of all.

The disappointingly limited evidence that is available on this point in fact hints at the reverse being closer to the mark. In another 1991 survey carried out by Harris of Asian voters, 37 per cent reported that the question of racial attacks was the most important issue they faced (BBC/Harris 1991). For this group at least, race and racism were not political issues in any general sense, however much they may have felt themselves to be the victims of racial hostility either individually or collectively. Race and racism for them were priorities in the sense that their ethnic group membership left them especially vulnerable to a particular form of violence and intimidation. It would certainly be safe to infer that this concern amounted to a racialised dimension of issues relating to crime and law and order; it may be less safe to claim that their perception of violence being directed at them on the basis of visible appearance necessarily led them to interpret race and racism in broader political terms. At another, related, level, one might ask: does survey data showing that over a third of a specific group are anxious about 'racial attacks' tell us something about the racial significance of their concerns or something about perceptions about individual and collective security? Table 8.2 below tells the story.

Table 8.2   *Most significant issue among Asian voters, 1991*

Issue	Per cent
Education	41
Racial attacks	37
Health service	29
Housing	25
Immigration	17
Poll tax	11
Mother tongue teaching	10
Separate schools	4

Source: BBC/Harris (1991)

Liberal values and opinions among non-white voters and leaders

Another common presumption is that ethnic minorities themselves necessarily hold liberal or progressive views on race relations issues. Again, the limited evidence on this point usually ends up clouding matters and seldom gives much reason to back conclusively such a claim. A 1991 NOP survey revealed that 12 and 15 per cent of Asians and blacks, respectively, disagreed with the suggestion that immigration had enriched the quality of life in Britain; furthermore, 5 and 7 per cent of each respective group felt that British laws against racial discrimination were in fact too tough (Kellner and Cohen 1991). These figures, while fairly modest, would presumably be met by some commentators with a large dose of politically-correct denial.

A similar pattern is seen when considering the old chestnut of ethnic minority support for the principle of ethnic minority political representatives. Only a very small fraction of Asian voters in 1991 said that they were more likely to vote for a candidate of the same ethnic origin as themselves (BBC/Harris 1991). The same note of ambivalence, possibly even scepticism, is arguably at play when it comes to political leaders taking up positions on issues in order to influence votes along ethnic lines. However, the ethnic background of certain leaders, rather than matching putative 'ethnic issues', may turn out to undermine and blur claims made by such leaders: for example, both Keith Vaz's and Max Madden's similar responses to the Rushdie affair were heavily driven by their perceived constituency interests and seemed unaffected by the fact that one of them was an Asian MP and the other was not!

More typically perhaps, suggestions that a race agenda characterises the political orientation of ethnic minorities are commonly expressed by activists and leaders who both have a stake in such a claim and who also hold a normative commitment to such an agenda. Partial support among the ethnic minority electorate for a race agenda will usually mean that these voters at least are undecided whether political participation can be understood in exclusively racial terms. We might predict that such voters would not particularly want to rule out the existence of, and subscription to, a race agenda but, at one and the same time, would fail to give much more than nominal support to race agenda political activists. In a sense then, critics might argue that these voters want to have things both ways. To be fair, this criticism has some weight since the normally race-free texture of everyday British politics ensures that such stark opposing choices are seldom forced upon minority voters.

On the evidence, therefore, it would be simplistic to the point of being naïve to assert that minority voters are motivated by racial concerns alone. What may be taking place is an unusual and specific way of looking at politics. A hard-line perspective based on racial divisions is of course one, perhaps crude, illustration of this phenomenon, but it may not be particularly representative of ethnic minority voters in general. An attractive alternative to this might be the suggestion that ethnic minority cultures create a sufficiently distinct approach to politics and political activity (Field 1984). At first glance, the cultural link displayed by many Asian and Caribbean voters seems to provide plentiful evidence for such an agenda, though it would be only fair to describe this as a cultural rather than racial approach to politics. In any case, however attractive this line of argument may seem (and it is regularly exploited by the media and politicians alike), the question remains as to whether this agenda shapes ethnic minority political participation in any exclusive or near-exclusive sense. Whatever the strength of the cultural basis of, say, Asians' political outlook may be, the argument is undermined if this factor is one of several shaping political behaviour. Arguably, this is perhaps as much as can be said about the theme of culture in modelling non-white electoral behaviour.

Conclusion

The central argument that has been advanced in this chapter is that non-white and white agendas are both the same and distinct at one and the same time. This does not, however, tell us much about why priorities may differ across ethnic lines. To meet this task we need to refine our understanding of causal relationships underpinning inter-ethnic variance (something that is beyond the remit of this chapter).

That said, it is worth commenting on one line of argument that is frequently espoused and that is something of a red herring. The role of ethnicity itself is often emphasised in explaining different priorities. However, it misses the key point, namely that ethnic minorities are more likely to be Labour supporters in any case. Identification with Labour, both at a party political level and in terms of general principles and philosophy, means that they are more likely in turn to attach priority to certain types of issues rather than others. Issues such as housing, health and education are the staple diet of Labour supporters and this is much the same for ethnic minority, Labour-inclined voters. Thus, different priorities have really very little to do with ethnically-related fundamentals.

Other lines of argument appear to have more to offer in contrast. One well-documented approach has highlighted the contribution made by objective socio-economic differences between the white and non-white electorates (Crewe 1983). For example, the substantially younger age profile of the latter, and the heavier middle-class concentration of the former, both serve to give ethnic minority voters a rather different stake in certain issues over others in comparison with their white counterparts.

It is not uncommon to observe that the age and class characteristics of any electoral subgroup shape their general orientation to key issues such as housing and taxation. Residential patterns are another example of orientation towards issues and, in turn, votes for political parties (McAllister and Studlar 1984: 147).

Finally, there is a slim chance of overdoing things by concentrating excessively on white versus non-white distinctions. For example, Labour Force Survey-derived analysis by Robinson (1990) correctly draws attention to fairly wide variations in the socio-economic profiles of Asian subgroups, ethnic Indians and ethnic Bangladeshi being prime examples at opposite ends of the spectrum. Data from the 1991 Census reinforce the same picture (ONS 1996). The upshot of such intra-Asian differences is that there are likely to be different underlying orientations toward political issues which may, in some cases, outstrip differences between white and non-white electors. An additional risk associated with a social demographic-linked explanation is that it still begs the question of how much convergence is probable over time. Ethnic minority voters in that sense are just another illustration of a sectional electorate which, for reasons to do with migration and labour market participation, looks rather different from the rest of the electorate. So much is clear. However, patterns of convergence – as well as some tendency toward greater divergence – are the key to understanding why certain issues count for more than others. Rather greater empirical research along these lines is sorely needed if we are to unpick the mystery of issue salience, and its relationship to issue voting, among ethnic minorities.[3]

Acknowledgements

An adaptation of this chapter appears in Saggar (1997). I am indebted to the following colleagues for their written and verbal comments: John Crowley (FNSP, Paris), Anthony Messina (Tufts University, USA), David Sanders (University of Essex), and Ken Young (QMW). In addition, pre-publication drafts and/or adaptations of this chapter were presented at departmental seminars at Salford University and QMW (both February, 1995), and at the 1995 annual meeting of the American Political Science Association (Chicago, September 1995). I am grateful for feedback provided on those occasions. Finally, deep thanks also goes to Rita Alfred for her supportive criticism.

Notes

1. The term 'ethnic minority' is used to denote people whose recent origins lie in South Asia, Africa and the Caribbean. The term is used more or less interchangeably with 'non-white' and 'black'. These terms are designed to encompass a wide range of non-white groups in contemporary Britain. Departures from these terms are properly identified in the chapter and are usually used in reference to specific component subgroups, for example

'Asians' and 'Afro-Caribbeans'. Readers are reminded that no particular sociological or political inference should be drawn from the use of these primarily descriptive terms, though the author accepts fully that recent intellectual debates in Britain and elsewhere have centred on the question of terminology and nomenclature in the study of race and ethnicity and political participation.

2. In a recent televised examination of the parties' responses to Britain's million-plus Asian voters, it was striking that none of the three major party leaders was successful in conveying the argument that (a) ethnicity did not feature in shaping Asians' voting choice, or (b) ethnicity counted alongside a range of mainstream factors. It is possible that one or more of the interviewed leaders holds either of these perspectives, and indeed there is reason to think that intra-party discussions are rather more pluralistic in their approach. However, as yet, none of the major parties appears willing officially to breach the principle that ethnicity overrides other concerns in shaping minority voting behaviour (see BBC 'East' 1996).

Part 4

Ethnic relations and religious diversity

The importance of the religious factor in the 'ethnic consciousness' of Moroccan immigrants in Belgium

Albert Bastenier

A sort of taboo has for a long time now been attached to the use of the concept 'ethnicity' in Belgian social science. Although this is astonishing in a country that has faced 'ethnic community' based conflicts for many years, researchers in Belgium have only very recently begun to admit that the question of ethnicity could play a role in the construction of social relations between the 'native majority' and the 'immigrant minority'.

To date, however, all such scientific work has remained limited to speculative theorisation regarding the effects of ethnicity on the relations between indigenous Belgians and diverse sections of the immigrant population. Aside from one or two notable exceptions (for example the anthropological work of Roosens 1989), we are thus faced with a grave lack of concrete empirical research on the question. The following reflections are therefore presented as the fruits of ongoing empirical research into the 'ethnic consciousness' of immigrants of Moroccan origin in Brussels.[1]

In this research, the immigrant population are taken to be an 'ethnic minority', confronted by an 'ethnic majority' who make up the indigenous population. This is because, in reality, the assertion of 'ethnicity' by a group never takes place in isolation, but is rather part of an ongoing, reciprocal series of such assertions by majority and minority alike, which respond in reaction to one another. The complementarity of such assertions of ethnicity often goes unobserved. This is quite simply because the majority group has no need to define or state its own identity when establishing its difference from others. Its numerical superiority allows it to enjoy an invisible 'abstract identity': that is one not defined in terms of any identifying particularities (such as being labelled 'foreigner' or 'Arab'). Indeed, the majority population can always assert its identity in terms of 'universal' cultural attributes, for example identifying itself simply with the uncontestable idea of representing 'modernity'.

With these interrelations in mind, this chapter focuses on the emergence of an 'ethnic consciousness' among the immigrant Moroccan population. We set off with the hypothesis that 'ethnicity' is – like gender or class – one of the possible forms of social self-differentiation, aimed at the production of lines of demarcation between different social groups. Indeed, it represents a means of social closure by which social actors effect a hierarchical classification of themselves and others within a social environment in constant recomposition (Barth 1969). The following questions thus become central to our enquiry. Which specific actors or subgroups among the Moroccans made reference to ethnicity as part of their own social self-positioning? Under what circumstances did they do so, how did they do it and what were their goals?

Identity and consciousness

Before moving on to the results of our research, it is first necessary to clarify the distinction used here between 'ethnic identity' and 'ethnic consciousness'. The concept of 'identity' is essentially understood here to be a response to the question social psychologists would pose: 'Who am I?' It would be based around the cultural, political and economic traits that actors recognise in themselves or see attributed to them. Identity is thus first and foremost an expression of social belonging, of the attachment of an individual to a group. The concept of 'consciousness', meanwhile, while not separable from that of identity, goes beyond it in its meaning and scope. Consciousness, as we use it, is about more than just belonging in a group. It situates belonging – and therefore the process of social self-differentiation – in the context of wider social relations. The notion of consciousness therefore fits with the question: 'Who am I distinct from and to whom am I opposed in this hierarchically organised social situation?' An ethnic consciousness is thus founded on the subdivision and classification of individuals into hierarchical groupings, rather than the construction of isolated, self-contained groups. In other words, it actively positions groups in relation to one another, ordering them into a particular set of relations.

Such consciousness of one's status in a hierarchical order is not limited to an actor's awareness of his or her absolute inequality or deprivation *vis-à-vis* others. Actors are as much defined by what mobilises them, by actions that may place them in opposition to others. It follows that 'ethnic consciousness' defines and brings into existence the actor as a specifically immigrant actor within the wider Western society. In other words, ethnic consciousness is what brings into existence this particular type of social relation described as an 'inter-ethnic relation'. Indeed, to be exact, it is the ethnic consciousness itself that constitutes the social relation.

Ethnic consciousness: immigration's sensitive side effect

It would, however, be wrong to think that all immigrants necessarily acquire an ethnic consciousness. In fact, within the same society, different subsections of the immigrant population can display different types of consciousness, or may not even display any kind of ethnic consciousness at all. What we need to look at therefore are the reasons for the appearance and potential development of an ethnic consciousness of this type among certain parts of the immigrant population.

The emergence of an ethnic consciousness may well be a sensitive historical side effect of immigration in Europe over the last 30 years. Being a post-colonial nation, Belgium, like other countries, is forced to deal with immigrants from its former colonies, though to a lesser extent than other post-colonial societies. However, the existence of an ethnic consciousness does not mean that it is the 'true' or only reaction to the experience of immigration, or indeed a necessary product of the historical logic of immigration in Europe. We speak of it being a sensitive side effect, and of the challenge it poses, because the emergence of an ethnic consciousness is indicative of a rearrangement of the kinds of social representations the members of an increasingly homogenous Western society (both indigenous and immigrant) now use to interpret and understand their own history. A symptom of this is that 'social problems' today are not always found to have an economic explanation at root (they are not always symptoms of a capitalist class system), but are increasingly ethno-cultural in nature (caused by segregation along lines of ethnic origin, whether by birth, nationality or religion). It is these categories that are often now the source of the social classification – or indeed declassification or even exclusion – that some members of society have to suffer.

This means that the emergence of an ethnic consciousness brings into existence a specific type of social conflict. It involves those in the indigenous majority as much as the immigrant minority and is not primarily socio-economic in nature. To engage in this conflict, the social actors call upon a cultural reference with which to mobilise their action. One powerful example of this is the reference to religion. In this sense, ethnic consciousness has caused immigration to become a wholly different kind of public problem in Western society in recent years.

This ethnic consciousness can only be shown explicitly by studying the actual practices and opinions provoked by the situations members of ethnic minorities experience. This experience is predominantly one of stigmatisation, caused by the ethno-stratification of Belgian society. The source of this ethnic consciousness thus rests in their perception of belonging with others to a social category or milieu that is experiencing the same obstacles to participating in the benefits of the wider society.

It is on these practices and opinions that our enquiry seeks to cast light. To do this, we brought together the results of around 60 in-depth interviews made with three types of Moroccan immigrant living in Brussels: (1) old men who frequently attend the mosque, nearly all over 60 years old; (2) men of between 30 and 50 who own shops and form part of the social wave of people involved in so-called 'ethnic businesses'; (3) young people aged between 15 and 25 who represent the different educational and professional paths taken by the young generation of immigrant origin. This chapter uses some of the results of this enquiry to focus on the specific importance of the religious factor in the construction of an ethnic consciousness.

The religious dimension of ethnicity

We can now examine the place and role of the religious element in building the ethnic consciousness of immigrant Moroccans. We should, however, bear it in mind that this is not the only (or even the principal) element involved in building such a consciousness.

Older immigrants

Not surprisingly, the religious element is most apparent among the older immigrants who attend the mosque. These people use the religious element in a most systematic manner to construct an ethnic consciousness. For a long time, any reference to Islam among this group, generally first-generation migrants in the 1960s and now almost all over 60 years' old, had been unapparent, if not entirely absent. It was as if it had been buried in the memories and baggage they never really unpacked, so strong was the presence of the idea of returning to their country of origin. Their real-life, subjective experience of migration, which they believed to be temporary, also continuously acted in such a way as to render their invocation of Islam unnecessary, at least in the public arena. The religious point of reference was not forgotten or abandoned. It was placed in reserve for the moment of the great return to the country of origin, which was itself bound up with their idea of the 'land of Islam'.

These people are, however, well aware of what their migratory state has progressively become. Their permanent residence in the country of immigration has been objectively (if not subjectively) accepted and, from this, has grown the need for a more explicit religious link with other Moroccans, who must all reconcile within themselves their present state of unwanted exile. This exile is also, in a certain manner, as much an indication of the failure (at least relative) of their initial project as the social segregation they endure. In this regard, it is above all a question of dignity and honour. For these older men, a new form of self-identification was felt to be necessary. This identification is as much an issue of class as of culture. In their eyes, it is because their community belongs to the former Arab colonies that they suffer rejection in Belgium.

This re-identification, because it combines both a sense of injustice and contempt for the host society, is ethnic in nature. The religious element plays a structuring role. This is understandable, for culture and religion work closely together in producing the social link of community belonging on the basis of genealogy, which may or may not be imaginary. Religion and ethnicity, in this instance, go hand in hand because together they build a compensatory foundation for what 'we' lost in the hazards and setbacks of immigration. The increased visibility of a Muslim community of Moroccan immigrants in Brussels is therefore like a religious reaffirmation that bestows dignity on a community with a common destiny. This community, which has a common destiny and which identifies itself in an ethnic manner, seeks to testify to the injustice it suffers. From the point of view of older Moroccans, it is evidence of what is in fact a policy of integration, which is not spoken about much in Belgium other than to blame the immigrants themselves for its failure. Ethno-religious consciousness, which exalts ideas of peace and justice, morality and order, allows them to distinguish themselves more from the surrounding society, which is the object of their failure and, according to them, is 'leading their children astray'.

The community recomposition to which the older immigrants are turning is undoubtedly a defensive strategy. Nonetheless, it contributes towards giving back pride to these immigrants who are confronted by a Western society they perceive as aggressive, false, perverse, even corrupt. Current international events in the Muslim world have enhanced the role of the religious element in building this consciousness, especially since Islam has been portrayed as a conquering religion in recent decades, while Christianity is seen to be on the decline.

This type of ethnic consciousness is mostly interpreted by native populations and even by the social sciences as a regression to tradition and old community strictures. For this reason, it is regularly perceived as a threatening form of 'religious fundamentalism'. This perception does not sit well with the results of our interviews. Without doubt it is true that immigration caused a defensive ethno-religious re-identification. This re-identification is being constructed in a new context which no longer has the village, the region or even the country of origin as its goal. It cannot therefore be purely and simply reduced to an anachronistic cloning of the old parochial and traditional peasant Islam, which are indeed the origins of the majority of these immigrants.

Within the ethno-religious consciousness of the Moroccans in our study, there is an adaptation to the supranational status of contemporary society, of which immigration is itself an essential part. The greater free movement of people, ideas, goods and symbols, which accompanies the establishment of religious networks and solidarity groups, deterritorialises symbolic references and enables their members to preserve themselves from the physical and spiritual contamination of a world 'under the domination of the infidel'. To make these networks work, they may seek the support of organisations with universalist pretensions, such as the World Islamic League or the Tabligh (Dassetto 1996). An important characteristic of the new situation is that it is no longer confined within state borders (aided above all by easier access to international television programmes). This is why we believe the majority of the Moroccans we interviewed identified themselves with Islam from a much more global perspective than before. The large number of *hadj* (Muslims who have gone on a pilgrimage to Mecca) among the older people interviewed in our study is tangible evidence of this evolution. This religious practice, which has become increasingly commonplace, unites Muslims from different countries. Embarking on a religious pilgrimage at least enables them to experience a situation in which Muslims from all countries can meet each other. They perceived the experience as having a transcultural dimension that broke down local and national peculiarities. It gives a certain consistency to the *Oummah* (the community of believers), which, imaginary though it is, nonetheless orients individuals towards something altogether different from ethno-community confinement as it is typically understood. We should perhaps speak about a 'neo-ethnic' consciousness in these immigrants, for theirs is an ethnic identification with a much sought after universal orientation, and no longer one based strictly on belonging to a community.

When speaking of older immigrants one must emphasise the paradox of their ethnic consciousness. It is at the same time both defensive and in the process of producing a new form of internationalism, which far from breaking down their ethnic consciousness in fact only strengthens and enhances it. The problems Westerners feel in relation to these 'new Muslims' is that they encounter an assertion by these 'others' of a kind of universalism that is different from theirs. It is obviously difficult for Westerners to accept an ethnicity with universal pretensions, which, despite being different from theirs, may also contribute to the modernisation of consciousness. This is an indication of one of the main difficulties that will be encountered in future ethnic relations.

The ethnic businessmen

The new class of ethnic businessmen have only recently rediscovered Islam's potential. In contrast with their predecessors, many of them explain that for the first part of their lives they were relatively indifferent to and distanced from the religion of their community of origin. They say that they only learnt through the immigration experience that religion is a powerful link between men, which secures and inspires mutual confidence. They have therefore also returned to religion.

What these businessmen have undoubtedly explored is not so much the religious and spiritual truth of Islam in their personal lives, as some of the potential social functions of the religion. These become apparent when a religion enters an ethnic group's public arena, which Islam did for the Moroccan immigrants in the 1980s and 1990s. This arena has opened up opportunities. There is a place for ethnically-oriented businesses in a predominantly Moroccan socio-cultural environment, with its shared language and history. Apart from the mosques, these businesses belong to the rebuilt network of solidarity in which religion plays an obvious social role that cannot be ignored, as it is certainly not by the businessmen themselves (local or otherwise).

One could say that these ethnic businessmen have seized an opportunity. Their original social backgrounds have provided them with a favourable environment in which to develop their commercial ventures. And their cultural resources (in this case religious) have given them a context in which to establish the reputation and confidence every businessman needs. In other words, they have found an instrumental use for the religious element.

This interpretation is, however, somewhat partial and rather simplistic, though not totally incorrect. It fails to take account of the encompassing significance of the new ethno-religious consciousness of these businessmen. There is a certain congruence between the new transnationalism of the migrants' Islam and the transnationalist characteristics the ethnic businessmen acquire through their dealings in imports and exports.

From a sociological point of view, the construction of a migratory ethnic community corresponds to the creation of a new form of belonging, whose challenge to Western modernity is at both expressive and instrumental levels. The ethnic community (and the consciousness that forms it) creates a complex network of relationships. Through these relationships, which hinge around the transfrontier movement of people, ideas and goods, these groups both preserve themselves from the risks of a changing and hostile world (a defensive stance) and assert the dignity of a distinct identity (the embryonic form of an offensive stance). These businessmen function equally well when participating in the expressive dimension of loyalty to 'the community of believers', represented by the mosques and religious associations, as they do when engaged in the economic activities that allow the community to prosper materially by creating its own resources. By so doing, these businessmen contribute towards the putting in place of a response to the effects of economic segregation and social exclusion that detrimentally affect migrants. These two aspects express a communal 'reality' that is perceived to be an alternative form of solidarity to that offered by the dominant society.

The ethnic businessmen thus participate both in the reactive strategy of immigrants who see obstacles hindering their ambitions of upward social mobility, and in the progressive creation of a 'community reality' in which different ethno-cultural symbols appear (for example the goods that are bought and sold in their community and the public emphasis on religious life). From this angle, we are better able to understand the double origins of these actors in ethnic business. Sometimes they are the representatives of an emerging ethnic middle class, where religious reconversion corresponds to the search for an ethno-religious substratum for their commercial businesses. At other times, however, they approach it from the religious side: they are the people who see a need to place religion – if they want to see it expand- in direct contact with the modernity of transnational business networks.

The type of ethnic consciousness at work at this level, even if it is reacting to the domination the 'native majority' exercises over the 'ethnic minority', takes place inside the group of belonging. It is grounded in a mobilisation of the symbolic resources of the ethno-religious community. It remains, however, visibly oriented towards strategies of individual social mobility (economic, religious or both) rather than towards a policy of global transformation of the native social order that detrimentally affects immigration.

The young generation

Despite social scientists often having studied young second-generation immigrants for their alleged social deviance, empirical knowledge of the religious dimension of their self-identification remains limited. Research into the impact of the religious element on the eventual construction of an ethnic-consciousness is, not surprisingly, the most confused.

Many sociologists have been content to reproduce common-sense assertions that assume, along with what is habitually said of the younger indigenous generation, that young immigrants are increasingly displaying a marked distancing from religious issues. It would be better to recognise that we still know very little about the processes at work in the generational change between the Islam of parents and the Islam of sons and daughters. It is clear, however, that this is not occurring in an identical manner to that displayed by younger generations of Christians (Dassetto 1996).

The theoretical 'problematic of loss of religion', as described and defined by Hervieu-Léger (1993), is completely inadequate, for it merely reproduces the widespread and well-known thesis of the 'cultural backwardness' of religion in comparison with 'Western Modernity'. This thesis does no more than state, in a naïve ethnocentric manner, that ultimately the best thing that could happen to young people of Moroccan origin is for them to begin to resemble in all respects their native counterparts. This thesis has, in the past, confused sociologists dealing with the Christian religion, who, as a result of being enclosed in the paradigm of secularisation, rendered themselves incapable of seeing anything other than the inexorable erosion of the religious reference. We know today that the reality is rather more complex. How can we use the same explanatory schema for young Maghrebi women who adopt the 'modern political uniform' (Lacoste-Dujardin 1992) of the *hijab* (the Muslim veil) as for those who refuse to submit to religious or paternal domination and become actors in the extra-domestic arena. With regard to these women, there is something more complex at work than mere family conformity. It would be better to accept once and for all that the social uses both immigrants and indigenous populations make of their cultures and religions, are less simple and unequivocal than this thesis seems to imply.

We were struck at first that, however distanced our young interviewees may have held themselves to have been from the Islam of their parents, in elaborations of their social consciousness they always took filiation and the family structure into account. The latter appears to be omnipresent in their minds – in answering questions on the family, they will always reintroduced religion into their discussions. We can state on this basis that, in the majority of cases, they must increasingly maintain the appearance of accepting family conventions, which are for the most part religious conventions, even if they are regularly the object of many compromises/transactions that are more or less accepted or hidden.

In the process of identity building, religion remains, despite everything, an important soldering element between generations. This is why in opinion polls (in particular the confidential/multiple choice polls and questionnaires) the verbal distancing of the young from Islam may be deceptive. Their concrete actions are a better indicator of reality and should be the object of researchers' attention.

Having made this statement, we must guard against the ease with which social scientists often consider young Moroccans as a monolithic group. In reality, they differ quite a lot between themselves according to their family, social and professional trajectory, history and background. These initial experiences do not appear to be irrelevant to the manner in which religious references affect the construction of their social identity. In any event, on the basis of our survey it is empirically evident that, in the quest for their identity, they have to undergo complex compromises with their environment. This process is so complex that it not easy to state at this point what the final result will be. The only certainties to have emerged so far are that they do not have a single trajectory, and that there is no predetermined future for the religious element laid down by the journey from the 'traditional' to the 'modern'.

Once it is observed that these young people have different types of links with religion, and that the impact of the latter on the possible emergence of an ethnic consciousness is far from being homogenous, it is even more true that a complex alliance always arises between the cultural-symbolic references these young Arab Muslims inherited on the one hand and the concrete forms of their economic, social and political inclusion in the local society on the other. It is important to highlight these issues in order to understand the forms of consciousness these young people may achieve. Deep down in themselves they believe that they are equally and contradictorily at one and the same time the heirs to a piece of the Third World transplanted into the heart of Europe, and the sole heirs of developed Western society. In addition to their family environment, that of their primary socialisation and by which they have been strongly influenced, their secondary socialisation is essentially the result of European social and cultural orders. School, the media, urban environments and belonging to 'adolescent culture' have profoundly shaped their imaginary social world. A great transition has occurred between generations of Moroccan immigrants in Belgium, especially among boys. For a variety of reasons, the young have opted for the social world of the street rather than for family life, which represents the funda-mental arena of the older generation. This priority granted to street life in the relationships they establish between the private and public arenas of their lives distances them from the family codes, even if this priority does not extinguish the family codes (Bensalah 1995). The cultural conformity they generally share with their young native counterparts also indicates that their social habits are primarily European. Moreover, they them-

selves never cease to repeat this by underlining that the demands continuously addressed to them to integrate are to them incomprehensible or
anachronistic.

Their demonstrations of discontentment or at times outrage towards
the local society do not arise because they are turning their backs on
consumption and social mobility. On the contrary, they arise because they
are being denied full integration into that society because of the stigma of
being Arab. If they forge for themselves an ethnic-consciousness, it is
essentially reactive: it is the consciousness of an arbitrary denial of the
means to participate truly in that society.

Various sociologists have suggested that recourse to the ethnic argument is most frequently encountered among the group of young people
who feel confined by the most hopeless social situations. This would
explain the urban riots of young Maghrebis in certain areas of Brussels
and other European cities against the police, whom the former see as a
tangible manifestation of domination. In the eyes of these young
Maghrebis, the police most explicitly symbolise the contempt from which
they suffer and the denial of access into the society to which they aspire.
By the same reasoning, it would seem logical that as already hopeless
situations get worse, recourse to the moral significance of Islam (as a
catalyst for an ethnic consciousness that expresses a ridiculed dignity)
would increase. The religious argument would also feed the protests of
the rioters in their revolt against the social decay of the underclass into
which some of them sink.

Our study, however, appears to indicate that this does not necessarily
occur. Among the interviewees most profoundly marked by the stigma of
scholastic or professional failure, Islam is more often invoked with reluc-
tance, for it is incapable of creating a proud consciousness. They say that
Islam could have ..., Islam should have ..., but alas Islam has become
debased and weakened by the hypocrisy of its superficial rituals. If one
participates in a riot, it is not 'for Islam or because of Islam, but against
racists'. They perceive Islam as having waned (become decomposed) in
its inability truly to mobilise its energies. Religion is no longer for them
anything other than a convention and a code they pretend to respect,
especially at a family level, so as not to aggravate family conflicts or, perhaps, sink any lower. We have therefore moved far from the ideas put
forward by certain researchers in which one possible strategy for Arab-
Muslim minorities experiencing difficulties integrating into society in
Europe is to attenuate their third-world Arab identity in favour of their
more universal Muslim identity (Roy 1996).

Not all the youths in our survey sensed this erosion of their religion, so
one should not rule out the emergence of other political, cultural and

religious actors capable of giving the riots an ethno-religious significance. However, this does not appear to be the case for the moment. The present rioting may be viewed as the embryonic form of an expressive display of a sense of belonging to a same community of young Moroccans – a sort of 'Intifada culture' – that bestows on excluded young Moroccans a new power that had been ignored in the public arena of the different districts of the town. It is a spectacular but wavering action around which the 'cop' is adopted as the symbol of 'racist' domination. Even if it does signify the social fracture of the society (brought about by ethno-stratification and the presence of a third-world identity inside even Belgian society), the rioting will not continue indefinitely. So far, these riots have neither given rise to an ethno-religious consciousness nor created actors with such a consciousness.

This first concrete observation does not in itself sum up the use (or non use) young Moroccans made of the religious element. The most important group in our survey in terms of numbers – those with a conformist relationship with the practices of a very formalised religion – was also the most difficult to quantify. At first sight, the use these youths made of religion, which was limited to facilitating their relationships within the family environment and social group from which they saw no great advantage in freeing themselves, seemed to have nothing in common with ethnic consciousness. Their religious behaviour reminds one of what Hoggart (1986) said about the 'culture of poverty' being a culture that finds its axis in the feeling of irrevocably belonging to an unchangeable group, a rigid and conformist culture which constitutes the elementary code of rules to be followed by those who know they have no other perspectives of mobility. It is not seen as their means of emancipation.

This simple reading of the phenomena may well, without being false, be inadequate and may dissimulate the importance of the contribution of young 'religious conformists' to the future development of an ethno-religious consciousness. How else can one understand the fact that the religious element – the body of rigid rites and precepts individuals limit themselves to endorsing – acts almost in the intemporal manner of a code instead of being a dynamic and mobilising culture overflowing with meanings and linked to social convictions about current events? While it does not indicate a reawakening of religious conviction in these youths, it may well be a sign of an ethnification of the religious element, for it tends more and more to have no function other. than to assure the continued survival of the community entity, for one does not wish to cut oneself off definitively in a precarious social situation (Roy 1996)

In this case, under the guise of their adhesion to the community and religious demands, the youths hide from the fears they associate with an increasingly individualised future in a world that is hostile to them. By formally accepting that 'this type of behaviour is Muslim' and 'that type is not', in an uncertain context they are agreeing to use religious signs to define a spirit of belonging. After all, the other forms of belonging are crumbling. The religious element thus allows them to retain a minimum identity as they lose their cultural points of reference. Learning to be Muslim by manifesting the rigid signs of religiosity is, of course, a defensive way of acting and one that ethnicises the arena of social exclusion. It also creates future opportunities for an ethnic consciousness that is thoroughly fundamentalist in nature.

Finally, we can pick out in Moroccan youths a small group of individuals who display a declared interest in Islam. These youths manifest a will to get to know the religion of their group of origin better and, in it, to rediscover its fundamental requirements. They are, however, very few of them – Tribalat (1995) estimates 10–15 per cent of all youths. Though it may be excessive to perceive of them as the heralds of a 'reislamification' (Kepel 1987) of the younger generation, their spiritual quest nonetheless appears to be quite strong, certainly stronger than that of young indigenous Christians (Muxel 1988). These youths build their identity by asserting that they wish to place religion in the new post-traditional society in which they live. We see appearing in them a religious identification that leaves more room for personal and free pursuits. We can also add to this the influence of the ongoing transformation of Islam, which is at the same time both more subjective and more universal. In this regard, we also observe among the young the emergence of the internationalist type of religious individual previously described in older generations.

The young Moroccans in this last category follow an inverted religious trajectory compared with that of the first group of old men to whom we referred. Here, Islamic universalism helps the entry into a modernity that attenuates distinctive Arab features. The blurred or decomposed identity of their origins is not denied but is recomposed. Insofar as it seeks to mark itself off from Western society and to construct an alternative universalism, this religious identity can easily link itself to an oppositional stance already existing among the segregated minority.

We did not often encounter a frank consciousness of this latter type among our young interviewees. However, this modernised 'Islamic action' could be at work among the young Muslim women who voluntarily wear the *hijab*, for these 'Muslims by filiation' (Lacoste-Dujardin 1992) are clearly doing something quite different from behaving passively. We believe that this latter group is likely to emerge in an ethno-religious consciousness, in which exclusion will be reread in terms of a 'third-world philosophy' that uses Islam as its medium of protest.

Conclusion

Ethnic consciousness should only become the object of sociological enquiry when it can be shown to be present in the behaviour and/or opinions that reveal the conceptual framework social actors give to their actions. We may ask then whether an ethnic consciousness of this kind is indeed present among Moroccan immigrants in Belgium. On the basis of the preliminary research presented, our response is that it is indeed very strongly present.

Our research tends to show that the immigrant Moroccans' experience of being disadvantaged, segregated or rejected by Belgian society is insufficient to engender an ethnic consciousness. For this to happen, these negative experiences need to be combined with some affirmation of personal dignity – affirmation that they share a basic human condition that Western society, cut in two between indigenous and immigrant populations, scorns and ridicules. In this way, they no longer see themselves as simply victims of an unchangeable social system, which hierarchically and unequally divides up social goods (both material and symbolic). Rather, they see themselves as a unique group of actors in a society in which tensions and conflict about rights that are attached to the human dignity of all its members are being played out. It is from this moment on that immigrant Moroccans bring into existence a specific kind of relation with the indigenous population, what we can call an 'inter-ethnic relation'.

The new migrations into Europe created a situation that amounted to a new kind of social stratification and hierarchy between indigenous people and North African immigrants in Belgium. Their emergent ethnic consciousness has, for its part, conferred a 'social identity' on this group of immigrants who, by this means, give a meaning to their historical situation and thereby begin to organise it for themselves. Relying on economic, political and cultural factors that are latent in their situation, this consciousness traces the line between the minority immigrant group and the majority indigenous group, drawing on assumptions about the nature of the ethnic conflict at stake. This then enables actors, from both groups, to explain to themselves the new social situation in which they find themselves. The experience of these actors thus goes beyond the simple passive reception of the given social experience, and becomes one of reflection about the functioning of society itself. From this moment on, a conception of the overall nature of society is created in the minds of the actors, and defines what they see at stake in their place in it. It is important to note that the ethnic consciousness itself is what creates this understanding. By enabling the interpretation and expression of conflictual social relations in a society perceived as unjustly organised, the consciousness itself thereby confers a meaningful framework on a situation which, until then, was just something passively received.

Ethnicity thus only really exists from the moment individuals give it a concrete content that corresponds to their actions. In this chapter I have tried to show that the kind of consciousness that comes out of these actions is far from being homogenous in nature. Ethnic consciousness need not necessarily be identified with a resolute commitment to transform the social relations between indigenous and immigrant populations. In fact, this is virtually absent as a motivation among Moroccans in Brussels. The will to transform social relations by mobilising politically behind an ethnic consciousness rarely appeared in this radical form among our interviewees. Must we conclude then that ethnic consciousness is weak and not very widespread, if not non-existent? Not at all. If we came to that conclusion we would be reducing the notion of ethnic consciousness to a specific kind of political consciousness, and be reading it as the one and only 'true' type of ethnic consciousness. In fact, immigrants have a whole range of strategic choices about ethnicity available to them.

We found that consciousness sometimes led to a shared identity oriented towards the expression of dignity by a simple community turned in on itself, and sometimes to more or less successful attempts to solder collective action. It is either defensive, building itself in opposition to the social environment in which it finds itself, or it is turned towards values that claim a social status different from the one the dominant society imposes. The consciousness can also create more individualistic strategies (either internal to the group or aimed at enabling individuals to distance themselves from their origins), or it may cause initial ambitions to be scaled down, decomposed or dissolved in resignation.

Because the ethnic consciousness does not result in constant, radical, politicised action does not mean we have to conclude that such a consciousness does not really exist or that it does not have long-term effects that transform social relations. Although we have not seen radically ethnicised political action in Belgium, it would be impossible to claim that the ethnic consciousness present has had no affect on questions such as education, the law, the right to free speech, the media, urban planning, political solidarity, social policy, or religion in the public sphere. These are precisely areas of society where the remodelling of social relations is in transformation today, as they will be in future.

Ethnically motivated action is also sporadic. It is only clearly visible at certain moments of social tension, when such action reveals the new divisions that cut across Western society. Rather than saying that ethnic consciousness is weak or non-existent, the real question ought to be whether it is becoming a fundamental determinant of social action in post-colonial Western societies, alongside class and gender. This is why it is necessary to learn how to recognise manifestations of ethnic consciousness in social behaviour. If no effort is made to deal with this new cause of social divisions, Europe risks finding itself with an ethnic problem of the kind seen so spectacularly in recent riots in the USA.

In this chapter, I have sought to show the importance of the religious factor in ethnic consciousness. It is, of course, far from the only one at work, but it would be wrong to underestimate its importance in the reconstruction of a Moroccan immigrant ethnic identity. Indeed, it should be seen in the light of the old reference points of Marxism and socialism having broken down, both in the West and in the former Arab societies, which drew heavily on these ideologies during the economic and political process of decolonisation. Although some have already announced the failure of political Islam (Roy 1992), Islam is now able to play the role of third-world ideology in its own right. This is undoubtedly aided by the present need, not merely for an economic and political ideology, but for something that assists the process of cultural decolonisation (Burgat 1995). Islam is central to the ethnic consciousness of immigrants because it alone is able to draw together culturally – that is to say symbolically – individuals who are suffering social exclusion. It does this by giving them a meaningful form of belonging to a society other than the one from which they are isolated and excluded. The imaginary *Oummah* of Islamic fundamentalism or political Islam reinserts these individuals into another history.

Finally, is ethnicity – the forms of social classification based on certain cultural traits that are more or less imaginary but that are taken to characterise individuals and communities – nothing more than a provisional residue of the past? Or will it remain one of the most fundamental beliefs of contemporary society? The belief in the existence of ethnicity is just as effective today in a post-colonial context, as it was in the colonial situations of the past. If ethnicity is to stay so fundamental, the real question for future research will be not how immigrants are ethnic communities, but how they become ethnic communities.

Note

1. I wish to thank at this point Nouzha Bensalah who collected the empirical data for the investigation on which this chapter is based.

Accommodating religious pluralism in Britain: South Asian religions

Steven Vertovec

Despite commonplace rhetoric hailing Britain as a multicultural society, politicians, leading Anglican churchmen and a host of other public figures regularly insist on describing the country as Christian and calling for an uplifting of society by way of reinvigorating Christian values. And despite HRH Prince Charles's wish, when King, to be 'defender of [many] faiths' – rather than, as per tradition, 'defender of *the* faith' – the formal Establishment of the Church of England can be seen as symbolically placing all other religions in a secondary or even inferior position (Modood 1994). This is evident in the *ex officio* presence of dozens of Anglican bishops in the House of Lords, where they reiterate the characterisation of Britain as first, foremost and ideally Christian.

The creation of visible, sizeable, organised South Asian religious communities has, of course, contributed significantly to Britain's pluralistic – rather than wholly Christian – religious landscape. A wide range of communities of South Asian origin, now in their second and third generation in Britain, are in the position of having to undertake introspective initiatives such as to look at their own beliefs and practices considering which are the features that link them to or separate them from other traditions both in the UK and in India, Pakistan and Bangladesh; to decide which features are central to the faith (and hence which must be preserved) and which are based on local cultural traditions of the subcontinent (thus possibly allowed to attenuate in Britain); and ultimately, to establish which are the rites, tenets, symbols and social forms critical to the maintenance of a collective identity, which must be passed on to and reproduced by the young, now absolutely British, South Asians.

Over time, the heightening of consciousness among South Asian religious communities has entailed a bolstering of confidence by way of dealing with British state authorities and the wider society in general. Subsequently, these communities have become increasingly organised and articulate in their calls for the recognition of minority rights and fair treatment in a variety of public arenas. The forms of ethnic-religious mobilisation have called for the broad acceptance and accommodation of practices, values, moralities and legal systems quite different from long-standing British traditions. The struggle to achieve these accommodations has consolidated and galvanised many communities, while the allowance of many of them has often proved to demonstrate Britain's openness towards true multiculturalism (flying in the face of the Christian-centred public discourses and structures, as well as running against other trends of xenophobia and racism). Following a brief description of the South Asian religious presence in Britain, this chapter outlines some of the key issues and areas surrounding public accommodation.

South Asian religions in Britain

For more than 200 years a variety of South Asian religious traditions were present in Britain among small numbers of sailors, students, emissaries and others. However, such a presence did not have much social or public impact. It has only been by way of the large-scale, post-Second World War migration of South Asian peoples to Britain that the transplantation of such traditions has had major effects within both the South Asian communities and wider British society (Ballard 1994; Clarke, Knott 1991; Parsons 1993, 1994; Peach and Vertovec 1990; Vertovec 1996d and 1996e).

Following the Second World War, British industry sustained a period of recovery and growth, which necessitated a large injection of additional manual and semi-skilled labour. Although various schemes saw to the importation of European labour, long imperial connections with certain parts of the Indian subcontinent facilitated the recruitment of a substantial workforce, particularly from the (by then Indian and Pakistani) Punjab, an area which had a large cadre of indigenous ex-British army men and a long history of migration to East Africa and other parts of the subcontinent. Thus Punjabis, together with Indians from certain parts of Gujarat and Bengalis from Sylhet district (in what is now Bangladesh), were drawn – indeed, invited – to come to and work in Britain. Systems of 'chain migration' saw to the establishment of settlement patterns and social networks in each locale largely characterised by groups from specific cultural, religious and linguistic backgrounds.

By the late 1950s and early 1960s, thousands of South Asian Muslim, Hindu and Sikh men had found industrial employment predominantly in the conurbations of northern England (especially Leeds, Bradford and Manchester), the Midlands (Birmingham, Coventry, Leicester and Nottingham), and Greater London. At this time the South Asian population in Britain was almost entirely comprised of men, whose guiding intention was to labour (usually under conditions of great hardship) for a number of years in order to accumulate, on behalf of their entire family back in the subcontinent, some given sum of money before returning to their home villages or towns. Eventually, however, many chose to remain in Britain and – despite increasingly tight immigration legislation in the late 1960s and early 1970s – they decided to reunify their families. Also in this period, the 'Africanisation' policies of some East African states made the substantial South Asian communities there feel most unwelcome, leading to a growing exodus from that region to Britain (in fact, culminating in the wholesale expulsion of South Asians from Uganda in 1972). In this way, entire families of 'East African Asians' (mostly of Gujarati origins) arrived *en masse*. As described below, it is especially the establishment of families among Muslims, Hindus and Sikhs in Britain that has had the most far-reaching implications for South Asian religions in Britain and their impacts on the wider society.

Within the total current population of nearly 55 million, the 1991 Census provides a figure of 1,479,645 for the South Asian categories (Peach 1996). This number, in turn, is comprised of 840,255 Indians (56.8 per cent of all South Asians), 476,555 Pakistanis (32.2 per cent) and 162,835 Bangladeshis (11 per cent). The numbers by religious affiliation are especially difficult to derive, however, since official sources do not include a 'religion' question (Knott and Toon 1982; Peach 1990). It is estimated that the total British South Asian population is comprised of around 44 per cent Muslims (two-thirds of which are Pakistanis, the balance being made up of near equal numbers of Gujarati Indians and Bangladeshis), 28 per cent Hindus (well over two-thirds of which are Gujaratis, the balance being made up of equal numbers of Punjabis and other Indians), 21 per cent Sikhs (practically all of whom are Punjabi), and 6 per cent Christians and Others (from all over the subcontinent). A sizeable proportions of each of these groups, it should be noted, is comprised of 'East African Asians' (and smaller numbers of Indians from Mauritius, Fiji and the Caribbean) whose social, cultural and economic patterns may differ from their counterparts who came directly from the subcontinent.

The differing regional and linguistic origins of each religious community within the British South Asian population indicate some of the social and cultural complexities inherent in such a diaspora. Some religious traditions (including specific rites, roles, texts, lore, calendars, focuses of worship and patterns of deference) characteristic of local contexts in the subcontinent have been reproduced in Britain, especially where large numbers of persons from such a former local context have settled: these include Sufi practices and collectivities centred around specific *pirs* (saints or holy men) among Mirpuri Muslims, and worship groups and rites devoted to certain goddesses or deified saints among Gujarati Hindus. Still other parochial traditions have been refined or amalgamated in Britain in order to create essentially new religious rites and congregations, notably in places where smaller numbers from mixed origins (especially Gujarati and Punjabi Hindus) have settled.

Further, several 'sects' or schools of thought and teaching within South Asian religions are now found in Britain, including Barelwi, Deobandi and Ahl-i-Hadith traditions among Muslims (Robinson 1988), and Swaminarayan and Pushtimarga among Hindus (Vertovec 1996d). Numerous 'minor' religious traditions within, or historically linked to, the 'major' traditions are to be found throughout Britain as well, including Jains, Valmikis, Ravidasis, Radhasoamis, Namdharis, Nirankaris, Ahmadiyyas, and Nizari Isma'ilis.

Caste also sometimes continues to affect the organisation of communities and the reproduction of religious traditions: although no caste 'system' exists in any form (by way of structuring relations of exchange), corporate caste identities persist as status groups within many South Asian communities in Britain such that various organisations and congregations are comprised of, or controlled by, members of certain castes. Despite a great variety of backgrounds, however, each South Asian religious group in Britain has organised itself (including considerable efforts at fund-raising from within each respective ranks) and liaised with local government bodies to gain specific forms of accommodation. Organising places of worship was usually the first item on the agenda of each.

Patterns of institutionalisation

In the 1950s and early 1960s, when the British South Asian population consisted mainly of pockets of men whose day-to-day existence was centred solely on working and saving money, religious life was little organised, mostly individualistic and often – when on occasion formal and collective – drew believers from a range of differing regional, linguistic or other backgrounds. With the settlement of family groups in the late 1960s and early 1970s, South Asian religious organisations of all kinds rapidly proliferated, while congregational and communal activities became key features of religious life. In so doing, such organisations and congregations consolidated around regional, linguistic and 'sectarian' (and sometimes caste) attributes. The 'fusion' of persons from varied origins was succeeded by a 'fission' into specific groups. When the South Asian population was comprised almost solely of men, ritual under-takings were unembellished and overseen mainly by a few lay individuals who knew the procedures; with the settlement of complete families, priests and other religious specialists were brought from the subcontinent so that ritual activities could take their prescribed forms – sometimes, eventually, becoming more elaborate than in their home settings. Finally, the presence of families meant that the domestic sphere, arguably the fun-damental realm of all South Asian religious practice and religious nurture, could take its rightful place within each of the traditions in Britain.

The settlement of families marked the emergence of viable South Asian religious communities in Britain, and coincided with a decline of the 'myth of return' in which migrants had looked to return after a few years of work (though to this day remittances have continued to be sent to extended family members in the subcontinent). Particularly, then, with the presence of children whom South Asian parents wanted educated and eventually employed in Britain, there arose among Muslims, Hindus and Sikhs (and members of the smaller South Asian religious communities) alike, a concern for collectively maintaining key aspects of their religious traditions. It has been especially for this purpose that South Asian religious organisations have proliferated especially since the early 1970s. The *raison d'être* of most such organisations on the local level has been to raise funds to build and maintain public places of worship.

The first Sikh gurdwara in Putney in 1911; first mosque in Britain was established in Woking in 1912; the first reported Hindu temple did not appear until 1969, in Leicester, although Hindu festivals were celebrated in rented public halls in the 1950s. Subsequently, the number of places of worship in Britain grew, in each case, from a mere handful in the 1960s to presently 304 Hindu temples, 248 Sikh gurdwaras, and no less than 849 Muslim mosques. The prominence of mosques is due not only to the greater number of Muslims in Britain, but to the fact that congregational worship is a central tenet of Islam – in contrast with Hinduism and Sikhism. Since mosques require nothing except space for praying, many if not most are simply converted houses, whereas Hindu temples and Sikh gurdwaras are more often large structures meant to receive and provide meals for large numbers on special religious occasions.

There are now, in addition to places of worship, some 391 Hindu, 191

Sikh, and 849 Muslim associations around Britain. Most of these associations and places of worship reflect the varying migration histories as
well as the regional, linguistic and sectarian backgrounds of each local
South Asian population.

Unlike in Belgium, religious institutions receive no direct support from
the state. They can, however, qualify as charities for tax advantages, and
sometimes may receive local government grants for assisting broadly
based community centres or festivals. In some cities, local religious
organisations of the same faith have made links with each other in an
attempt to provide common representation to local government authorities in order to gain funding, to make requests or demands, to protest, or
to call for the recognition of certain civic rights. However, most such
link-bodies have often succumbed to personality clashes among leaders
of associations, factionalism and other forms of divisiveness.

A number of national associations have been created by Muslims,
Hindus and Sikhs respectively, yet to this date none has achieved a
wholly representative status for each faith. One recent, prominent
example is the Muslim Parliament, founded in January 1991 and
modelled to some extent on the General Synod of the Church of England
and the Board of Deputies of British Jews: though gaining prominent
media coverage, the Parliament's 155 members are drawn from four
manifesto groups, rather than local Muslim associations, and many are
hand-picked. Still, there is growing need for national bodies representing
South Asian faiths, and doubtless in the years to come, some such
effective organisations will emerge. On a broader scale, currently some
British South Asian organisations are also associated with international
religious organisations (sometimes propounding political ideologies),
such as the Vishwa Hindu Parishad for Hindus, the International Sikh
Youth Federation and Damdami Taksal Jatha for Sikhs, and Jama'at-i-
Islami and Tabligh-i-Jama'at for Muslims.

South Asian religious associations in Britain can be described according to the following rough typology, in categories that are by no means
mutually exclusive (Shadid and van Koningsveld 1995; Vertovec and
Peach 1997):

- those that arose as 'grass-roots' organisations to serve perceived
  needs of a local community – including those specific to certain
  neighbourhoods, kinship groups, Muslim minority traditions (for
  example, Ismailis), national or regional origins, linguistic groups, or
  social groups such as youths, women, or students;
- those that were set up as an extension of organisations in a country of
  origin (for example among Hindus the Vishwa Hindu Parishad, which

is linked to organisations of the same name and other temple groups in Britain; or among Muslims Jamaat-i-Islami, a prominent Islamicist political party in Pakistan tied closely with Muslim organisations in Britain – specifically the Islamic Foundation, the UK Islamic Mission, Young Muslims UK and Dawat-ul-Islam);

- those that have benefited financially from contributions by the government of another country – no political or other ties are known to have derived, for instance, from Saddam Hussein's contribution of £2 million for a mosque in Birmingham, which still bears his name, or from Saudi Arabia's supposed investment of some £50 million in British Islam during the 1980s (*The Economist*, 26 January 1991);
- those that are attached to an international mystical fraternity or religious movement (such as Tabligh-i-Jama'at for Muslims, Rama-krishna Mission for Hindus, Namdharis for Sikhs); and
- those that have been set up, coordinated or backed by national or local government agencies (there is no example of the former in Britain – in contrast with the Islamic Cultural Centre in Belgium, while an example of the latter is the Bradford Council of Mosques (Lewis 1994)).

Other kinds of religious organisations have been established within Britain as fund-raising outposts of movements elsewhere. As described among Muslims in a feature article in the *Guardian* (7 February 1994), these are exemplified outside the Regent's Park mosque in London every Friday where numerous groups gather donations for various Muslim causes in Algeria, Palestine, Iraq, Egypt and, increasingly, Bosnia. Among the active overseas groups are Al Muntada al Islami (linked with the Middle Eastern Salafi movement), Muslim Welfare House (said to be linked with the Algerian *Front islamique du Salut*, or FIS), and the Palestine and Lebanon Relief Fund (believed to be linked with the Palestinian Hamas movement).

Each effort in mobilising and lobbying – whether successful, unsuccessful or still in process – has brought new experience and, thereby, new confidence in Muslim organisational efforts. This, in turn, has encouraged the engagement in recent years of new spheres of concern and activity around *access to resources* and *social service provision*. Examples of such activity can be seen in applications by Muslim women's groups seeking public funding for education and community activities, the rise of Muslim housing associations and employment advice centres, and calls by Muslims for special promotion of health awareness campaigns and programmes and the provision of suitable hospital facilities.

On the national level, important networks or boards have emerged which facilitate the expression of the needs and concerns of South Asian religious communities (as well as other faiths). Foremost are the Inter-Faith Network of the United Kingdom, which promotes dialogue and research on religious minorities in Britain, and the Inner Cities Religious Council, established by the Department of the Environment in 1992 as part of its 'Action for Cities' initiative. The latter consists of 11 representatives of different faiths, brought together as a consultative body to consider policy issues affecting religious communities throughout Britain. It holds regional conferences and promotes dialogue within given regions and between regional groups and central government.

Another important avenue of institutionalisation and representation is conventional politics. In contrast with immigrant-descent minorities in the majority of European countries, most blacks and Asians in Britain today are citizens (that is, in actual British terms, subjects of the Crown), having originally entered as members of the Commonwealth or having gained the legal status after being born in the country. (In 1981 the British Nationality Act removed the right to automatic citizenship of those born in Britain to immigrant parents; this must now be applied for.) They have full voting rights in local and national elections.

The political route has been particularly important to British Muslims. In Britain, the size and impact of 'the Muslim vote', especially in local elections, is not insubstantial, but often it is exaggerated. Nevertheless, local politicians are always sure to liaise with designated Muslim leaders who promise to deliver 'the Muslim vote'. In 1991, the Islamic Party of Great Britain contested its first seat: however, it has never received much support. The Labour Party receives the bulk of Muslim voters' support in Britain, and this is particularly evident in the success of Muslim candidates for Labour in local government elections. For example, in 1981 only three of Bradford's 90 councillors were Muslim; by 1992 there were 11 Muslim councillors, including the deputy leader of the ruling group (Lewis 1994). The city also boasted the country's first Asian, and Muslim, Lord Mayor in 1985/6. The city of Leicester not only has produced a number of Muslim city and county councillors, but also a Muslim chief executive alongside a Muslim police superintendent (Vertovec 1994). In June 1994, Waltham Forest produced the first Muslim woman to be elected mayor. A Muslim Labour candidate for Glasgow Gowan was elected to the House of Commons in the 1997 general election. He faced charges of corruption immediately after his election and had to resign.

Today, minority religious organisations are in many British cities regularly included in local government consultations about community relations matters. On both local and national levels, there have been efforts to create forums, boards or other umbrella organisations to provide a common front in dealing with political authorities (Lewis 1994; Vertovec 1994, 1996c). The range of their concerns is considerable, as outlined in the following sections.

Concerns surrounding education

Since the 1970s, the growth in size and prominence of South Asian religious communities (especially the presence of large numbers of children thereof) has led to several fundamental changes in educational philosophy and provision. Essentially, this has taken the form of wide-spread debate on the nature and content of 'multicultural education', a controversial concept which had its landmark expression in the Swann Report published by the Department of Education and Science in 1985.

With regard to religion itself, 'multicultural education' has come to involve teaching all children – in ways equally positive, rather than judgmental – the basic beliefs and practices of 'world faiths', especially those represented among South Asians in Britain. Further, particularly in schools characterised by a substantial proportion of South Asians, this approach has been accompanied by endeavours to ensure that pupils need not have to act in ways, or participate in activities, contrary to their and their parents' religious beliefs and cultural traditions. Key areas of concern for South Asian parents include:

- expressed preference for single-sex education, especially for girls;
- modesty in dress and in physical education activities (such as swimming, showers, changing rooms) – again, especially for girls;
- specifically among Muslims, allowing for prayer times and religious holidays in the school timetable and calendar;
- also for Muslim children, provision of *halal* food in school cafeterias;
- providing for collective worship among religious minority pupils – especially on important religious festivals – or excepting them from Christian-oriented collective worship;
- being sensitive to parents' concerns about aspects of curriculum, including sex education, aspects of art, dance and music and, of course, the entire subject of religious education;
- again, especially for Muslims, exemption from fund-raising activities involving lotteries and gambling; and
- more staff members and schools' governors from minority communities.

Such sensitivities and concerns about establishing provisions in the education system for South Asian religions and, ultimately, for creating and sustaining a totalising religious 'ethos', has led some South Asian religious organisations to call for state ('voluntary aided') funding to support separate schools. Such organisations point to similar, existing state support for Jewish and Roman Catholic schools, thereby insisting on fair and equal treatment. The government has yet (at the time of writing) to grant such support, a stance which consequently continues to pose serious questions regarding what some see as institutionalised forms of religious-cum-racial discrimination evident in a number of public domains.

While there has been some limited call for the establishment of independent Hindu schools, the issue of state-funded schools has largely been one developed within Muslim communities in Britain. In only a few European countries have Islamic schools received state support (Shadid and van Koningsveld 1995). Claire Dwyer and Astrid Meyer (1995) observed that the outcome of such calls has been strongly conditioned not only by national legislation but by the variable strength of local (Muslim and non-Muslim) support for such schools, the effectiveness of lobbying efforts by local Muslim groups and, not least, the influence of constructed representations of 'Muslims' on the local non-Muslim population. Regardless of whether Islamic schools – state or privately funded – exist, in most places for most Muslims, Islamic education takes place in supplementary schools, which run at mosques or in private homes during evenings and weekends.

Since the bulk of educational matters in Britain are decentralised to local education authorities, it is on this level that Hindu, Sikh and Muslim associations have had most to do – and most success. The nature of accommodations vary, therefore, from city to city (even from school to school around the country).

Resistance to the Conservative government's drive to ensure Christian hegemony has also been undertaken on local levels. The 1988 Education Reform Act (ERA) posed a potential problem for schools with significant numbers of pupils from South Asian and other religious minority groups. The 1944 Education Act required that schools should begin the day with collective worship: while it was originally presumed this would be of a Christian character (as the numbers of non-Christian pupils was then negligible), in more recent decades this has been more loosely interpreted to accommodate assemblies comprised of pupils from a range of faiths. The 1988 ERA, however, restated this provision with a qualification that there should be daily acts of worship 'wholly or mainly of a broadly Christian character'. This upset many educationists, who saw it as a measure retrograde to advances in multicultural education. Yet, within the framework of this latter Act, if any county school believes that this requirement is inappropriate – given its proportion of non-Christian pupils – it can apply to the local Standing Advisory Council for Religious Education, or SACRE, for a 'determination' to have this requirement lifted or modified. This enables the school basically to forego the 'Christian' character of assemblies and to arrange for alternative acts of worship to be provided, including those of non-Christian faiths. In these ways British schools have generally provided a range of accommodations for South Asian religious concerns, perhaps more so than in any other sphere of public life.

Legal and governmental acceptance of South Asian religious practices

A number of other areas of concern surrounding specific practices, values and traditional institutions have been voiced (or defended following some form of public condemnation) among South Asian religious communities in Britain. In recent years, there have arisen cases in which these issues were debated in court, in Parliament, in local government, or in the media (Charlton and Kaye 1985; Nielsen 1988; Parekh 1991, 1994; Pearl 1987; Poulter 1990; Vertovec and Peach 1997). These include:

- polygamy (multiple marriage partners) is practised by some Muslim communities. Polygamous marriages are, on the whole, banned in Britain, though they are permitted among persons domiciled in the UK but resident elsewhere (Parekh 1994);
- *talaq*, a form of Islamic divorce initiated by so pronouncing three times; the call for acceptance of this in British law is still highly contested;
- a wide range of forms of arranged marriage practised by a variety of South Asian communities. These are generally accepted in the eyes of British authorities, unless considerable coercion (on occasion evidenced by kidnapping or deceit) is demonstrated;
- marriages within various degrees of relationship – for instance, among first cousins; this is widely practised among Pakistani Muslim families in Britain, for instance;
- accommodating prescribed modes of dress – especially Sikh forms. Under the Motor-Cycle Crash-Helmets Act 1976, turban-wearing Sikhs are excused from wearing crash helmets. Similarly, the Construction (Head-Protection) Regulation of 1989 specifically exempts turban-wearing Sikhs from having to wear safety helmets on building sites. In the police force and armed services, Sikhs are entitled to wear turbans as well. Within the 1988 Criminal Justice Act the law on carrying knives in public places exempts Sikhs carrying them for religious reasons;

- demands for time off work for religious purposes (such as visiting mosques to participate in Friday prayer) or for appropriate prayer facilities in the workplace. Such demands are addressed by specific employers concerned; in factories with large numbers of Muslims, prayer facilities are often allocated. The Commission for Racial Equality has been approached on several occasions where discrimination is suspected in cases of refusal of demands in this area;
- for Muslims, provision of *halal* (sanctioned) food in schools and other public institutions such as prisons and hospitals; associated with this are issues surrounding:
- Islamic ritual slaughter (*dhabh*), which has been abhorred by many non-Muslims since it is often interpreted as prescribing that the animal remain conscious when its throat is slit. The most vocal opponents to *halal* food provision and *dhabh* emerged as the unlikely pairing of animal rights activists who were against the method of slaughter, and right-wing nationalists who were against accommodating seemingly alien customs of minorities. Following the Slaughter of Poultry Act 1967 and the Slaughterhouses Act 1979, Jews and Muslims may slaughter poultry and animals in abattoirs according to their traditional methods. The right to engage in ritual slaughter in inspected abattoirs was maintained, largely through the political lobbying of Jewish rather than Muslim groups, and provision of *halal* food has become standard practice in British public institutions of many kinds, especially schools;
- matters surrounding burial, such as gaining designated areas of public cemeteries for specific religious communities, obtaining permission for burial in a cloth shroud instead of a coffin, urging speedy issuing of death certificates for burial within 24 hours, and immersion in water the ashes of cremated persons. The latter has been addressed in the Water Act 1989, which allows persons to do so provided they obtain a licence and that the ashes are disposed of in tidal or estuary waters or in the sea within 12 miles of the coastline; most of the former matters are considered – often with eventual approval – by local government authorities;
- taking oaths on scriptures. Under the Oaths Act of 1978, Muslims may swear on the Koran, Hindus on the Bhagavad Gita or the Vedas, Sikhs on the Guru Granth Sahib or Gutka, and Parsees on the Zendavesta; and
- altering work and school uniform codes to allow South Asian women to wear traditional forms of dress (including head scarves) in the interest of modesty.

Beyond aspects of practice, values and traditional institutions, however, many members of South Asian religious communities have called for legal measures to protect their rights and help safeguard against discrimination.

Anti-discrimination measures

In Britain, although there exist legal frameworks surrounding discrimination with regard to gender, 'race' and ethnicity, which are some of the most far-reaching in Europe, at present religious minorities *per se* are not protected from discrimination. An important ruling by the House of Lords in 1983 (*Mandla v. Dowell-Lee*, following a head teacher's refusal to allow a Sikh boy to wear a turban in school) established that Sikhs are considered an 'ethnic group' (given such determinants as common geographic provenance, common language and culture, visible traits) and are thus protected by the 1976 Race Relations Act. However, a case in 1988 (*Nyazi v. Rymans Ltd.*, concerning an employer's refusal to allow an employee time off to celebrate Eid al Fitr) ruled that Muslims do not constitute such a group – and therefore, are not protected by the Act – since their regional, linguistic and cultural origins are more diverse.

The implications of this ruling were evident in a 1991 case (*Comission for Racial Equality v. Precision Engineering Ltd.*) after an employer blatantly stated that he refused to employ Muslims because he considered them 'extremist': he was found guilty only of 'indirect discrimination' against Asians (since most British Muslims are of such descent), while his anti-Muslim sentiments were unassailed. More recently, Muslim workers in Yorkshire mills have alleged that Muslims are treated worse than other employees with respect to tasks, pay and holiday benefits (*Guardian*, 15 March 1993; *Q-News*, 2–9 April 1993).

Tariq Modood (1993: 516–17) has pointed to a number of other related areas in which forms of disadvantage affecting Muslims still need to be addressed. These include:

> same-race adoption and fostering policies which place black Muslims with black Christians, and Asian Muslims with Hindus and Sikhs; social work based on Asian needs which can lead to a Muslim being given a Hindu home-help who does not know about Muslim sensitivities or whose own inhibitions (about meat for example) prevent her from fulfilling her duties; the recent decision by the Housing Corporation to reverse its policy of registering housing associations catering for religious communities in favour of race; recruitment monitoring and targeting in terms of 'Black' or 'Asian' statistics which obscure the level of Muslim disadvantage and under-representation and fail to measure whether the equal

opportunity policies are making any difference to the Muslim position; arts funding for anti-Muslim but not Islamic artists; racial harassment figures which fail to register that the majority of victims are Muslims and that there is a specific anti-Muslim harassment which even white Muslims suffer.

Among leading intellectuals, throughout the media and in much popular opinion, the main issue surrounding the notorious 'Rushdie affair' was freedom of expression (although this was often posed without reference to authors' responsibilities). The issues that many British Muslims raised surrounding the affair included the notion of blasphemy (what kinds of offences were included and, most importantly, which religions it covered) and whether offences to religious groups (slander, incitement to hatred) were akin to offences relating to 'race' and ethnicity. It has been particularly since the 'Rushdie affair' that the rise of specifically anti-Muslim forms of racism has been marked, leading to calls for new or extended legislation (CRE, 1989, 1990a, 1990b; Modood 1993).

With the support of Muslim organisations and Muslim newspapers, the Commission for Racial Equality has advocated measures to redress the situation (CRE 1992). This includes a call for legislators to consider enacting special laws (as there are in Northern Ireland) on religious discrimination and on incitement to religious hatred, similar to existing laws with regard to racial discrimination and incitement to racial hatred. It also sees the need for change in law concerning blasphemy: at present, only Christianity is protected under such law. The CRE and others believe that either the blasphemy law should be extended to other faiths, or that it should be abolished altogether. (Many Muslims prefer the former option, since this, they say, would therefore remove *The Satanic Verses* from British book shops.) In its *Second Review of the Race Relations Act 1976*, the Commission (CRE 1992: 60) concluded that:

> While the blasphemy law is concerned with certain forms of attacks on *religion* as such, a law of incitement to religious hatred is concerned with stirring up hatred against persons, identified by their religion. Arguments that freedom of speech should include the right to stir up hatred against persons inevitably seem limp, and the more so when this is done on grounds of religion, since the freedom to practise the religion of one's choice is itself recognised in international law. No country can be said to guarantee the freedom to practise the religion of one's choice if, at the same time, it permits others lawfully to stir up hatred against those doing just that.

In line with these views, in July 1993 the UK Action Committee on Islamic Affairs (UKACIA) submitted to the Home Secretary a memorandum entitled 'Muslims and the Law in Multi-Faith Britain: Need for

Reform'. The document called for legislation in three areas affecting Muslims (and other religious minorities). There is pressing need, it proposed, for laws concerning (a) vilification of religious beliefs and practices as well as group defamation, (b) incitement to religious hatred, and (c) discrimination on religious grounds. The Home Office has yet to respond concretely to such calls.

Conclusion

The depth and breadth of any society's vision of multiculturalism can be gauged by its treatment of traditions and values most dissimilar from long-standing norms. 'Equality requires a rejection of arbitrary or irrelevant differences,' Bhikhu Parekh (1994: 306) points out, 'and a full recognition of legitimate or relevant differences. A society committed to it must know how to be discriminating without being discriminatory.' Arguably, South Asian religions have posed the greatest forms of difference, in practices, values and traditions, from Britain. On the whole, accommodation of many specific tenets and traits of these religious minorities has been considerable and progressive: disregarded as irrelevant to the functioning of certain institutions, as Parekh suggests, or recognised as legitimate and therefore seen as grounds for institutional change.

It is unfortunate that these myriad accommodations – indicating substantial frameworks for multiculturalism – have not had the cumulative effect in changing public attitudes among the majority British population. In other words, although Britain demonstrates many such exemplary forms of multicultural accommodation, popular opinion – bolstered by politicians, churchmen and certain quarters of the media – still considers Britain to be monocultural with exceptional pockets of migrant deviation. Accommodation is a necessary, but insufficient, means towards creating a society truly multicultural in practice and identity.

Conclusion: convergence and divergence between Belgian and British multiculturalism

Adrian Favell and Marco Martiniello

This volume has set out to provide a representative selection of perspectives on multiculturalism in two ethnically diverse contemporary European societies: Belgium and Britain. In our conclusion, we aim to supplement this picture with a wider, comparative discussion of the issues at stake. First, we hope to provide a brief synthesis of some of the most important areas of comparison presented: raising some of the most salient issues about state multicultural policies, the political representation of ethnic minorities, and the importance of religious diversity in the two countries. And second, we aim to take a step further, going beyond the content of the volume to address some of the substantive issues raised by the very question of comparing two countries as distinct as Belgium and Britain: a comparison in which the differences are perhaps as interesting as the similarities.

Comparing and miscomparing

Although there are a number of clear reasons – set out in the introduction – why the coupling of Belgian and British multiculturalism is a highly appropriate and timely comparison, bringing them together in a single comparative focus is in fact not as straightforward as it might seem. As was indicated by Steve Vertovec's contribution in the first part of the volume, 'multiculturalism' in a country such as Britain is never a single, homogenous 'form of politics'. This observation indeed holds for other national settings such as Belgium. There is, in other words, no 'essence' of multiculturalism that can be read into different countries, even relatively close neighbours like Belgium and Britain, without contextual translation. There is at best an uneven 'family resemblance' between these different single cases. As John Rex reminds us in the first chapter, there are obvious factual reasons – of history, politics and geography – why Belgium and Britain will always be an asymmetrical kind of pairing in any comparison. To bring the underlying comparative issues into focus, then, we are interested here in distinguishing the various elements of convergence and divergence between the two national cases. From this, it is then possible to make sense of these observations by situating them in terms of the two countries' rather distinct relation to wider European questions.

As always, at the heart of the comparative problem are very basic linguistic issues of understanding and translation. The source of some of the differences in perspective about multiculturalism in the two countries – well represented by the selection of contributions in this volume – in fact lies in the rather uncomfortable application of the very British, but dominant, social scientific language about the management of 'racial' or 'ethnic' diversity and conflict, onto a continental situation characterised by its own, rather different legal and constitutional system. Indeed, Belgians traditionally are far more comfortable with Francophone forms of political discussion, which, on the question of ethnic relations or multiculturalism, sit very badly with the kind of commonplace terms and language used by Anglophone observers. Typically, this can create problems with understanding the category of 'race' and 'racial discrimination' as a channel for social policy, or the supposed 'communitarian' nature of British multiculturalism. The Francophone reflex – often dictated by the dominant forms of discussion among Parisian intellectuals – is, in fact, to reject talk of 'ethnicity' or 'multiculturalism', equating them with the perceived nightmare scenario of racial and ethnic breakdown associated with the USA in the wake of the Los Angeles 'race' riots. Britain is thus lumped with the USA into a generic *modèle anglo-saxon*, which is in some ways insensitive to the distinctiveness of British multiculturalism and race relations. Moreover, Belgians have often imported the distinctly French *problématiques* of the *banlieues* (violence and deprivation in suburban housing projects) or the *affaire du foulard* (the problem of Muslim girls wearing veils in secular public schools), even though the political and social situation in Belgium does not always correspond very well with that in France over these cases.

In this volume, however, our Belgian contributors have paid rather more attention to these matters of translation and contextualisation than the British. Belgian political discourse, because of its geographical and political situation, in fact finds itself at the confluence of various different international influences, whereas the British often find it very difficult to break out of the taken-for-granted island-bound ways of thinking about the questions at stake. As we will go on to point out, there are a series of questions which British observers need to rethink in terms of the wider European experience.

There are several examples of this problem of translation and contextualisation in the contributions. A genuine comparison is often made very difficult when the same issues in both national settings are approached from very different perspectives. For example, this is certainly the case in the fourth part of this volume dedicated to the issue of religious diversity. Whereas the contribution by Steve Vertovec emphasises how the South Asian religions have been accommodated and 'managed' within the British context, Albert Bastenier's contribution on Belgium highlights the social importance of the religious factor in the proactive formation of an ethnic consciousness among Moroccans in Brussels. Both chapters provide a valuable insight, but they do not yet easily open a way to a deeper comparison. We hope to provide a context for this kind of comparison in the following reflections.

Points of convergence

To start with, it would be helpful to point out the clear points of convergence that have emerged from the various contributions to this volume. First, it should be underlined how, in both countries, the question of ethno-cultural diversity brought on by the new migrations of the postwar period was perceived as a problem requiring reactive measures. Traditionally, both states had conceived of themselves as homogenous ethnically and culturally, and while not being heavily intolerant towards the new cultures that immigrants brought, there were sharp limits to the degree of cultural and ethnic difference that was felt to be tolerable in the new situation. The ethno-cultural difference was thus perceived as a potential 'threat' to the integrity of the nation-state. And this, despite the fact that both nations are founded on the coexistence of distinct 'national' minorities or 'founding' nations, and are therefore far from being ideal-typical, homogenous nation-states (in the manner of France, for example).

Both countries have therefore maintained a strongly assimilationist undercurrent in their approach to ethnic minorities. Multicultural diversity, even if permitted, has always been kept in bounds by an assimilationist preservation of the dominant elite social and political system in the two countries. Furthermore, in Belgium, the full social incorporation of new immigrants was for a long time resisted by the implementation of a guestworker system, which refused to consider migrants as anything more than temporary additional workers who would one day 'return home'. It has taken a long time, both in Britain and Belgium, to recognise what could be called the 'diversification of ethno-cultural diversity', beyond the official definitions of multicultural diversity grudgingly given to the new immigrants at the outset. Britain on the whole has recognised these questions earlier than Belgium: something we will return to later. Still, in both countries, a proactive long-term project for a genuinely multicultural society (rather than a multiculturalism subordinate to a dominant mono-cultural elite vision) remains a problematic and vulnerable possibility. This is clearly highlighted in the discussion of state policies by Jan Blommaert and Malcolm Cross in the second part of the volume.

A further point, not picked out by many of the contributions, is the common impact of colonialism on multicultural policies in both countries. It would seem that the colonial experience of Belgium and Britain is crucial to explaining how both countries have gone on to manage their immigrant ethno-cultural diversity in the post-colonial era. In some ways, it would be true to say that the peripheralisation of race relations in Britain is in fact the colonial idea of indirect rule applied to the new context of immigration. Similarly, the paternalist management of the Belgian colonies was translated into domestic Belgian politics when the country had to deal with immigration in recent years. The question then arises: why have both states turned to their specific colonial experience to find a solution to the problem of immigrant ethno-cultural diversity, instead of trying to extend or adapt their long-standing models of multinational statehood to the new situation? Why are the problems with Scottish– or Irish–English relations, or Flemish–Walloon relations, never associated or applied to the problem of ethnic relations between immigrant and indigenous populations in Belgium or Britain?

A third point of convergence is the management of the specific question of religious diversity – in particular the question of Islam – in the two countries. Indeed, the mismanagement of this question in both Britain and Belgium brings into doubt the degree of genuine multicultural opening offered to new ethnic minorities. On the one hand, it is generally accepted that the presence of Islam in both societies is recognised and stable, and that therefore some degree of accommodation for this religion needs to be found officially. In Belgium, the religion is indeed recognised and given an official status by the state; in Britain, meanwhile, representatives of the religion have often been co-opted into the implementation of multicultural policies at local levels. However, on the other hand, the 'new' religion is not accepted easily because it implies a deep revision of the Belgian and British Christian heritage so deeply implanted in the state and political structures of the two countries. There is in fact strong popular resistance to recognising Islam on a par with Protestantism or Roman Catholicism, despite its numerical strength in comparison with these declining denominations. Is this inequality over the recognition of religions really compatible with the 'official' multiculturalism espoused in Belgium and Britain? This question has been a live debate in the two countries in recent years, and will continue to be so in the near future.

A final point of convergence is worth noting. Up until the late 1980s, the question about the potential political force of ethnic minorities was very different in Britain and Belgium. While legal immigrants in Britain have always gained immediate access to voting rights, many immigrants in Belgium were for a long time deprived of any voting and eligibility rights, despite being legitimately resident in the country. The situation has changed in recent years, for access to Belgian nationality has been facilitated. The ethnic electorate has therefore been growing, and has become a potential stake for mainstream political parties. To them, the question is how can we get the ethnic vote without giving much open credit to specifically ethnic claims? In both Britain and Belgium, as both Marco Martiniello and Shamit Saggar underline in their chapters, political parties seem to anticipate an ethnically-based political behaviour among ethnic minorities, although this behaviour is far from being proven (Taylor 1996). However, the parties' ambiguous strategies to collect the ethnic minorities' votes may indeed create this outcome unintentionally.

How far 'advanced' is Britain? How far 'behind' is Belgium?

Beyond these points of convergence, a full comparison needs also to take account of the various divergent or distinct characteristics of multi-culturalism in the two countries. These differences indeed are inscribed in the comparisons that are often made between the two countries. One frequently made Belgian self-criticism – applicable also to other conti-nental European countries – is how poor its track record and legal provisions are in comparison with the 'advanced' and 'long-standing' British experience in handling racial and ethnic diversity. Some British scholars indeed rather un-self-critically echo this sort of perspective in their self-evaluation relative to 'Europe' (that foreign place across the sea). There are certainly three reasons for thinking there is some truth in this stance.

First, on paper at least, Britain certainly does have more sophisticated and long-standing legislation for dealing with racial discrimination. The first Race Relations Act dates back to 1965, and from 1976 there has been in place a fairly effective and widely recognised law against both direct and indirect discrimination in the public arena (Layton-Henry 1992). The first and only specific anti-racist law in Belgium, the so-called *Loi Moureaux*, was only passed in 1981. Second, Britain can fairly claim that it has achieved an advance in social attitudes and the self-recognition of being a 'multicultural society' during the last 25 years, that is indeed probably better established than in other European countries. From an early date, it was accepted that black and Asian immigrants in Britain were 'here for good', and – in most urban areas at least – that they would have a distinct and beneficial contribution to make to the cultural diversity of the nation. In Belgium, the idea of the 'multicultural society' – often referred to in terms of the distinct national communities – is still not unproblematically extended to the immigrant ethnic communities, and is often a matter of live debate. Third, there does appear to be in Britain a dominant consensus on the ills of racism and the reality of multiculturalism (meaning here the basic recognition of demographic and cultural diversity) as basic givens in mainstream British political life, together with the somewhat exceptional absence of any significant extreme-right 'racist' party. Even rather traditionalist sections of the Conservative Party in Britain are careful to be politically correct about racial and ethnic issues, and little capital these days is made from 'playing the race card' against the established ethnic minorities. In Belgium, by contrast, political recognition of *de facto* multiculturalism remains more problematic and a significant extreme-right 'racist' party is now a stable part of the political spectrum: the Vlaams Blok has indeed become the largest party in the city of Antwerp.

Some of these British 'achievements' might indeed provide direct lessons or inspiration for other national cases, an experience that can be granted because of the disjunction in time and type of immigration faced by the two countries, and because of Britain's much earlier 'institutional solution' to the problem of the integration of immigrants. Taken on their own without a full portrait of multicultural race relations in Britain, however, these positive 'facts' can be quite misleading. Without the right qualification, they may indeed be examples of a mistranslation that has not yet been through the kind of contextualised conversion necessary, if they are applied instructively to other less 'advanced' national cases. To turn the issue round (in perhaps an equally misleading way), Belgian scholars could quite fairly compare the management of the Flemish-Walloon conflict with that of Northern Ireland, and claim a much higher efficacy and peacefulness for the Belgian institutional 'model' of conflict management. They could also point out that there were no 'race riots' in Belgian inner cities comparable with the Brixton or Toxteth disturbances of the early 1980s. Compared with these, the first 'ethnic disorders' in

Belgium, the 'Forest disorders' of 1991 (Martiniello 1991), seemed to be smaller and much less violent. It might be claimed therefore that the Belgian 'model' allows for more peaceful urban race and ethnic relations.

What has been left out of the British self-portrait?

These positive 'facts' about British multicultural race relations have therefore to be reinterpreted as part of the overall British 'solution' to its problems of racial, ethnic and cultural diversity: that is, as a complex institutional structure rather distinct to anything that might be found in mainland Europe. Progressive, idiosyncratic and regressive aspects of this picture can this way be seen to be interlinked and structurally inter-dependent. Any account that puts an accent on the happier and creative side of multiculturalism should be supplemented by a recognition of the costs by which this particular positive effect has been achieved. Only by seeing the whole picture can any kind of comparative evaluation with other countries begin.

First, it must be said that the 'progressive' idea of multiculturalism and advanced race relations mechanisms were only secured at the expense of a much tougher immigration regime than anywhere else in Europe. The systematic closing of the doors of immigration through a series of legis-lation through the 1960s, 1970s and 1980s, clearly worked as a politically and socially expedient 'trade off' with the progressive legislation also being developed during this period. The shutting and securing of the doors was thus a prior structural condition to any more liberal internal policies, which enabled the two questions of immigration and integration henceforth to be kept as strictly separate policy areas. Obviously, this was only made possible by Britain's peculiar geographical situation. Shutting the doors gave time and space to ethnic minority groups already there to settle, establish a presence and – localised and concentrated in certain urban areas – develop an accepted visibility in public life. In general, they, as much as the ruling establishment, are hostile to the idea of open doors and undifferentiated new immigration, because they fear any change in the status quo would undermine their hard-won privileged status. The British version of multicultural tolerance is thus delimited within strict bounds of predefined national responsibility, exclusively based on old colonial ties. It is therefore not such an enlightened or open philosophy, but rather a conception of 'multiculturalism in one nation', a conception that has no real component of multinationalist or inter-nationalist ideals, as multiculturalism is generally taken to embody.

In Belgium, meanwhile, immigration control was until recently rather less restrictive than in Britain, due partially to the geographical location of the country. A worked out integration policy was non-existent as a coherent set of legislative and administrative provisions. The issues of migration flows and integration are therefore often conflated together, both by policymakers and politicians. This, at least, has made Belgium more sensitive to the issues surrounding new types of migration in recent years. It is important to note that in the new federal state, immigration policy is a competence of the 'central' state, whereas integration policy is now devolved as a competence of the different national communities (more precisely the regions).

Further, British multicultural race relations are now pretty much devoid of any substantive idea that assuring the welfare levels or rectifying socio-economic inequalities experienced by immigrant groups is the key to successful 'integration'. These elements were present in the social policy at the outset in the 1960s, but over time have diminished in favour of an accent on cultural representation and recognition. This tendency has been encouraged by the relative numerical strength of the Asian lobby in Britain (who outnumber black West Indians 2:1), and are more interested in securing control over issues involving religion or separate education than anti-discrimination or inner-city poverty. Britain would certainly compare badly on this scale with other European countries, where welfare provision, social rights and more egalitarian standards of living are still strongly preserved. In Belgium, migrant workers and their families have to a large extent been included in the very protective (and expensive) welfare state system, whose fundamental reform is now under discussion.

Finally, British multicultural race relations do not constitute a philosophy based on the granting of constitutional 'minority rights' to ethnic groups. The much vaunted link between the progressive 1960s legislation and the US civil rights movement is in fact misleading in this respect. In the context of Britain's idiosyncratic common-law tradition, where judgements are made according to legal precedence rather than constitutional right, the concessions granted to minority groups are in fact strictly delimited in legal terms. The Race Relations Act has allowed for the incremental recognition of different types of ethnic groups bringing anti-discrimination claims, but none of the judgements made institute irrevocable rights for ethnic groups that could not be later taken away or compromised. Moreover, the management of ethnic tensions is designed to keep ethnic minority issues peripheralised at local levels, well away from the main arena of national political life, and frame them specifically in terms that do not raise fundamental constitutional issues. As a philosophy, then, it is difficult to read the idea of integration in Britain as one that enables access to full participatory 'citizenship', whether we conceive citizenship in terms of a full-blown classically French idea of *citoyenneté*, or even the incremental progress of rights and membership envisaged in T. H. Marshall's famous narrative about social incorporation (Marshall and Bottomore 1992). As this suggests, the formal status of ethnic minority groups in Britain remains predominantly symbolic in nature, and is in a way rather precarious – for example, the occasionally mooted suggestion that the CRE (Commission for Racial Equality) and its legislation should be wound up in favour of a general 'Commission for Equality'. Representatives of ethnic minorities are forced to act defensively and to lobby within the existing framework, something which has created a good deal of vested interests and directed attention away from the shortcomings of the institutional framework.

In Belgium, as in other continental European systems, ethnic minority members could in theory make anti-discrimination claims as individuals in constitutional law. As distinct groups, however, there is no such coverage. Regions and communities defined as the 'national ethnic groups' enjoy constitutional recognition, whereas immigrant ethnic communities do not enjoy any collective minority rights either in the constitution or elsewhere. It may seem paradoxical that the sophisticated Belgian model of multiculturalism, which has been pragmatically created to accommodate Flemish, Walloon and Germanophone identities and claims has so far not been extended to immigrant ethnic communities (Martiniello 1996).

Other significant 'facts' about Britain relative to the rest of Europe

A number of other facts peculiar to Britain's situation modify the picture of its 'advancedness' *vis-à-vis* the rest of Europe. Britain, it should be pointed out, has had to deal with a fraction of the migrants and asylum seekers that the rest of the continent has seen in recent years, particularly in the years since 1989. There is also a deep rooted resistance in Britain to thinking through the issues that these new migrations pose to the established terms of diversity and ethnic relations. These channels are reserved exclusively in the British picture for the management of existing post-colonial ethnic minorities who are said to be totally distinct from these new groups.

This self-styled exceptionalism is partly behind the fact that Britain has opted out of cooperative European steps and measures that have begun to face up to these new challenges, such as the Schengen accords. It takes the attitude that issues of immigration and ethnic relations are exclusively internal domestic matters, that can be dealt with by the nation-state alone.

This amounts to a short-sighted refusal to face up to the fact that these new migratory phenomena are all part of international political economy currents, and thoroughly interconnected. The maintenance of conceptual national borders in this respect is anachronistic, if not absurd. It is then surely artificial to draw such a distinction between the original immigration of the 1950s and 1960s and the new migrations, simply because of the time scale difference. The integration and discrimination problems at base remain the same. On the contrary, there is a strong pro-European tradition in Belgian governments. Belgium was a founding member of the Schengen group, and its representatives are in favour of a coherent and international European immigration policy.

These differences are also at the root of other distinctly British problems. Within the British picture, it would be inconceivable to find nonnational residents unproblematically (in some cases over a lifetime) enjoying full rights and social status without holding national citizenship; yet this is commonplace in Belgium, among its Italian or Spanish populations, for example. It is in fact easy to find lifelong Belgian residents still holding full Italian citizenship who barely speak a word of their 'native' language! This apparent curiosity of Belgium in this respect is in fact indicative that the country is already dealing with the fact of 'postnationality' in an international context, and developing *de facto* new forms of citizenship and social belonging (Soysal 1994). Indeed, the issue of managing ethnic diversity or racial tensions on the one hand, and the issue of developing new categories of status and residency within a nonnational idea of citizenship or social membership on the other, are increasingly inseparable for continental European countries, which do not have the British luxury of island status. Whereas some other countries such as Germany also seem to be facing up to this issue, others such as France are still trying to find their own way of preserving their distinct national borders and self-sufficient policies on immigration and integration, albeit less stubbornly than Britain (Favell 1998).

Put another way, Belgium could in fact be read as more advanced than Britain in these matters. In a country such as this, where the attributes of formal political and social status – such as freedom of movement, residency, official identity card and welfare rights – are not necessarily connected to holding full nationality; where there have been strongly institutionalised forms of devolution of responsibilities up to the European level or down to the communities and regions; and where, therefore, immigration and integration cannot be divided off as wholly separate problems as in the British 'trade-off' – then it might be said that the Belgian political system is already struggling with 'post-national' issues at the same time as national 'integration–disintegration' issues that are likely to become very widespread within fragmenting European nation tates in coming years. The British attitude of national exceptionalism and self-sufficiency in these matters – despite its inescapable involvement in these shared currents of European political change and international migration – leaves it lagging behind badly in facing up to the new situation. It would appear then that Britain's early solution of the problem of immigration (in the 1960s and 1970s) has in fact made it proportionately difficult for it to face up to the Europeanisation of these problems. Belgium, meanwhile, is well placed to respond, which is ironic given the lack of concerted policy solutions to migrant integration problems in the past (Rea 1993). It is now an open question how long Britain can resist facing up to these new realities connected with contemporary immigration politics.

The European question

As the internationally embarrassing party political attitudes towards the EU over the 'European question' in British politics testify, Britain has a hard time realising what the nub of the European question raised here is all about. It is not whether or not a European regulatory or legislative framework is a kind of imposed, 'strap-on' additional set of rules that have to be adapted to by proudly distinct nation-states. It is rather that all this talk about the 'nation-state' is already in many ways anachronistic and irrelevant. In the context of international political economy and mobility, the degree of European political and legal cooperation (harmonisation) achieved to date has already transformed internal national political systems, by changing the powers of government, law and economy and their relation – particularly by creating new institutional venues for politics. When the British go on about 'sovereignty', it is difficult to see what they are talking about any more. This is as true for immigration and integration issues, as it is for many other international political problems, even if the British refuse to see them from a common European perspective. Challenges to the restrictiveness of British immigration practices and claims that find no outlet in the rather limited scope of British race relations legislation are now commonly taken to the European Court of Justice or the European Court of Human Rights, and challenged using 'foreign' human rights or EU communitarian logic. It is regrettable that such 'progressive' outlets are viewed by the predominantly Euro-phobic public and political class in Britain in generally negative, threatening terms (Favell and Tambini 1995).

Meanwhile, British representatives have been exceedingly slow in their comprehension that the last thing Europe needs is a generalisation of

British race relations to the continent's new and rather different migration problems. Instead of offering full cooperation for the European 'Forum for Migrants' set up to consider these matters, they typically opted out, instead setting up a rival organisation SCORE (Standing Conference on Racial Discrimination in Europe). Yet the British mechanisms of race relations make little sense outside the nationally peculiar institutional context within which they were devised. They cannot be meaningfully translated into European constitutional rights-based terms. The euphemisms of 'ethnic minorities' or 'community relations', which are the symbolic shorthand of the British version of multiculturalism, are likewise problematic. A serious leap of perspective and comparative imagination would seem to be required on the part of these lobbyists. The idea of citizenship of the European Union remains a rather empty category, an insubstantial and forlorn ideal (Martiniello 1995a). The intergovernmental conference of 1996–97 and the Amsterdam Summit of 1997 did not lead to relevant progress on this issue. But even in its minimal conception of freedom of movement, settlement and residence, and partial franchise, it flies in the face of the British idea of 'low threshold' citizenship, which fixes membership in terms of right of entry and abode, and makes any other kind of residency problematic. Some non-nationals, such as EU citizens, do have the right to residency, work and (limited) welfare, yet the obvious connection with the older question about the integration of ethnic minorities is avoided. Time will tell whether Britain can indeed adapt its legendary pragmatism to the European situation, although it is difficult to see an end to its Euro-scepticism and political feet dragging. But the extraordinary amounts of divergence and rhetorical misunderstanding that are found at the official discursive level – not to mention the rather hypocritical fact that there is in fact a strong tendency of convergence in *de facto* policy practices (CCME 1996) – does suggest that dramatic changes in Britain's treatment of immigration and integration questions might be just around the corner.

Conclusion: Belgium as a guide to Europe's (and perhaps Britain's) future?

Several things in fact suggest that Belgium could be a very interesting guide to future Euro problems about nationality and citizenship. These concern issues of transnational mobility and migration, which will be set in the context of the dissolution of the previously coterminous ideas of state–nation–community–ethnic culture, with the faltering construction of a cooperative European sphere as a backdrop. State and nation already do not coincide in Belgium; and the clash between the representation of 'ethnic' versus 'community' minorities in its political life cannot be ignored any longer, despite the continual official denial of there being any connection (Martiniello 1996). The question is where will citizenship be located in this shifting backdrop of political contexts? Will it become a transcending, overarching membership status in a newly constituted super-nation of Europe? Or will be disaggregated and its functions distributed unevenly to different levels of a federal system (nation, state, community, region, ethnic group or city)?

On this question, Belgium's famous cross-cutting political formations and their ongoing tribulations are in fact a rare guide to the problems of how a genuinely European political system might look. Such a system is caught between post-national coalitions of ideology and interest, and regressive pockets falling back on circumscribed ethno-cultural communities (possibly nations) that reject the ongoing internationalisation and federalisation. Moreover, the crisis over solidarity and the welfare state that is currently such a dramatic issue in Belgium – Who pays? Who is responsible? To whom do we owe a living? – is also a likely harbinger for European-wide dilemmas everywhere. By definition, immigrants, migrants and ethnic minorities (being problematic groups that fall across the different cross-cutting lines of community, solidarity and membership) may well fall between the cracks. Belgium today might be a good indication of how Europe as a whole might look in a few years' time. With a little imagination, it may prove to be a good guide to Britain's fragmented future, if Britain also finds itself going down the Belgian path. Is this so unthinkable? If, as it seems, some extraordinary developments concerning a constitutional crisis over Scotland and Northern Ireland are just around the corner, Britain may well be forced to federalise its own proudly protected nationalist political system and begin to relocate political powers at regional and supra-national levels. If this happens, then British ideas about nationality, citizenship and the integration of immigrant minorities may indeed prove to be as anachronistic and ineffective as we have suggested throughout.

References

Ali, A. and Percival, G. (1993) *Race and Representation: Ethnic Minorities and the 1992 Elections*, London: Commission for Racial Equality

Alibhai, Y. (1989) 'Satanic betrayals', *New Statesman and Society* 24 February: 12

Ålund, A. (1995) paper presented for the workshop nationalism and ethnicity, Bern, March

Ålund, A. and Schierup, C. (1991) *Paradoxes of Multiculturalism: Essays on Swedish Society*, Aldershot: Avebury

Anon (1993) *Schola Europaea 1953–1993*, Brussels: Schola Europaea

Anthias, F. (1993) 'Rethinking categories and struggles: racism, anti-racisms and mc', paper presented to the European Workshop on Racism and Anti-Racist Movements, University of Greenwich, London, September

Anthias, F. and Yuval-Davis, N. (1992) *Racialized Boundaries*, London: Routledge

Appadurai, A. (1990) 'Disjuncture and difference in the global cultural economy' in M. Featherstone (Ed.) *Global Culture: Nationalism, Globalization and Modernity*, London: Sage, 295–310

Appignanesi, L. and Maitland, S. (1989) *The Rushdie File*, London: Fourth Estate

Asad, T. (1990) 'Multiculturalism and British identity in the wake of the Rushdie affair' *Politics and Society* Vol. 18: 455–80

Australian Law Reform Commission (1991) *Multiculturalism: Criminal Law*, Sydney: Australian Law Reform Commission

Ballard, R. (1994) (Ed.) *Desh Pardesh: The South Asian Presence in Britain*, London: Hurst

Ballis Lal, B. (1990) *The Romance of Culture in an Urban Civilisation: Robert E. Park on Race and Ethnic Relations in Cities*, London: Routledge

Banks, S. P. (1995) *Multicultural Public Relations*, London: Sage

Barber, B. (1995) *Jihad vs. McWorld: How Globalism and Tribalism are Reshaping the World*, New York: Ballantine Books

Barth, F. (1969) *Ethnic Groups and Boundaries: The Social Organization of Cultural Difference*, Boston: Little Brown

Battle, D. E. (1993) *Communication Disorders in Multicultural Populations*, Boston: Andover

Bauböck, R. (1995) *Transnational Citizenship*, Aldershot: Edward Elgar

Bauman, G. (1994) 'Dominant and demotic discourses of culture', paper presented at conference on Culture Communication and Discourse: Negotating Difference in Multi-Ethnic Alliances, University of Manchester, December

BBC 'East' (1996) *A Power in the Land*, BBC2 broadcast, 23 May

BBC/Harris (1987) 'Political attitudes among ethnic minorities', commissioned by *Caribbean/Africa/Asian Times* unpublished data set JN98746, Richmond: The Harris Research Centre

BBC/Harris (1991) 'Asian poll 1991', commissioned by BBC Pebble Mill, unpublished data set JN99245, Richmond: The Harris Research Centre

Bensalah, N. (1995) (unpublished) *La Signification sociale de l'Enfance chez les Familles d'origine Turque et Marocaine en Immigration*, Louvain-la-Neuve: UCL/GREM

Bhabha, H. (1994a) *The Location of Culture*, London: Routledge

Bhabha, H. (1994b) 'Subaltern Secularism', *Women Against Fundamentalism Journal* Vol. 6

Billiet, J., Carton, A. and Huys, R. (1990) *Onbekend of Onbemind? Een Sociologisch Onderzoek naar de Houding van de Belgen Tegenover de Migranten*, Leuven: Sociologisch Onderzoeksinstituut

Björklund, U. (1986) 'World-systems, the welfare state, and ethnicity', *Ethnos* Vol. 34: 285–307

Black, J. (1989) *Child Health in a Multicultural Society*, London: British Medical Journal

Bleidt, B. (Ed.) (1993) *Multicultural Pharmaceutical Education*, Binghampton, NY: Pharmaceutical Products Press

Blommaert, J. (1996) 'Power and semantics: the politics of the concept of "integration" in Belgium', paper presented at Fifth International Pragmatics Conference, Mexico, July

Blommaert, J. and Verschueren, J (1992) *Het Belgische Migrantendebat: De Pragmatiek van de Abnormalisering*, Antwerp: IprA

Blommaert, J. and Verschueren, J. (1994) 'The Belgian migrant debate', *New Community* Vol. 20, No. 2: 227–51

Bonnett, A. (1993) *Radicalism, Anti-racism and Representation*, London: Routledge

Bottomley, G. (1993) 'Culture, ethnicity and the politics/poetics of representation', *Diaspora* Vol. 3: 303–20

Bouamama, S. (1994) *Contribution à la Mémoire des Banlieues*, Paris: Éditions du Volga

Bourne, J. and Sivanandan, A. (1980) 'Cheerleaders and ombudsmen: the sociology of race relations in Britain', *Race and Class* Vol. 21, No. 4: 331–52

Boyd, A. (Ed.) (1995) *Guide to Multicultural Resources 1995/1996*, Fort Atkinson, Wisconsin: Highsmith Press

Brah, A. (1991) 'Difference, diversity, differentiation', *International Review of Sociology* Vol. 2: 53–72

Burgat, F. (1995) *L'Islamisme en Face*, Paris: La Découverte

Byram, M. and Leman, J. (Eds) (1990) *Bicultural and Trilingual Education: The Foyer Model in Brussels*, Clevedon/Philadelphia: Multilingual Matters

Cain, H. and Yuval-Davis, N. (1990) '"The equal opportunities community" and the anti-racist struggle', *Critical Social Policy* Autumn

Cammaert, M.-F. (1985) *Migranten en Thuisblijvers: Een Confrontatie. De Leefwereld van Marokkaanse Berbervrouwen*, Leuven: Leuven University Press/Assen: Van Gorcum

Caplan, R. and Feffer, J. (Eds) (1996) *Europe's New Nationalism: States and Minorities in Conflict*, Oxford: Oxford University Press

Cashmore, E. E. (1989) 'The Dawkins case: official ethnic status for rastas', *New Community* Vol. 16, No. 1: 158–60

Castles, S. (1987) 'Multiculturalism', Woolongong: Centre for Multicultural Studies, *Occasional Papers Series* No. 4

Castles, S. (1993) 'Migration and minorities in Europe: perspectives for the 1990s: eleven hypotheses' in J. Wrench and J. Solomos (Eds) *Racism and Migration in Western Europe*, Oxford: Berg, 17–34

Castles, S. (1995) 'How nation-states respond to immigration and ethnic diversity', *New Community* Vol. 21, No. 3: 293–308

CCME (1996) *The Comparative Approaches to Societal Integration Project*, Brussels: Churches Commission for Migrants in Europe/Migration Policy Group

Chan, B. J. (1993) *Kid Pix around the World: A Multicultural Computer Activity Book, Reading*, New York: Addison-Wesley

Charlton, R. and Kaye, R. (1985) 'The politics of religious slaughter: an ethno-religious case study', *New Community* Vol. 12, 490–503

Chhachhi, A. (1992) 'Forced identities, the state, communalism, fundamentalism and women in India' in D. Kandiyoti (Ed.) *Women, the State and Islam*, London: Macmillan, 144–75

Chicago Cultural Studies Group (1994) 'Critical multiculturalism' in D. T. Goldberg (Ed.) *Multiculturalism: A Critical Reader*, Oxford: Blackwell, 114–39

Clarke, S., Peach, C. and Vertovec, S. (1990) (Eds) *South Asians Overseas: Migration and Ethnicity*, Cambridge: Cambridge University Press

Costa, J. A. and Bemossy, G. J (Eds) (1995) *Marketing in a Multicultural World*, London: Sage

CRC (1975) *Participation of Ethnic Minorities in the General Election of October 1974*, London: Community Relations Commission

CRE (1980) *Votes and Policies: Ethnic Minorities and the General Election 1979*, London: Commission for Racial Equality

CRE (1989) *Law, Blasphemy and the Multi-Faith Society – Report of a Seminar*, London: Commission for Racial Equality and the Inter-Faith Network for the UK

CRE (1990a) *Britain: A Plural Society*, London: Commission for Racial Equality and the Runnymede Trust

CRE (1990b) *Free Speech – Report of a Seminar*, London: Commission for Racial Equality and the Policy Studies Institute

CRE (1992) *Second Review of the Race Relations Act 1976*, London: Commission for Racial Equality

CRE (1994) 'Don't take them for granted', *Connections* No. 1, London: Commission for Racial Equality, 5–8

Crewe, I. (1983) 'Representation and ethnic minorities in Britain' in N. Glazer and K. Young (Eds) *Ethnic Pluralism and Public Policy*, London: Heinemann

Cross, M. (1991) *Racial Equality and the Local State: Monographs in Ethnic Relations*, (NS) No 1, University of Warwick (with H. Brar and M. Mcleod)

Cross, M. (1992a) 'Black workers, recession and economic restructuring in the West Midlands' in M. Cross (Ed.) *Ethnic minorities and industrial change in Europe and North America*, Cambridge: Cambridge University Press

Cross, M. (1992b) 'Race and Ethnicity' in A. Thornley (Ed.) *London: City in Crisis*, London: Routledge

Cross, M. (1993a) 'Generating the "new poverty": a European comparison' in R. Simpson and R. Walker (Eds) *Europe: For Richer or Poorer?*, London: CPAG, 5–24

Cross, M. (1993b) 'Migration, the city and social change' in R. King (Ed.) *The New Social Geography of Migration in Europe*, London: Belhaven Press, 116–34

Cross, M. (1994a) *Ethnic Pluralism and Racial Inequality: A Comparison of Colonial and Industrial Societies*, Utrecht: ISOR, University of Utrecht

Cross, M. (1994b) 'Generating the new poverty' in R. Walker (Ed.) *Poverty and Social Policy in Europe*, London

Cross, M. (forthcoming) 'Racial inequality and public policy: Britain in a European context' in Z. Layton-Henry and C. Wilpert (Eds) *Racism and Discrimination in Britain and Germany*, Basingstoke: Macmillan

D'Andrade, R. (1992) 'Cognitive anthropology' in T. Schwartz, G. White and C. Lutz (Eds) *New Directions in Psychological Anthropology*, Cambridge: Cambridge University Press, 47–58

D'Hondt, P. (1992) 'Jeugdwerk in intercultureel perspectief', speech in Leuven, 23 October

Dacyl, J. W. (Ed.) (1995) *Management of Cultural Pluralism in Europe*, Stockholm: UNESCO and CEIFO

Dassetto, F. (1996) *La Construction de l'Islam européen: Approche socio-anthropologique*, Paris: L'Harmattan

Department of Education and Science (1985) *Education for All*, Report of a Committee of Enquiry into the Education of Children from Minority Groups Vol. 2 (Chairman Lord Swann) (Cmnd 9453) HMSO

Dieckhoff, A. (Ed.) (1996) *Belgique: La Force de la Désunion*, Brussels: Éditions complexe

Dirlik, A. (1990) 'Culturalism as hegemonic ideology and liberating practice' in A. R. Jan Mohamed and D. Lloyd (Eds) *The Nature and Context of Minority Discourse*, New York: Oxford University Press, 394–437

Ditchfield, C. (1987) *Better Science: Working for a Multicultural Society*, London: Heinemann Education

Drew, D. (1995) *'Race', Education and Work: The Statistics of Inequality*, Aldershot: Avebury

Duncan, C. G. (1988) *Pastoral Care: An Antiracist/Multicultural Perspective*, Oxford: Blackwell

Dwyer, C. and Meyer, A. (1995) 'The institutionalisation of Islam in the Netherlands and in the UK: the case of Islamic schools', *New Community* Vol. 21: 37–54

Edwards, J. E. and Batley, R. (1978) *The Politics of Positive Discrimination*, London: Tavistock

Enloe, C. (1990) 'Women and children: making feminist sense of the Persian Gulf crisis', *Village Voice* Vol. 25, September

Favell, A. (1998) *Philosophies of Integration: Immigration and the Idea of Citizenship in France and Britain*, London: Macmillan

Favell, A. and Tambini, D. (1995) 'Britain: clear blue water between "us" and "Europe"' in B. Baumgartl and A. Favell (Eds) (1995) *New Xenophobia in Europe*, The Hague: Kluwer

Feldblum, M. (1993) 'Paradoxes of ethnic politics: the case of Franco-Maghrebis in France', *Ethnic and Racial Studies* Vol. 16, No. 1: 52–74

Feuchtwang, S. (1990) 'Racism: territoriality and ethnocentricity' in A. X. Cambridge and S. Feuchtwang (Eds) *Anti-Racist Strategies*, Aldershot: Avebury, 3–25

Field, S. (1984) 'The attitudes of ethnic minorities: myth and reality', *Home Office Research Study* No. 80, London: HMSO

Finkielkraut (1994) 'Eloge des frontières' in H. Corijn (Ed.) *Van Wereldburger tot 'Bange Blanke Mani'*, Brussels: VUBPress, 67–76

FitzGerald, M. (1984) *Political Parties and Black People*, London: Runnymede Trust

FitzGerald, M. (1985) 'Preliminary report on GLC sponsored survey of ethnic minority political attitudes in London', unpublished discussion paper, January

FitzGerald, M. (1987) *Political Parties and Black People,* 2nd edn, London: Runnymede Trust

Fitzgerald, M. (1988) 'There is no alternative ... black people and the Labour Party', *Social Studies Review* Vol. 4, No. 1: 20–3

Foblets, M.-C. (1994) *Les Familles maghrébines et la Justice en Belgique: Anthropologie juridique et Immigration*, Paris: Karthala

Friedman, J. (1994) *Cultural Identity and Global Process*, London: Sage

Fryer, P. (1984) *Staying Power: The History of Black People in Britain*, London: Pluto

Fuller, J. H. S. and Toon, P. D. (1988) *Medical Practice in a Multicultural Society*, Oxford: Heinemann Medical

Furnivall, J. S (1948) *Colonial Policy and Practice*, London: Cambridge University Press

Gates, H. L. (1992) *Loose Canons*, New York: Oxford University Press

Geddes, A. (1993) 'Asian and Afro-Caribbean representation in elected local government in England and Wales', *New Community* Vol. 20, No. 1: 43–57

Geertz, C. (1963) 'Primordial sentiments and civil politics in the new states' in C. Geertz (Ed.) *Old Societies and New States: The Quest for Modernity in Asia and Africa,* New York: The Free Press

Giroux, H. A. (1992) *Border Crossings*, New York: Routledge

Giroux, H. A. (1993) *Living Dangerously,* New York: Peter Lang

Giroux, H. A. (1994) 'Insurgent multiculturalism and the promise of pedagogy' in D. T. Goldberg (Ed.) *Multiculturalism: A Critical Reader*, Oxford: Blackwell, 325–43

Glazer, N. and Moynihan, D. P. (1993) *Beyond the Melting Pot*, Cambridge: Harvard University Press

Goldberg, D. T. (1994a) 'Introduction: multicultural conditions' in D. T. Goldberg (Ed.) *Multiculturalism: A Critical Reader*, Oxford: Blackwell, 1–41

Goldberg, D. T. (Ed.) (1994b) *Multiculturalism: A Critical Reader*, Oxford: Blackwell

Gordon, J. (1994) *Managing Substance Abuse in a Multicultural Society*, London: Sage

Gunzburg, J. C. (1993) *Unresolved Grief: A Practical, Multicultural Approach for Health Professionals*, London: Chapman and Hill

Gutman, A. (Ed.) (1992) *Multiculturalism and the 'Politics of Recognition'*, Princeton: Princeton University Press

Gyford, J. (1985) *The Politics of Local Socialism*, London: George Allen & Unwin

Haegen, H. van der et al. (1996) *Bruxelles multiculturel*, Brussels: Le Secrétaire d'Etat flamand chargé de la recherche scientifique non-économique de la Région de Bruxelles-Capitale

Hall, S. (1991a) 'Ethnicity: identity and difference', *Radical America* Vol. 13, No. 4: 9–20

Hall, S. (1991b) 'Old and new identities, old and new ethnicities' in A. D. King (Ed.) *Culture, Globalization and the World-System*, Basingstoke: Macmillan, 41–68

Hall, S. (1992) 'The new ethnicities' in J. Donald and A. Rattansi (Eds) *'Race',
Culture and Difference*, London: Sage, 252–9
Hall, S. (1993) 'Culture, community, nation', *Cultural Studies* Vol. 7: 349–63
Halstead, M. (1988) *Education, Justice and Cultural Diversity*, London: Falmer
Press
Hannerz, U. (1992) *Cultural Complexities: Studies in the Social Organization of
Meaning*, New York: Columbia University Press
Heath, A. et al. (1991) *Understanding Political Change: The British Voter 1964–
87*, Oxford: Pergamon Press
Hermans, P. (1992) *Opgroeien als Marokkaan in Brussel*, Brussels: Cultuur en
Migratie
Hervieu-Léger, D. (1993) *La Religion pour Mémoire*, Paris: Cerf
Hobsbawm, E. (1995) 'The new world disorder', paper presented at the
International Conference 'Dialogues Européens', Brussels, ULB, 24–25
February
Hobsbawm, E. and Ranger, T. (1983) (Eds) *The Invention of Tradition,*
Cambridge: Cambridge University Press
Hoggart, R. (1986) *La Culture du Pauvre*, Paris: Minuit
Hollinger, D. (1995) *Postethnic America: Beyond Multiculturalism*, New York:
Basic Books
Home Office (1977) *Policy for the Inner Cities* (Cmnd 6845) London: HMSO
Honeyford, R. (1988) *Integration or Disintegration*, London: Claridge Press
Hood, R. (1992) *Race and Sentencing*, Oxford: Clarendon Press
Horowitz, D. (1985) *Ethnic Groups in Conflict*, Berkeley: University of
California Press
Hughes, R. (1993) *Culture of Complaint: The Fraying of America*, New York:
Oxford University Press
Hunter, J. D. (1991) *Culture Wars: The Struggle to Define America*, New York:
Basic Books
Huntington, S. (1996) *The Clash of Civilizations and the Remaking of the World
Order*, New York: Simon & Shuster
Hutnik, M. (1991) *Ethnic Minority Identity: A Social Psychological Perspective*,
Oxford: Clarendon Press
Institut national de statistique (1996) *Annuaire de Statistique*, Brussels: Institut
national de Statistique
Ivey, A. E. and Ivey, M. B. (1993) *Counselling and Psychotherapy: A Multi-
cultural Perspective*, London: Allyn & Bacon
Jackson, B. W., LaFasto, F., Schultz, H. G. and Kelly, D. (1992) 'Diversity',
Human Resource Management Vol. 31, Nos 1/2: 21–34
Jacobs, B. D. (1986) *Black Politics and Urban Crisis in Britain*, Cambridge:
Cambridge Universiy Press
Jakubowicz, A. (1981) 'State and ethnicity: multiculturalism as an ideology',
Australia and New Zealand Journal of Sociology Vol. 17, No. 3
James, W. (1993) 'Migration, racism and identity formation: the Caribbean
experience in Britain' in W. James and C. Harris (Eds) *Inside Babylon: The
Caribbean Diaspora in Britain*, London: Verso, 231–88
Jaspaert, K. and Verlot M. (1992) 'Taalkundige en culturele gevolgen van een
multi-etnische samenleving voor het Nederlandstalig onderwijs', *Ons Erfdeel*
Vol. 2: 213–21 (Koninklijk Commissariaat voor het Migrantenbeleid)

Jayasuriya, L. (1990) 'Multiculturalism, citizenship and welfare: new directions for the 1990s', paper presented at the 50th Anniversary Lecture Series, Department of Social Work and Social Policy, University of Sydney

Jenkins, R. (1967) *Essays and Speeches*, London: Collins

Johnson, M. R. D. (1994) 'Health and social services', *New Community* Vol. 20: 309–16

Joris, C. (1991) *Vrouw Worden op Sicilie: Een Culturele Levenscyclus*, Leuven: Leuven University Press

Kalka, I. (1991) 'Striking a bargain: political radicalism in a middle-class London borough' in P. Werbner and M. Anwar (Eds) *Black and Ethnic Leaderships in Britain*, London: Routledge, 203–25

Kearney, H. (1991) 'Four nations or one?' in B. Crick (Ed.) *National Identities: The Constitution of the United Kingdom*, Oxford: Blackwell

KCM (1989) *Integratie (Beleid): Een Werk van Lange Adem*, 3 vols, Brussels: KCM/INBEL

KCM (1993) *Tekenen voor Gelijkwaardigheid*, Brussels: Inbel

Kellner, P. and Cohen, N. (1991) 'Racism: someone else is to blame', *Independent on Sunday*, 7 July

Kepel, G. (1987) *Les Banlieues de l'Islam*, Paris: Seuil

Kessler, G. E. (Ed.) (1992) *Voices of Wisdom: A Multicultural Philosophy Reader*, Belmont, Ca: Wadsworth

Khan, V. S. (1975) in S. Allen and D. Barker (Eds) *Sexual Divisions and Society: Process and Change*, London: Croom Helm

Knopfelmacher, (1984) 'Anglomorphism in Australia', *The Age*, 31 March, Melbourne

Knott, K. (1991) 'Bound to change? the religions of South Asians in Britain' in S. Vertovec (Ed.) *Aspects of the South Asian Diaspora*, Delhi: Oxford University Press, 86–111

Knott, K. and Toon, R. (1982) 'Muslims, Sikhs and Hindus in the UK: problems in the estimation of religious statistics', Leeds, Department of Sociology, University of Leeds, *Religious Research Papers* No. 6

Kobayashi, A. (1993) 'Multiculturalism: representing a Canadian institution' in J. Duncan and D. Ley (Eds) *Place/culture/representation*, London: Routledge, 205–31

Koontz, C. (1986) *Mothers in the Fatherland*, London: Jonathan Cape

Kymlicka, W. (1995a) *Multicultural Citizenship*, Oxford: Oxford University Press

Kymlicka, W. (Ed.) (1995b) *The Rights of Minority Cultures*, Oxford: Oxford University Press

Lacoste-Dujardin, C. (1992) *Yasmina et les autres de Nanterre et d'Ailleurs: Filles de Parents maghrébins en France*, Paris: La Découverte

Lambert, P.-Y. (1996) 'Candidats et élus d'origine extracommunautaire aux élections européennes, communales, régionales et législatives de 1994 et 1995 en région bruxelloise', *L'année sociale*, 267–91

Laszlo, E. (Ed.) (1993) *The Multicultural Planet: The Report of a UNESCO International Expert Group*, Oxford: Oneworld

Layton-Henry, Z. (1992) *The Politics of Immigration*, Oxford: Blackwell

Lohe, M. le (1996) 'Ethnic minority participation and representation and the British electoral system' in S. Saggar (Ed.) (1997) *Race and British Electoral Politics*, Hemel Hempstead: Prentice Hall

Lee, J. Y. (1995) *Marginality: The Key to Multicultural Theology*, Minneapolis: Fortress Press

Leman, J. (1987) *From Challenging Culture to Challenged Culture: The Sicilian Cultural Code and the Socio-Cultural Praxis of Sicilian Immigrants in Belgium*, Leuven: Leuven University Press

Leman, J. (1993) 'Hoe de scholenslag winnen? Beleidsperspectieven inzake onderwijs aan allochtonen in de vlaamse gemeenschap', *Tijdschrift voor Onderwijs en Onderwijsbeleid*, 151–61

Leman, J. (Ed.) (1995) *Sans Documents: Les Immigrés de l'Ombre. Latino-Américains, Polonais et Nigérians clandestins*, Brussels: De Boeck University

Lewis, P. (1994) *Islamic Britain: Religion, Politics and Identity among British Muslims*, London: I.B.Taurus

Lynch, F. R. (1993) 'Whose diversity? Whose consensus?', *Society* Vol. 30, No. 5: 36–40

Lynch, J., Modgil, C. and Modgil, S. (Eds) (1992) *Cultural Diversity and the Schools* (4 vols) London: Falmer Press

Lyon, M. and West, B. J. M. (1995) 'London Patels: caste and commerce', *New Community* Vol. 21, No. 3: 399–419

McAllister, I. and Studlar, D. (1984) 'The electoral geography of immigrant groups in Britain', *Electoral Studies* Vol. 3, No. 2: 139–50

McCrudden, C., Smith, D. J. and Brown, C. (1991) *Racial Justice at Work: Enforcement of the Race Relations Act 1976 in Employment*, London: Policy Studies Institute

McLennan, G. (1995) *Pluralism*, Milton Keynes: Open University Press

McNeill, W. H. (1986) *Polyethnicity and National Unity in World History*, Toronto: Toronto University Press

Marshall, T. H. and Bottomore, T. (1992) *Citizenship and Social Class*, London: Pluto Press

Martens, A. (1976) *Les Immigrés: Flux et Reflux d'une Main-d'oeuvre d'Appoint*, Louvain: PUL Editions Vie Ouvrière

Martens, A. (1993) 'De Integratieproblematiek binnen een multiculturele samenleving: het verzuilingsmodel als hypothese' in F. Demeyere (Ed.) *Over Pluralisme en Democratie: Verzuiling en Integratie in een Multiculturele Samenleving*, Brussels: VUBPress, 39–50

Martin, J. (1991) 'Multiculturalism and feminism' in G. Bottomley, M. de Lepervanche and J. Martin (Eds) *Intersections*, Sydney: Allen & Unwin, 110–31

Martiniello, M. (1991) ''Turbulences à Bruxelles' (mai 1991)', *Migrations Société* Vol. 3, No. 18: 19–29

Martiniello, M. (1992) *Leadership et Pouvoir dans les Communautés d'origine immigrée*, Paris: CIEMI–L'Harmattan

Martiniello, M. (1994) 'De communautaire kwestie en het migrantenvraagstuk in België' in R. Detrez and J. Blommaert (Eds) *Nationalisme: Kritische Opstellen*, Berchem: Epo, 172–82

Martiniello, M. (1995a) 'European citizenship, European identity and migrants: towards the post-national state?' in R. Miles and D. Thränhardt (Eds) *Migration and European Integration: The Dynamics of Exclusion and Inclusion*, London: Pinters Publishers, 37–52

Martiniello, M. (1995b) 'The national question and the political construction of immigrant ethnic communities in Belgium' in A. Hargreaves and J. Leaman

(Eds) *Racism, Ethnicity and Politics in Contemporary Europe*, London: Edward Elgar Press, 131–44

Martiniello, M. (1996) 'La question nationale belge à l'épreuve de l'immigration' in A. Dieckoff (Ed.) *Belgique: La Force de la Désunion*, Bruxelles: Éditions Complexe, 85–104

Maruyama, M. (1994) *Mindscapes of Management: Use of Individual Differences in Multicultural Management*, Aldershot: Dartmouth

Massey, D. (1994) *Space, Place and Gender*, Cambridge: Polity Press

Mercer, K. (1988) (Ed.) *Black Film/British Cinema*, ICA\documents, British Film Institute

Messina, A. (1989) *Race and Party Competition in Britain*, Oxford: Clarendon Press

Miles, R. (1978) 'Racism, Marxism and British politics', *Economy and Society* Vol. 17, No. 3: 428–60

Min-ha, T. T. (1989) *Woman, Native, Other*, Bloomington: Indiana University Press

Ministère de l'Education de la Communauté française (1992) *Rapport communautaire sur l'Éducation interculturelle en Communauté française de Belgique*, Brussels: Secrétariat du Ministère de l'Education de la Communauté française

Modood, T. (1993) 'Muslim views on religious identity and racial equality', *New Community* Vol. 19: 513–19

Modood, T. (1994) 'Political blackness and British Asians', *Sociology* Vol. 28: 859–76

Mullard, C. (1984) *Anti-Racist Education*, London: National Association for Multi-Racial Education

Muxel, A. (1988) 'Les attitudes socio-politiques des jeunes issus de l'immigration maghrébine en région parisienne', *Revue Française de Science Politique* Vol. 38, No. 8: 925–40

Nanton, P. (1989) 'The new orthodoxy: racial categories and equal opportunities', *New Community* Vol. 15, No. 4: 549–64

Nelli, H. S. (1983) *From Immigrants to Ethnics: The Italian-Americans*, Oxford: Oxford University Press

Nelson, D., Joseph, G. G. and Williams J. (1993) *Multicultural Mathematics*, Oxford: Oxford University Press

Nie, N. et al. (1976) *The Changing American Voter*, Cambridge: Harvard University Press

Nielsen, J. (1988) 'Muslims in Britain and local authority responses' in T. Gerholm and Y. G. Lithman (Eds) *The New Islamic Presence in Western Europe*, London: Mansell, 53–77

Norris, P. and Lovenduski, J. (1995) *Political Recruitment: Gender, Race and Class in the British Parliament*, Cambridge: Cambridge University Press

Office of Multicultural Affairs (1988) *Towards a National Agenda for Multiculturalism*, Canberra: Australian Government Publishing Service

ONS (1996) *Ethnicity in the 1991 Census*, London: Office for National Statistics, HMSO

Parekh, B. (1991) 'British citizenship and cultural difference' in G. Andrews (Ed.) *Citizenship*, London: Lawrence & Wishart, 183–204

Parekh, B. (1994) 'Equality, fairness and limits of diversity', *Innovation* Vol. 7, No. 3: 289–308

Parsons, G. (1993) (Ed.) *The Growth of Religious Diversity: Britain from 1945. Volume I – Traditions*, London: Routledge

Parsons, G. (1994) (Ed.) *The Growth of Religious Diversity: Britain from 1945. Volume II – Issues*, London: Routledge

Patterson, O. (1978) *Ethnic Chauvinism: The Reactionary Impulse*, New York: Stein & Day

Patterson, S. (1965) *Dark Strangers: A Study of West Indians in London*, Harmondsworth: Penguin

Peach, C. (1990) 'The Muslim population of Great Britain', *Ethnic and Racial Studies* Vol. 13, No 2: 414–19

Peach, C. (1996) (Ed.) *Ethnicity in the 1991 Census Vol 2. The Ethnic Minority Populations of Great Britain*, London: Office for National Statistics/HMSO

Pearl, D. (1987) 'South Asian communities and English family law, 1971–1987', *New Community* Vol. 14: 161–9

Phillips, A. (1995) *The Politics of Presence*, Oxford: Oxford University Press

Portes, A. (1993) 'The new second generation: segmented assimilation and its variants', *Annals of the American Academy of Political and Social Sciences* Vol. 530, November: 74–96

Portes, A. and Rumbaut, G. (1990) *Immigrant America: A Portrait*, Berkeley: University of California Press

Poulter, S. (1990) *Asian Tradition and the English Law*, London: Trentham Books

Radtke, F. (1992) 'Multiculturalism: a fitting ideology for the postmodern nineties?', paper for the German Association for American Studies Regional Conference, Munich

Radtke, F. (1994) 'The formation of ethnic minorities and the transformation of social into ethnic conflicts in a so-called multi-cultural society: the case of Germany' in J. Rex and B. Drury (Eds) *Ethnic Mobilisation in a Multi-Cultural Europe*, Aldershot: Avebury, 30–8

Rafiq, M. (1992) 'A comparison of Muslim and non-Muslim owned Asian businesses in Britain', *New Community* Vol. 19, No. 1: 43–60

Rath, J. (1991) *Minorisering: De Sociale Constructie van 'Etnische Minderheden'*, Amsterdam: SUA

Rattansi, A. (1992) 'Changing the subject? racism, culture and education' in J. Donald and A. Rattansi (Eds) *Race, Culture, Difference*, London: Sage

Rea, A. (1993) 'La Politique d'intégration des populations d'origine étrangère' in M. Martiniello and M. Poncelet (Eds) *Migrations et Minorités ethniques dans l'Espace européen*, Brussel: De Boeck, 143–66

Reeves, F. W. (1989) *Race and Borough Politics*, Aldershot: Avebury

Rex, J. (1986) 'The concept of a multicultural society', Coventry, Centre for Research in Ethnic Relations, University of Warwick, *Occasional Papers in Ethnic Relations No. 3*

Rex, J. (1988) *The Ghetto and the Underclass: Essays on Race and Social Policy*, Aldershot: Avebury

Rex, J. (1991) 'The political sociology of a multi-cultural society', *Journal of Inter-cultural Studies* Vol. 2, No. 1: 7–19

Rex, J. (1995) 'Ethnic identity and the nation state: the political sociology of multi-cultural societies', *Social Identities* Vol. 1, No. 1: 21–31

Rex, J. (1996) *Ethnic Minorities in the Modern Nation State: Working Papers in the Theory of Multi-culturalism and Political Integration*, Basingstoke: MacMillan

Rex, J. and Drury, B. (Eds) (1994) *Ethnic Mobilisation in a Multi-cultural Europe*, Aldershot: Avebury

Rex, J. and Tomlinson, S. (1979) *Colonial Immigrants in a British City*, London: Routledge & Kegan Paul

Ritzer, J. (1993) *The McDonaldization of Society*, Thousand Oaks: Pine Forge

Robbins, B. (1991) 'Tenured radicals, the new McCartyism, and "PC"', *New Left Review* Vol. 188: 151–7

Robinson, F. (1988) 'Varieties of South Asian Islam', Coventry, Centre for Research in Ethnic Relations, University of Warwick, *Research Paper* No. 8

Robinson, V. (1990) 'Roots to mobility: the social mobility of Britain's black population, 1971–87', *Ethnic and Racial Studies* Vol. 13, No. 2: 274–86

Roosens, E. (1989) *Creating Ethnicity: The Process of Ethnogenesis*, Newbury Park (Calif.): Sage Publications

Roosens, E. (Ed.) (1992) 'The insertion of allochthonous youngsters in Belgian society', *Migration* Vol. 15, No. 3

Roosens, E. et al. (1993) *Beelden van Immigrantenkinderen bij Leraren*, Brussels: Diensten voor Programmatie van het Wetenschapsbeleid

Roosens, E. (1994) 'The primordial nature of origins in migrant ethnicity' in H. Vermeulen and C. Govers (Eds) *The Anthropology of Ethnicity: Beyond 'Ethnic Groups and Boundaries'*, Amsterdam: Het Spinhuis, 81–104

Roosens, E. (Ed.) (1995) *Rethinking Culture, 'Multicultural Society' and the School*, Oxford: Pergamon Press

Roy, O. (1992) *L'Échec de l'Islam politique*, Paris: Seuil

Roy, O. (1996) 'Le néo-fondamentalisme islamique ou l'immaginaire de l'oummah', *Esprit*, April

Saggar, S. (1992) *Race and Politics in Britain*, London: Harvester–Wheatsheaf

Saggar, S. (1993) 'Can political parties play the "race card" in general elections? The 1992 poll revisited', *New Community* Vol. 19: 693–9

Saggar, S. (Ed.) (1997) *Race and British Electoral Politics*, Hemel Hempstead: Prentice Hall

Sahgal, G. and Yuval-Davis, N. (1992) (Eds) *Refusing Holy Orders: Women and Fundamentalism in Britain*, London: Virago

Scarman Report (1981) *The Brixton Disorders 10–12 April 1981: Report of an Inquiry by the Rt Hon. Lord Scarman, OBE*, Cmnd 8247, London: HMSO

Schierup, C. (1992) 'What agency should we be multi about? The multicultural agenda reviewed', *European Journal of Intercultural Studies* Vol. 2, No. 3: 5–23

Schierup, C. (1995) 'Multiculturalism and universalism in the USA and EU Europe', paper for the workshop on Nationalism and Ethnicity, Bern, March

Schierup, C. and Ålund, A. (1987) *Will they Still be Dancing? Integration and Ethnic Transformation among Yugoslav Immigrants in Sweden*, Stockholm: Almqvist & Wiksell

Schlesinger Jr, A. M. (1991) *The Disuniting of America: Reflections on a Multicultural Society*, New York: W. W. Norton & Company

Seyd, P. et al. (1992) *Labour's Grassroots: The Politics of Party Membership*, Oxford: Clarendon Press

Shadid, W. A. R and van Koningsveld, P. S (1995) *Religious Freedom and the Position of Islam in Western Europe*, Kampen, The Netherlands: Kok Pharos

Shohat, E. and Stam, R. (1994) *Unthinking Eurocentrism: Multiculturalism and The media*, New York: Routledge

Shukra, K. (1990) 'Black Sections in the Labour Party' in H. Gouldbourne (Ed.) *Black Politics in Britain*, Aldershot: Avebury

Shweder, R. (1992) *Thinking through Cultures: Expeditions in Cultural Psychology*, Cambridge, Mass.: Harvard University Press

Singer, M. and Spyraw, M. (1989) *Textile Arts: Multicultural Traditions*, London: A & C Black

Smith, A. D. (1994) 'Polyethnicity in history', *International Journal of Comparative Race and Ethnic Studies* Vol. 1, No. 1: 1–13

Solomos, J. (1993) *Race and Racism in Britain*, 2nd edition, London: Macmillan

Sowell, T. (1991) 'A World View of Cultural Diversity', *Society* Vol. 29, No. 1: 37–44

Soysal, Y. (1994) *Limits of Citizenship: Migrants and Postnational Membership in Europe*, Chicago: Chicago University Press

Squires, A. (Ed.) *Multicultural Health Care and Rehabilitation of Older People*, London: Edward Arnold

Srinivasan, S. (1992) 'The class position of Asian petit-bourgoisie', *New Community* Vol. 19, No. 1: 61–74

Stolcke, V. (1995) 'Talking culture: new boundaries, new rhetorics of exclusion in Europe', *Current Anthropology* Vol. 36, No. 1: 1–24

Studlar, D. (1983) 'The ethnic vote 1983: problems and analysis and interpretation', *New Community* Vol. 11: 92–100

Study of Dance Conference (1986) *Dance: A Multicultural Perspective*, Guildford: Centre for Dance

Suarez-Orozco, M. (1995) 'Anxious neighbors: Belgium and its immigrant minorities' in W. Cornelius, P. Martin and J. Hollifield, *Controlling Immigration: A Global Perspective*, Stanford: Stanford University Press, 237–68

Swyngedouw, M. (1991) 'Het Vlaams Blok in Antwerpen: een analyse van de verkiezingsuitslagen sinds 1985' in H. de Schampelheire and Y. Thanassekos (Eds) *L'Extrême droite en Europe de l'ouest*, Brussels: VUBPress: 93–114

Taguieff, P.-A. (1990) 'The new cultural racism in France', *Telos* Vol. 83: 109–22

Taguieff, P.-A. (1988) *La force du préjugé*, Paris: La Découverte

Tastenhoye, G. (1993) *Naar de Multiculturele Samenleving?*, Leuven: Davidsfonds

Taylor, C. (1994) 'The politics of recognition' in A. Gutman (Ed.) *Multiculturalism*, Princeton: Princeton University Press, 25–73

Taylor, R. (1996) 'Political science encounters "race" and "ethnicity"', *Ethnic and Racial Studies* Vol. 19, No. 4: 884–95

Thompson, N. (1996) 'Supply Side Socialism: The Political Economy of New Labour', *New Left Review* Vol. 216: 37–54

Timmerman, C. (1996) 'Onderwijs als diacriticum. Socioculturele praxis en etniciteitsbeleving bij jonge Turkse vrouwen; drie perspectieven', doctoral dissertation, Leuven, Department of Anthropology

Tribalat, M. (1995) *Faire France: Une Enquête sur les Immigrés et leurs Enfants*, Paris: La Découverte

Troyna, B. (1979) 'Differential commitment of ethnic identity by black youths in Britain', *New Community* Vol. 7, No. 3

Turner, B. S. (1990) 'Outline of a theory of citizenship', *Sociology* Vol. 24, No. 2: 189–217

Turner, T. (1993) 'Anthropology and multiculturalism: what is anthropology that multiculturalists should be mindful of it?', *Cultural Anthropology* Vol. 8: 411–29

Verba, S. and Nie, N. (1972) *Participation in America: Political Democracy and Social Equality*, New York: Harper & Row

Verhofstadt, G. (1992) *De Weg naar Politieke Vernieuwing: Het Tweede Burger-manifest*, Antwerp: Hadewijch

Verlinden P. (1991) 'Morfologie van extreem rechts binnen het Vlaams-nationalisme' in H. de Schampheleire and Y. Thanassekos (Eds) *L'Extrême Droite en Europe de l'ouest*, Brussels: VUBPress, 235–45

Vertovec, S. (1994) 'Multicultural, multi-Asian, multi-Muslim Leicester: dimensions of social complexity, ethnic organisation and local government interface', *Innovation* Vol. 7, No. 3: 259–76

Vertovec, S. (1996a) 'Berlin multikulti: Germany, "foreigners," and "world-openness"', *New Community* Vol. 22, No. 3: 381–99

Vertovec, S. (1996b) 'More multi, less culturalism: the anthropology of cultural complexity and the new politics of pluralism', paper for the British Sociological Association Annual Conference, Reading

Vertovec, S. (1996c) 'Multiculturalism, culturalism and public incorporation', *Ethnic and Racial Studies* Vol. 19, No. 1: 49–69

Vertovec, S. (1996d) 'Muslims, the state and the public sphere in Britain' in G. Nonneman, T. Niblock and B. Sjazkowski (Eds) *Muslim Communities in the New Europe*, London: Ithaca Press, 167–86

Vertovec, S. (1996e) 'On the reproduction and representation of Hinduism in Britain' in T. Ranger, Y. Samad and O. Stewart (Eds) *Culture, Identity and Politics: Asians and Afro-Caribbeans in Britain*, Aldershot: Averbury, 77–89

Vertovec, S. and Peach, C. (1997) 'Introduction' in S. Vertovec and C. Peach (Eds) *Islam in Europe: The Politics of Religion and Community*, Basingstoke: Macmillan

Viaene, W. (1996) *Stimuleren van Nederlandstalige Zelforganisaties van Migranten in het Brussels Hoofdstedelijk Gewest (Report)*, Brussels: Intercultureel Centrum voor Migranten

Waldron, J. (1992) 'Minority cultures and the cosmopolitan alternative', University of Michigan, *Journal of Law Reform* Vol. 25, No. 3: 751–93

Werbner, P. (1991) 'Black and ethnic leaderships in Britain: a theoretical overview' in P. Werbner and M. Anwar (Eds) *Black and Ethnic Leaderships: The Cultural Dimensions of Political Action*, London: Routledge

Wils, L. (1995) *Vlaanderen, België, Groot-Nederland. Mythe en Geschiedenis*, Leuven: Davidsfonds

Yeatman, A. (1992) 'Minorities and the politics of difference', *Political Theory Newsletter* Vol. 4, No. 1: 1–11

Young, I. M. (1990) *Justice and the Politics of Difference*, Princeton: Princeton University Press

Yuval-Davis, N. (1991a) 'Ethnic/racial and gender divisions and the nation in Britain and Australia' in R. Nile (Ed.) *Immigration and the Politics of Ethnicity and Race in Australia and Britain*, London: Institute of Commonwealth Studies, 14–26

Yuval–Davis, N. (1991b) 'The citizenship debate: women, ethnic processes and the state', *Feminist Review* No. 39: 58–68

Yuval-Davis, N. (1992) 'Fundamentalism, multiculturalism and women in Britain' in J. Donald and A. Rattansi (Eds) *Race, Culture and Difference*, London: Sage, 278–91

Yuval-Davis, N. (1994) 'Women, ethnicity and empowerment' in K. Bhavnani and A. Poenix (Eds) *Feminism and Psychology*, special issue *Shifting Identities Shifting Racisms* Vol. 4, No. 1: 179–98

Yuval-Davis, N. (1996/7) *Gender and Nation*, London: Sage
Yuval-Davis, N. and Anthias, F. (1989) (Eds) *Woman–Nation–State*, Basingstoke: Macmillan

Contributors

Albert Bastenier is a professor of sociology at the Université Catholique de Louvain, where he founded the GREM (Groupe d'Etude des Relations Interethniques et des Migrations). His latest books include *Immigration et Espace public: La Controverse de l'Intégration* (with Félice Dassetto) (L'Harmattan 1993), and *Immigrations et nouveaux Pluralismes* (edited with Félice Dassetto) (De Boeck 1990).

Jan Blommaert holds a doctorate in African Studies and works as a research director at the IPrA Research Center of the University of Antwerp. His research interests include language and ideology, political language, language politics and intercultural communication. Fields of application include migrant politics in Belgium, the practice of intercultural communication in institutional settings, and nationalist movements in Europe and Africa.

Malcolm Cross B.Sc. (Econ) (London) MA (East Anglia) Ph.D. (Utrecht), director of ERCOMER 1994–98, is an associate professor in the Faculty of Social Sciences, Utrecht University. He is an economic sociologist with research interests in the social and economic positions of ethnic minorities in cities, and in the analysis of ethnic conflict in Western and Eastern Europe. He is also interested in comparative research methodology. He is an advisor to a number of Western European governments in the field of ethnic minority policy and is the editor of the *Journal of Ethnic and Migration Studies* (*JEMS*) (incorporating *New Community*).

Adrian Favell is a Marie Curie Research Fellow at the European Research Centre on Migration and Ethnic Relations at Utrecht University. He was formerly *chercheur invité* at the Centre d'Études de la Vie Politique Française (CEVIPOF), Paris, and was during 1995/6 a Hoover fellow at the Chaire Hoover d'Éthique Économique et Sociale, Université Catholique de Louvain, Belgium. He is co-editor of *New Xenophobia in Europe* (Kluwer 1995) and author of *Philosophies of Integration: Immigration and the Idea of Citizenship in France and Britain* (Macmillan 1997).

Marco Martiniello holds a doctorate in social and political sciences (European University Institute, Florence). He is a research fellow at the Belgian National Fund for Scientific Research (FNRS). He also teaches politics at the University of Liège. He has been a visiting scholar/ professor at the University of Warwick, the European University Institute, Cornell University, and the Centre d'Études et de Recherches Internationales in Paris. His research deals primarily with the political aspects of migration, ethnic relations and nationalism. His latest books include *L'ethnicité dans les Sciences Sociales contemporaines* (PUF 'Que sais-je?' 1995) and *Migration, Citizenship and Ethno-National Identities in the European Union* (Avebury 1995).

John Rex is emeritus professor of sociology at the University of Warwick. He has been a visiting lecturer/professor to many European and American universities. His latest books include *Ethnic Minorities and the Modern Nation State* (MacMillan 1996), *Ethnic Mobilisation in a Multicultural Europe* (edited with Beatrice Drury, Avebury 1994) and *Ethnic Mobilisation in Britain* (1991).

Eugeen Roosens is professor and head of the Department of Social and Cultural Anthropology at the Katholieke Universiteit Leuven and *professor extraordinarius* at the Université Catholique de Louvain. He has frequently taken up the post of visiting professor at this same university. At present, he is holder of the National Francqui Chair 1996–7 at the Vrije Universiteit, Brussel. He has directed the long-term fieldwork project 'The Cultural Identity of Ethnic Minorities' since 1974. He is the author of *Creating Ethnicity: The Process of Ethnogenesis* (Sage 1989) and of several other books and articles on cultural change and ethnicity.

Shamit Saggar is currently a senior lecturer in government at Queen Mary and Westfield College, University of London. He has held several distinguished international posts and awards. In 1988 he was awarded the Stein Rokkan Postgraduate Fellowship of the International Political Association; in 1991 he held the Australian Bicentennial Research Fellowship of the Sir Robert Menzies Centre for Australian Studies, University of London; in 1993 he was a Harkness Fellow of the Commonwealth Fund of New York, held in conjunction with a visiting post in urban planning at the University of California, Los Angeles. His books include *Race and Public Policy* (Avebury 1991), *Race and Politics in Britain* (Harvester Wheatsheaf 1992), and an edited volume entitled *Race and British Electoral Politics* (Prentice Hall 1997).

Steven Vertovec is a senior research fellow at the Institute of Social and Cultural Anthropology, University of Oxford. He is author of *Hindu Trinidad: Religion, Ethnicity and Socio-Economic Change* (Macmillan 1992), editor of *Aspects of the South Asian Diaspora* (Oxford University Press 1991) and *Muslim European Youth: Reproducing Religion, Ethnicity and Culture* (Avebury forthcoming), and co-editor of *South Asians Overseas: Migration and Ethnicity* (with C. Clarke and C. Peach, Cambridge University Press 1990), *The Urban Context: Ethnicity, Social Networks and Situational Analysis* (with A. Rogers, Berg 1995) and *Islam in Europe: The Politics of Religion and Community* (with Ceri Peach, Macmillan 1997).

Nira Yuval-Davis is a professor and post-graduate course director in Gender and Ethnic Studies at the University of Greenwich in London. She has written extensively on nationalism, racism, multiculturalism and women. Among her books are W*oman–Nation–State* (MacMillan 1989); *Racialized Boundaries* (Routledge 1992); *Unsettling Settler Societies* (Sage 1995) and *Gender and Nation* (Sage 1997).

Index